FOUL & FAIR PLAY

FOUL
&
FAIR
PLAY

READING GENRE IN CLASSIC DETECTIVE FICTION

MARTY
ROTH

The University of Georgia Press
Athens & London

© 1995 by the University of Georgia Press
Athens, Georgia 30602
All rights reserved
Designed by Walton Harris
Set in 10/14 Linotype Walbaum by Tseng Information
Systems, Inc.
Printed and bound by Thomson-Shore

The paper in this book meets the guidelines for
permanence and durability of the Committee on
Production Guidelines for Book Longevity of the
Council on Library Resources.

Printed in the United States of America
99 98 97 96 95 C 5 4 3 2 1

Library of Congress Cataloging in Publication Data

Roth, Marty.
Foul and fair play : reading genre in classic detective fiction /
Marty Roth.
p.   cm.
Includes bibliographical references and index.
ISBN 0–8203–1622–9 (alk. paper)
1. Detective and mystery stories—History and criticism.
I. Title.
PN3448.D4R66 1995
809.3'872—dc20   93-30367

British Library Cataloging in Publication Data available

To Martha, Molly, Jennifer, and David—dear friends

The customs of a community, taken as a whole, always have a particular style and are reducible to systems. I am of the opinion that the number of such systems is not unlimited and that—in their games, dreams or wild imaginings—human societies, like individuals, never create absolutely, but merely choose certain combinations from an ideal repertoire that it should be possible to define.

—CLAUDE LÉVI-STRAUSS

To work from slight indications, as we constantly do in this field, is not without its dangers. There is a mental disorder called combinatory paranoia in which the practice of utilizing such small indications is carried beyond all limits.

—SIGMUND FREUD

We had long been at once attracted and repelled by that very modern form of the police novel or mystery story . . . attracted by its peculiar interest when done, and the peculiar difficulties that attend its execution; repelled by that appearance of insincerity and shallowness of tone, which seems its inevitable drawback. For the mind of the reader, always bent to pick up clews, receives no impression of reality or life, rather of an airless, elaborate mechanism; and the book remains enthralling, but insignificant, like a game of chess, not a human work of art.

—ROBERT LOUIS STEVENSON

CONTENTS

PREFACE

Classic detective fiction differs from other fiction in at least one way: it challenges us to read it faster than the words appear on the page. The challenge may be spelled out by an author like Ellery Queen, but even if not, it is covered by a rule that supposedly governs the analytic or puzzle-solving branch of this genre: "It was only by slow degrees that the most important principle of the modern detective story was isolated and generally accepted: the principle which we know as the 'Fair-Play Rule'" (Sayers 1947, 225). In theory, this rule—that the reader must have as much information relevant to the solution of the crime as the detective has—is played out according to a fantastic scenario by which various triumphant readers solve the mystery as they read page 64, 91, or 113, respectively, at which point the rest of the book becomes redundant for them.

I don't believe detective fiction works this way, but even if this is a deluded or overidealized view of the genre, it implies a kind of reading that is both highly gratifying and diminished—and a work not worth reading in itself. Pride and shame coincide in a golden text that certain highbrow readers claim to have found in their flirtation with detective fiction some decades ago, when making a fuss about popular fiction seemed to be an essential act of culture.

These readers confessed they were drawn back to read one after another of these meager texts. What were they reading that was at once so worthless and so fascinating? The simple answer is they were reading genre. I attempt to reread detective fiction in such a way as to avoid valorizing individual works and declaring them minor masterpieces of popular fiction and yet still find the genre full of the resonance, shadow, and play that I would prefer not to pack into any particular text. Nevertheless, although this study is based on a sample of 138 primary works, certain writers and books do tend to dominate the discussion.

Anyone who writes about mystery and detective fiction inherits a history of subdivisions that are expected to have a prescriptive force. Julian Symons, in his study of detective fiction, *Mortal Consequences*, laid down a law of differences: "It has been said already that crime fiction is a hybrid, and that too much categorization is confusing rather than helpful, but within the hybrid form detective stories and crime novels are of a different strain from spy stories and thrillers. The lines of demarcation are vague, but everybody recognizes their existence. It would be absurd to consider John Buchan and Eric Ambler together with R. Austin Freeman and Agatha Christie" (1973, 230). This book is Symons's absurdity. Although I acknowledge three general categories of detective fiction—the analytic, the hard-boiled, and the spy thriller—I not only consider Buchan, Ambler, Freeman, and Christie together, but also find they illuminate one another. There is much crossing back and forth across the few borders that remain: the strand of hair that James Bond lays across his door as a sign-in sheet for intruders is the same hair Dr. Thorndyke scrutinizes at the scene of the crime; the woman Peter Wimsey saves from execution in *Strong Poison* is the same woman Philip Marlowe condemns to death in *Farewell, My Lovely*. My critical task in this book has been one of *adjustment* rather than an institutional inscription of differences.

For almost a century, another group of popular culture critics who do *not* like detective fiction have dismissed all internal demarcations and insisted that detective and mystery fiction in all its generic permutations amounts to one extended repetition. I have tried to read my 138 fictions as if they were indeed a single story, as if no individual telling mattered that much. On the other hand, I have quoted lavishly, trying to create as much space as possible for the sound of these texts.

This book is an attempt to read classical detective fiction as a genre, that is, to read a range of separately authored stories (from Edgar Allan Poe's in the 1840s to the traditional detective novel written in the 1960s) as variations on a tight set of conventions. I conduct an ongoing investigation into the meaning of these conventions (that the detective must be an amateur, for example, or that one is led to the solution by curious signs called clues).

Whereas most of the chapters deal with conventions that constellate around a central topic like the detective, the crime, or the criminal, the first three chapters are devoted to issues that detective fiction shares with popular fiction generally. Chapters 3 through 5 treat the conventions of the hero detective and his investigation (for example, the detective as a thinking machine and other scientific or aristocratic personae, the investigation as a game, and forms of exhibitionism that characterize the detective's performance—assembling the community or dropping "bombshells"). Chapter 6 deals with the place of women in what is, classically, a masculine genre even when authored by women. Chapter 7 explores the conventions surrounding the crime, the criminal, and the community, and chapter 8 focuses on the convention of the solution and the meanings of that compulsive form of narrative closure. Chapters 9 and 10 examine the curious laws of exchange that operate in the realm where detective stories take place: how an order of sign that we commonly ignore (the clue, the trifle, and dirt) assumes extraordinary significance and how laws of coincidence and convolution govern behavior there. Chapter 11 creates a geology for the world of detective fiction, working through myths of the underworld and the frontier in order to anchor the paradigms that have been established.

My models for this book are two works by Tzvetan Todorov, his monograph on fantastic tales and his essay "The Typology of Detective Fiction," because I find them to be the most adept studies of genre.[1] However, I make no attempt, as he does, to keep structure uncontaminated by various orders of interpretation.

I do not historicize or contextualize detective fiction because I am still fascinated by its generic completeness, by how well it can be seen to work as a self-contained system. This may be a consequence of the extreme conservatism of the genre. Such a concentration has limitations, but then so does the concern with a linear history of development that occupies an excellent study like Martin Kayman's *From Bow Street to Baker Street*. On the other hand, the structures I discuss are historically bound to one another: I read from the prehistory of detective fiction in Edgar Allan Poe, Charles Dickens, Wilkie Collins, Robert Louis Stevenson, and H. G. Wells through the slow attenuation of what might be called the classical and baroque periods of the genre.

Readers have mildly or strenuously disagreed with my unwillingness to differentiate between men and women writers of detective fiction or male and female detectives. Despite the prominence of women writers in British analytic detective fiction (Agatha Christie, Ngaio Marsh, Margery Allingham, Dorothy Sayers, Josephine Tey), my controlling assumption is that in detective fiction gender is genre and genre is male; Jane Marple and Modesty Blaise are feminine notations that perform a masculine function. Janet Batsleer et al. state that Christie and Sayers work "in the 'masculine' genre of the detective story" (73). Nevertheless, readers have challenged me with the names of P. D. James, Amanda Cross, and Sarah Paretsky, as if traces of male fantasy and patriarchal ideology evaporated soon after I stopped looking—which may be the case.[2] The end of the classical period saw the end of an extremely conservative paradigm when many changes burst all at once upon this relatively static genre: "The detective is no longer an amateur, à la Peter Wimsey and Philo Vance, and is no longer wholly of the middle or upper class. He or she may be a Navajo (Tony Hillerman), an Afrikaner working with a Bantu (James McClure) . . . a Chicano (Rex Burns), a male homosexual (Joseph Hansen), a lesbian (M. F. Beal), a dwarf, a child, a machine. He (or she) may be evil" (Winks 8).

Many critics agree with me. Maureen T. Reddy wrote, "Even though women have been writing crime fiction for nearly a century, the genre seems a particularly problematic one for the woman writer because of its history. . . . Far too often, strong women detectives are found filling the (gum)shoes of strong male detectives, with only the gender changed" (5–6); Kathleen Gregory Klein claims that "not until the 1970s is there a consciously articulated response to social change by women writers who challenge the sexist assumptions of hero formation apparently required by the formulaic demands of the fiction" (5); and Lyn Pykett doubts that even the recent "space for a new breed of female protagonists in a traditional field of popular fiction" has altered "the politics, sexual or otherwise, of the genre itself" (49; see also Clover 213–18, Priestman 167).

I do not regret my inability to discover a buried feminist text in Christie's Miss Marple stories; I do regret that limitations of space dissuaded me from different kinds of gender hypothesis, such as David Lehman's hint that analytic detective fiction is female, hard-boiled is male (12) or Carlo Ginzburg's theory that the marginal epistemology on which detective fiction draws is female (see chapter nine of the present volume). The method that Sherlock Holmes opposes to the official means for solving crime is based on kitchen things. In a story by Susan Glaspell, "A Jury of Her Peers,"

> a man is murdered, strangled in his bed with a rope. The victim's wife, Mrs. Wright, formerly Minnie Foster, has been arrested for the crime. The men investigating—the sheriff, the county attorney, and a friend— think she is guilty but cannot imagine her motive. . . . When the three men go to the Foster house to search for evidence, two of their wives go along to collect some things for the jailed Minnie Foster. The men laugh at the women's attention to Minnie's kitchen and tease them for wondering about the quilt she was making, while the women speculate about whether she was going to quilt it or knot it. There is nothing here but kitchen things, the sheriff says. But would the women know a clue if they did come upon it? the other man scoffs. While in the kitchen, the women discover several things amiss. They find signs that allow them to solve the murder, determine the motive from "kitchen details." The men return later, mocking them about the quilt. She was going to—what is it you call it Ladies? We call it, knot it. Knot it also refers to the method of murder. Women's culture is "not it" to the men. (Andersen 222)

Detective fiction is as simple as the clever exercise in ratiocination it has always pretended to be and as complex as a timetable, a conundrum, or literature. It incorporates the complexity (even the impossibility) of its simplicities as successfully as it does their easy assurances. A criticism that notices only that a high order of narrative complications is inevitably dispelled in the press toward solution and does not try to account for its active presence in the first place can tell only a small part of the story of the power of genre.

Kent Bales, Michael Hancher, Gordon Hirsch, and Derek Longhurst were kind enough to read chapters in progress. Phil Furia was generous enough to read the whole book. Martha Roth has worked with me on every stage of this book, as editor, reader, and colleague.

FOUL & FAIR PLAY

1 ┃ Preliminaries

DETECTIVE FICTION HAS ALWAYS BEEN ANXIOUS ABOUT ITS CUL-
tural status. Even more than science fiction, it has been shadowed by
a drifting yet rigorous bar of judgment that the caretakers of culture
insert between a potentially good and a necessarily bad literature. The
special pleasure detective fiction generates, the compulsion to continue
reading it, and the shame associated with its reading have led to re-
current crises of sensibility in a vocal group of the cultural elite, and
detective fiction has long been the subject of apology and defense: "It
is read," Joseph Wood Krutch wrote in 1942, "either aggressively or
shamefacedly by nearly everyone, and it must be, at the present moment, the most popular of all literary forms" (41). Consequently, a
substantial literature of apologetics is available for reading alongside
detective fiction, and I begin by reading both this and a complemen-
tary body of writing that attacked detective fiction as worthless. The
first speculated, often grandiosely, about the cultural value of detective
fiction; the second exposed its sins, ranging from mindless repetition
to virtual toxicity.

An occasional writer was able to avoid this literary Manichaean-
ism. E. M. Wrong, for example, accused art fiction of only reporting its

I

masterpieces while reckoning contemporary "junk" fiction as a steady stream of inferior production (20). Making the distinction between art and popular fiction a matter of reporting sounds like a manageable way to handle the difference between the two kinds of fiction. In its developed form, this approach outlines two reading projects corresponding to two writing projects: art fiction is properly read within a myth of transcendent individual production, whereas popular fiction is read generically, and the way we tell the stories of these two cultural enterprises enshrines these practical differences.

Other writers found other ways to adjust the perceived discrepancy between detective fiction and literature. One was a recycling of J. G. Herder's argument that works of genius grow out of popular art forms—originally a strategy for explaining the relationship of folk to high art. According to Herder's argument, detective fiction, like all popular fiction, furnished a level of ordinary and ongoing narrative performance upon which, from time to time, a mountain peak arose. Art fiction consisted of a succession of peaks with, occasionally, works by the likes of Dashiell Hammett, Raymond Chandler, Georges Simenon, or John Le Carré cut into their midst.

This argument staked its credit on the occasional production of masterpieces in detective fiction, but arguing masterpieces is a sticky business. The impossibility of determining whether *The Maltese Falcon* is excellent of its kind but prevented by the limitations of genre from being a first-rate work of art, or whether it is a full-fledged work of art that transcends its genre, suggests something shaky about the concepts that hold this machinery of evaluation in place. Yet the masterpiece interval—the difference between *excellent* and *good of its kind*—was inscribed by Hammett and Chandler themselves. Late in their writing careers both authors attempted to go straight, to try their hands at literature, and in this late writing, interestingly enough, both authors lost their style. It was as if they were punishing themselves for transgression by losing their ability to write; they reproduced the bar of judgment on their own corpuses.

According to a second model, detective fiction was in an early stage of evolution into its own high art form. Some writers imagined this process as a repetition of earlier stories of generic growth: "The detective novel, now snobbishly cut off from the main stream of literature . . . may at this moment have within it secrets of what we are and shall be. And the future may look back to it . . . through great works engendered by it, as we look back . . . through Shakespeare to the crude horrors of the Tragedy of Blood" (Bogan 478). The ideal that detective fiction clumsily reflected would realize itself in a new form, a novel of crime comparable to such earlier works as *Oedipus Rex* or *Crime and Punishment*, already canonized as art. High orders of crime fiction wait both at the end and at the beginning of this trajectory: Ford Madox Ford claimed that "the great novels of the world . . . [have all] been mystery stories" (832), and much more recently Martin Kayman wrote, "the novel at its inception is haunted by this eminently secular topic [of crime]. Why was it then, as Lennard Davis puts it, that 'there seems to have been something inherently novelistic about the criminal, or rather the form of the novel seems to demand a criminal content'?" (31).

Philip Van Doren Stern felt there was nothing inherent in the mystery story to limit it as literature: "Its central core is almost always premeditated murder . . . and premeditated murder is one of the greatest themes in all literature: witness such works as *Electra*, *Hamlet*, and *Crime and Punishment*. . . . There is no reason why a tale concerning itself with the most soul-racking deed a human being can undertake should be a silly, mechanically contrived affair. The writer of murder mysteries holds high cards in his hand; if he does not know how to play them, that does not lessen their value" (529). Detective fiction compulsively chooses to treat murder, but fails to realize the values of that theme; detective fiction repeatedly trivializes death.

Like Stern, Sayers argued for the transmutation of detective fiction into literature, but she thought the process should go backward: "We also took occasion to preach at every opportunity that if the detective story was to live and develop it *must* get back to where it began in the hands of Collins and Le Fanu, and become once more a novel of manners" (1929, 31). Was the genre to move forward away from clumsy beginnings, or to return to an ideal moment of origination? Going forward and going backward are sometimes not sharply differentiated in popular fiction: in *The Time Machine*, for example, H. G. Wells proposed a journey into the future, but since the future of the species was a degenerative one, each next stage mirrored a corresponding stage in the past.

In 1972 Julian Symons published a study of detective fiction, *Bloody Murder*, that was devoted to an evolutionary thesis. Symons argued that what detective fiction lacks as literature is character. In 1941 John Peale Bishop wrote that "Simenon's originality was at once obvious to me, and it was not long before I discovered that he was a serious writer, serious in a way that Conan Doyle could never have dreamed of being. . . . [He] has created a form of detective fiction into which real characters can enter. For if his detective is convincing, his criminals are credible" (345).

The key words *character* and *serious* identify the enclosure of the nineteenth-century novel, and this defense recycles arguments designed to win supremacy for the novel over its competitor forms. In particular, it recapitulates a long and complex dialectic of evaluation that went on between the novel and its closest rival, the prose romance, in the early nineteenth century. According to this ranking (as opposed to the contrary adjustment proposed by Hawthorne in the preface to *The House of Seven Gables*), the romance was the lower form, devoted to plot or action, whereas the more evolved novel recentered itself in character.

The most specific form of the evolutionary thesis was couched not so much in terms of character as characters. Since only two are central to the plot, the remedy is simple: the detective failed to pay off in literary currency, so writers must invest in the murderer. Refocus the form on the criminal, and the potential for growth would be as various as in the novel itself. The groundwork was already there because every work of detective fiction contained, however implicitly, the story of a murderer and his or her crime; a story of psychological depth and intensity lay buried in the form.

This was the solution offered in 1935 by Sean O'Faolain in his article "Give Us Back Bill Sikes." The real crime in detective fiction was the narrative suppression of the criminal because the criminal was the only "true principal . . . the one *free* agent, the one person not circumscribed by the necessity of having to catch someone." The criminal was a character, O'Faolain argued, whereas the detective was only a plot function and a detached personality. The so-called character of the detective belonged to the paranoid climate in which alone detective fiction could prosper: "What should we think of him if he interrupted his work, for example, to discuss Blank Junior's doings at Oxford? I think we should very properly conclude, at once, that Blank Junior had a line on the criminal, and we should be very naturally chagrined to find that he had not" (243, 242). Franco Moretti played thematic variations on this opposition: "The difference between innocence and guilt returns as the opposition between stereotype and individual. Innocence is conformity; individuality, guilt. It is, in fact, something irreducibly personal that betrays the individual: traces, signs that only he could have left behind" (135).

According to a third model, detective fiction did not need to change because the form already realized its virtue: to preserve classical narrative, pure storytelling, in a fallen world. According to some writers, detective fiction was the last stronghold of a plain style that had been perversely abandoned by the prevailing literary culture in the 1880s and after. The art thesis is nominally the opposite of the evolutionary thesis: one says that detective fiction is the best art we have in the present decay of culture, the other says that detective fiction should go on (or back) to become art. The art thesis claims that detective fiction need not move in any direction; in a high culture that is rapidly changing, stability is its virtue.

In 1944 Bernard De Voto wrote a simple narrative of a half-century's production of fiction:

> Dissection of motive, exploration of psychological states, social analysis and criticism, economic theorizing, every conceivable variety of thesis and crusade . . . has greatly enriched the novel but also it has steadily diminished the element of narrative, of pure story. . . . [Narrative] expresses a deep and everlasting need which many people bring to literature, and if you heave it out the door it always comes back in through the window. Coming back in through the window it has produced the detective story. The detective story . . . is so popular right now because it is the only current form of fiction that is pure story. (37)

The art thesis was also put forward by an American academic, Marjorie Nicolson, as a repudiation of the avant-gardism of the 1920s: "we have revolted from an excessive subjectivity to welcome objectivity; from long-drawn-out dissections of emotion to straightforward appeal to intellect . . . from formlessness to form; from the sophomoric [that is, stream of consciousness] to the mature" (113–14). These terms are commonly accepted: the emergence of an avant-garde in the last half of the nineteenth century polarized culture and led to the codification of popular fiction; story was crucial to this antagonism.

The presence of story in detective fiction, however evident it was felt to be, was nevertheless problematic. In an essay called "Primitive Narrative," Todorov discussed the critical yearning for a golden age of simple narrative that is always felt to be lacking in contemporary fiction; Todorov, however, reread the *Odyssey*, "that first narrative which should, a priori, correspond best to the image of primitive narrative" and found it "an accumulation of 'perversities,' so many methods and devices which make this work anything and everything but a simple narrative" (1977, 53). The ideal of story answered, in a falsified retrospect, to a desire to resolve the conflict between chronology and logic implicit in narrative.

Edmund Wilson, who had no taste for detective fiction, also repudiated this claim: "It seems to me . . . perfectly fantastic to say that the average detective novel is an example of good story-telling" (1945: 395); and the announcement that the emperor was not wearing his proper clothes was often blurted out in commentary: "Little actually happens [in *The Maltese Falcon*] until the conclusion; why the narrative has been called fast-paced is itself something of a mystery" (Moss 33).

In his structural paradigm for analytic detective fiction, Todorov opposed the *story of the crime* to the *story of the investigation*: the first ends as the actual book begins; the second element is largely what we read. "But what happens in the second? Not much. The characters of this second story. . . do not act, they learn. . . . The hundred and fifty pages which separate the discovery of the crime from the revelation of the killer are devoted to a slow apprenticeship: we examine clue after clue, lead after lead" (1977, 44–45). We indulge in what Moretti called "a long *wait*" (148).

In the case of Ellery Queen's *French Powder Mystery*, there is a short opening unit that could be called the story of the discovery of the crime and a final unit, the solution or the retelling of the story of the crime. The intervening space consists for the most part of interviews conducted by the detective, interviews that go over the same material—the disposition and sequencing of small stretches of space and time—repeatedly. The book moves to a loose narrative beat, primarily governed by a repetition compulsion. The narrator of Roy Fuller's detective novel *With My Little Eye* begins a middle chapter by claiming, "It bores me to write it—it must be even more boring to read it. . . . My life was assuming the repetitive pattern of a compulsive neurotic's" (WMLE 86). An originating fiction would be Edgar Allan Poe's "The Mystery of Marie Rogêt," where various newspaper accounts of the crime and its investigation are compared and contrasted and made the subject of lengthy commentary. Narrative may be the category through which we habitually report gratification in fiction, but we need different terms for structures of this kind, which seem much more critical than narrative.

In contrast to the evolutionary model, what distinguished detective fiction in the art thesis was the absence of character and its attendant psychology: "Character—so worshipped by the psychological novelists—troubles us little. . . . Characters addicted to dependence upon the subconscious or upon the glands need not apply. . . . We grant that our characters are largely puppets, and we are delighted once more to see marionettes dance while a strong and adept hand pulls the string cleverly" (Nicolson 116). Character shifted from a concept of rich verisimilitude to one of post-Freudian perversity. It was an appropriate shift, however, because detective fiction is the last bastion of not one but two crucial cultural values, traditional narrative and sexual decency: The intelligent inquirer "is apt to point out that novels today take in their scope every aspect of human life, including many that our grandparents would not consider fit to be mentioned. Words are freely printed in modern books which a former generation of readers would not have allowed even to be hinted at. A detective story, on the other hand, is by comparison mealy-mouthed. It is, he will observe, favorite reading of the very classes who are most easily shocked by frankness in such matters as sexual behavior" (Hare 83).[1] The strong and adept hand that Nicolson praised is the hand of repression. Detective fiction rejects not only overt sexual reference but the erotic contract of narrative; it is a literature in which repression writes itself. This is the first of many identities of the criminal who is so central to the forms under investigation: he or she is the insider the detective seeks to exclude and the outsider the detective seeks to imprison—emotional perversity, sexuality, subjectivity, art itself.

The last defense of detective fiction replaced high and low with old and new, the art work of the past as opposed to that of the present: "Our evaluation of the world no longer depends . . . on the opposition between *noble* and *base,* but on that between Old and New" (Barthes 1975: 40). Used most often to legitimate science fiction, this position restricted serious art to a historical enclosure like Walter Benjamin's cult of the beautiful or Marshall McLuhan's Gutenberg culture. Such art may have had a positive function in its time but was now reactionary, kept in place by an archaic cultural elite. Accordingly, detective fiction would not evolve into conformity with the novel but had already, in its differences, replaced the novel as the appropriate contemporary form of fiction: "The novel is dying—and very properly—in face of the romance of crime" (Ford 831). Louise Bogan wrote of detective fiction, "Here is this new form, coldly opposed to everything literature stands for" (476). In this model, the cultural ideal was itself cold or cool, and the notion of the text as a puzzle and reading as the activity of filling in gaps resembled McLuhan's fiction of aesthetic response.

If the art defense was a response to high modernism, this defense harked back to the soft naturalism of writers like Robert Louis Stevenson and G. K. Chesterton, who argued that it was possible for fiction to treat its proper subject matter, the urban wasteland, in the spirit of romance. The detective novel attracted them because it promised to encompass this: "The first essential value of the detective story lies in this, that it is the earliest and only form of popular literature in which is expressed some sense of the poetry of modern life" (Chesterton 1902, 4).

There is also a critical mass of commentary that relished the cultural inferiority of detective fiction, and its descriptions and judgments were so unlike those just gathered that it is hard to accept them as statements about the same body of work. These writers reported all sorts of bad things about detective fiction; for example, it was "formulaic," by which they meant mechanical, or it was "conventional," by which they meant inert or dead. Detective fiction was also abjectly repetitive; it consisted of the same few stories written over and over—"Chandler's novels are all variations on this pattern, almost mathematically predictable combinations and permutations of these basic possibilities" (Jameson 647)—unquickened by the immanent values of literary fiction.

Notions of conventionality and repetition in fiction have been turned from their negative bias by the work of structuralist theorists like Vladimir Propp. A word like *formula*, however, still connotes debasement: Gardner's "books seem to have been manufactured rather than composed; they are assembled with the minimum expenditure of effort from identical parts that are shifted about just enough to allow the title to be changed from *The Case of the Curious Bride* to *The Case of the Fugitive Nurse*" (Macdonald 6). This would be bad enough, but the charge also tipped its object into the swamp of consumer capitalism: "Like other commercial products, thrillers require a brand image to promote brand loyalty" (Palmer 9). All art, however, is commerce, though it has been customary to see only popular fiction as commodified; works of literature are seen as valuable in themselves.

As opposed to advocates who believed that detective fiction was evolving into something better, critics hostile to mass fiction asserted that it neither developed nor matured:

> Perhaps the tempo has become a trifle faster and the dialogue a little more glib. There are more frozen daiquiris and stingers ordered, and fewer glasses of crusty old port. . . . But fundamentally it is the same careful grouping of suspects, the same utterly incomprehensible trick of how somebody stabbed Mrs. Pottington Postlethwaite III . . . just as she flatted on the top note of the Bell Song from *Lakmé* in the presence of fifteen ill-assorted guests . . . the same moody silence next day . . . while the flat-feet crawl to and fro under the Persian rugs, with their derby hats on." (Chandler 1944, 393)

Chandler's statement of the case was correct but not necessarily damning. *Development* is an evaluative bluff: you can find it if you have a stake in finding it. Nevertheless, Chandler's perception breaks the literary connection and associates detective fiction with other cultural forms that operate through patterned repetition, from basket weaving to myth-making and, Barthes would add, linguistic "repeating machines" like "school, sports, advertising, popular song, news," forms that do not value or protect individual difference (1975, 40).

The same repetitive process, conflation to a single story, applies to most popular fiction—science fiction, jungle adventure, the Western, the romance. The sameness is contractual and requires the writer to satisfy a desire for genre similarity. In detective fiction, however, as with literature, the sameness must hide behind nominal signs of change, what Freud calls a "date-mark" (1953 [1908b], 147); the reader not only wants the same Dick Francis, but the latest Dick Francis. Detective fiction even demands a kind of development (the development that is abdicated as force of genius is written into the sequence as detail): a different title, a different setting, the aging of the hero, a later set of contemporary references, etc. Holmes changed from a laboratory technician to a fin de siècle aesthete between *A Study in Scarlet* and *The Sign of Four,* and in later works he became more and more conservative, in keeping with Conan Doyle's own ideological shifts. Poirot aged between his first appearance in 1924 and his last—but his "last" appearance was actually written in the early 1940s and sealed in a vault, not to be published until 1975 under the title *Curtain* (Sanders and Lovallo 373).

Another way of saying the same bad thing was to charge detective fiction with being *conventional,* with depending too heavily on conventions or featuring them—as when, in Freeman Wills Croft's *Cask,* the wine barrel containing the corpse bears the return address of Rue de la Convention. In detective fiction as in art, conventions codify what most violates credibility. Detective fiction has been a frequent object of parody, and a list of what parodists seized on to release comic energy from the form would also be a list of its major conventions. In literature, conventions are regarded as scaffolding, indifferent elements of framework, whereas in detective fiction they are the crucial relays of meaning and pleasure.

Writing of the sensation novel, a reviewer in the *Quarterly* for 1863 wrote: "Every game is played with the same pieces, differing only in the moves" (quoted in Phillips 26). A century later Umberto Eco wrote:

We might compare a novel by Fleming to a game of football, in which we know beforehand the place, the number and the personalities of the players, the rules of the game, the fact that everything will take place within the area of the great pitch. . . . [Actually,] it would be more accurate to compare these books to a game of basketball played by the Harlem Globe Trotters. . . . We know with absolute confidence that they will win: the pleasure lies in watching the trained virtuosity with which the Globe Trotters defer the final moment, with what ingenious deviations they reconfirm the foregone conclusion, with what trickeries they make rings round their opponents. (58)

The deviations, ingenious or otherwise, that Eco referred to are the conventions in variant forms. Brigid Brophy speculated that the "countless stories we generically call 'the detective story' resemble a group of myths, inasmuch as there is really only one skeleton detective story, on which detective writers invent variations consciously . . . and more or less ingeniously" (12). Italo Calvino made this the condition of all literary works: "that is, they are 'modelled on fixed structures and we might almost say on prefabricated elements—elements, however, that allow of an enormous number of combinations.' Thus, 'what can be constructed on the basis of these elementary processes can present unlimited combinations, permutations and transformations'" (quoted in Hilfer xii). Many of these conventions are common to the tradition of male romance, high and low.

Within analytic detective fiction, for example, the convention that the detective be an isolated amateur may be satisfied through the fictions of a regular policeman on vacation or in a foreign country, an older policeman on his last case before retirement, or a mod or hippie policeman like Raven or Serpico. In hard-boiled detective fiction this convention takes the form of a detective who is in business for himself. The opening of Hammett's *Maltese Falcon* became paradigmatic when Sam Spade's partner, Miles Archer, was killed and Spade ordered his name scraped off the door. Although Spade used that as a reason for rejecting Brigid O'Shaughnessy, it was a crime committed by the form itself. In the espionage thriller, the convention of the isolated amateur may appear as character—like Leamas in Le Carré's *Spy Who Came In from the Cold* who is a cynical and alienated member of his intelligence section—or as structure—as when an agent is cut off from the authorizing agency because reasons of state determine that no official record of the agent or the mission may exist.

Cultural critics also charged analytic detective fiction with bad writing; the form lacks style, lacks the very thing that makes writing art: to the serious writer of fiction, writers of detective fiction "are ingenious illiterates, skilled in the devising of plots and puzzles but content to propound them in words shovelled together anyhow. Rhythm, texture, characterization lie outside their ken. Their figures are the crudest cutouts. . . . Even at the high crime level of the Queen's Awards there can be found stories so commonplace in texture that, were the subject anything but crime, one would not read beyond the opening phrases" (Strong 155). Such a charge, however, usually came from a critic of high culture who had gone slumming; George Elliott wrote, "whether Chandler will ever be elected into literary history is another question. The odd thing is that he is known and enjoyed by those who have the power to vote him in—critics, writers, scholars, literary historians" (354). Literature and popular fiction are in economic competition, and literary judgments also create or depress markets.

How do we picture the critic reading (or not reading) that bad text? Does she intuit the quality of the whole from an opening phrase or two, like the Jamesian novelist with her glimpse of a French family at table as she passes the door: it "lasted only a moment," but "she was blessed with the faculty which when you give it an inch takes an ell" (James 1956, 13). Or does he set his eyes in a dull stare and force his head to move mechanically over that cratered wasteland of prose? Whatever the technique, it is a great price to pay for truth: "It never seems worthwhile wading through all that terrible prose, the typecasting of the characters and the inane exchange of cliches that passes for dialogue in the average Agatha Christie" (Alvarez 169). By his own admission, Wilson did not read the books: Christie's "writing is of a mawkishness and banality which seems to me literally impossible to read. You cannot *read* such a book, you run through it to see the problem worked out" (1952, 326).

Some commentators made a division in the genre: analytic detective fiction might be well crafted but it definitely lacked style. Hard-boiled detective fiction, on the other hand, had style to give away; in a sense it was nothing but style. D. C. Russell claimed that "Chandler writes . . . with an artistry of craftsmanship and a realism that can rank him with many a famous novelist. In his hands, words do become beautiful and wonderful things" (123). André Gide wrote that Hammett's dialogues "can be compared only with the best in Hemingway" (quoted in Blair 303), but Hammett himself suggested that style may be another form of bad writing: "Asked why he had stopped writing he said that he found he was repeating himself. 'It is the beginning of the end when you discover that you have style'" (quoted in Symons 1981, 619). Thomas R. Edwards offered another sense of the situation: "It's hard for sophisticated people to like something simple without overrating it . . . [and] I'd recommend more caution in judging [detective novels]. . . . Even an addict can see that they follow a formula, are unevenly written and less than convincing in their efforts at social and psychological commentary. Yet the genre itself still pleases" (13).

Judgments about the relative merits of writing were wonderfully open: Wilson stated that "as a writer . . . [Hammett] is surely almost as far below the rank of Rex Stout as Rex Stout is below that of James Cain" (1952, 327). Definitions of good writing and style may be impossibly slippery, but insofar as style can also mean *signature* and implicates the author as a soulful presence in the work, analytic detective fiction was by and large a writing without style. Scandalous instances of the lack of style would include the marketing of several pseudonyms for a single author; the ending of Charles Dickens's *Mystery of Edwin Drood* (after it had been claimed by detective fiction) by other hands; the collaborative writing of a second Philip Trent mystery; and the production of additional Albert Campion and James Bond books after the deaths of their original authors.

But after all, detective fiction cannot be badly written because it is read with pleasure. "Fleming 'writes well'; in the most banal but honest meaning of the term. He has a rhythm, a polish, a certain sensuous feeling for words. That is not to say that Fleming is an artist; and yet he writes with art" (Eco 62). The dialectic of good and bad is always ready to collapse and reverse itself: George Orwell divided the field into good, bad, and "good bad"—a third category made necessary by the presence of popular art—when he attempted to articulate Kipling's virtue as a writer: "Most of Kipling's verse is so horribly vulgar that it gives one the same sensation as one gets from watching a third-rate music-hall performer recite 'The Pigtail of Wu Fang-Fu' with the purple limelight on his face, *and yet* there is much of it that is capable of giving pleasure to people who know what poetry means." By the end of the essay the "good bad" has swallowed up art: "Even his worst follies seem less shallow and less irritating than the 'enlightened' utterances of the same period, such as Wilde's epigrams or the collection of cracker-mottoes at the end of *Man and Superman*" (135, 139).

The distinction between popular and art fiction has been tied to a prior division between two kinds of reading: "Popular literature never seems the kind of literature that you are reading for the first time. It always seems like something you are reading for the second or third— or millionth—time" (Fiedler 200). Roland Barthes made almost the same distinction: "Whence two systems of reading: one goes straight to the articulations of the anecdote, it considers the extent of the text, ignores the play of language (if I read Jules Verne, I go fast: I lose discourse, and yet my reading is not hampered by any verbal *loss*—in the speleological sense of that word); the other reading skips nothing; it weighs, it sticks to the text, it reads, so to speak, with application and transport" (1975, 12). The distinction can be made in other ways: Harold Bloom, for example, differentiated between the text and the tale—"The tale somehow is stronger than its telling, which is to say that Poe's actual text does not matter." In a neatly folded example, he quoted C. S. Lewis on the fantasies of George Macdonald: Lewis defended Macdonald's work as myth—which "does not essentially exist in words at all"—as opposed to literature. When Lewis went on to apply the same test successfully to Franz Kafka's *Castle*, Bloom quickly set the record straight: "Clearly mistaken about Kafka, Lewis was certainly correct about [*Lilith*]" (23–24).

Here, then, were two different acts of inscription that seemed indistinguishable. Their packaging was virtually the same, and both were made of words and obeyed the same system of composition. Both presented worlds of men and women thinking, feeling, speaking, and behaving in various ways. Like England and America, they had nothing in common but language and not even that. Each provided a different kind of pleasure: art fiction was incapable of providing the pleasure that detective fiction afforded.

Once reading becomes plural, alternative models become available for the system of popular fiction, as, for example, Umberto Eco's metaphors of football and basketball. A writer in 1932 compared his reading of detective fiction to the game of "even and odd" that Poe offers in "The Purloined Letter" as a model for detection: "The experienced reader works by a sort of rule of contraries, and follows only the most unlikely clues, unless indeed he is dealing with a particularly wily writer, in which case he may find it convenient to turn on the limelight to the obvious and concentrate on that" (Adams 191). Stephen Leacock agreed: "from reading so many of these stories I get to be such an expert that I don't have to wait for the finding of the body. I can tell just by a glance at the beginning of the book who's going to *be* the body" (1938, 328).

Detective fiction is made out of writing that is somehow not meant to be read in the same sense as literature is read. Since the inside of this fiction reproduces its outside (an assumption examined in chapter 2), the unpacking of a conversation between a spy and his contact in Adam Hall's *Quiller Memorandum* may serve as a paradigm for readership. In the stressful situation depicted, speech consists of overlays of arbitrarily assembled linguistic mechanisms designed to operate in a binary manner; what is read is the final distribution: "Between us we set three quick traps and sprang them. . . . My leading trap had been set to find out if he were still testing me. He was. Otherwise he would have said, 'No. . . .' Instead, he had trapped me back at once with the one word—'yes'—to see if I'd spring it. I did: with 'Schultze.' Even then he wouldn't let me off the hook, because I had only gone half-way, telling him that I knew he would have drawn a blank at the box-office. That was how they hadn't found me; he wanted me to tell him how they had" (QM 10).

On the other hand, far from lacking style or good writing, detective fiction can only afford a little of either. The relaxation of style that reconstituted C. Day Lewis as Nicholas Blake, J. I. M. Stewart as Michael Innes, or Gore Vidal as Edgar Box represents an upper limit of style permissible to analytic detective fiction. Edmund Wilson "complains that he cannot go slow enough to read Agatha Christie for values because she forces him to hurry on and find out how the puzzle is solved" (in De Voto 36). It may be that detective fiction was only written badly for Wilson because Wilson read it too slowly. The reading of detective fiction is characterized by an overriding of syntactic pace. I suggest that a range of reading rates collaborates in the production of the kinds of detective fiction: at the slow end of the range are hard-boiled fiction and the spy thriller, from Ambler to Le Carré, which can provide a relatively elegant dance of treachery and deceit and ask to be read slowly enough for individual works to be hailed as existential masterpieces.

Critics hostile to popular fiction regarded a detective story as throwaway, or disposable, fiction. As such, analytic detection fiction contains what it is, for a specific charge made against that subgenre is that most of it is throwaway fiction, something between filler material and a false text—"as such-and-such is pronounced irrelevant, so-and-so a red herring, a large body of textual signifiers is exiled to a state of no status" (Miller 1979, 102). "It's odd isn't it . . . that it all began with a photograph which was a fake in the first place, and a fake that had really nothing to do with the murder in the second?" (MCH 245).[2]

On the other hand, detective fiction is charged with making extraordinary, though artificial, demands on the reader. Anthony Trollope complained of the reading program in the sensation novel, "I can never lose the taste of the construction. The author seems always to be warning me to remember that something happened at exactly half-past two o'clock on Tuesday morning; or that a woman disappeared from the road just fifteen yards beyond the fourth milestone" (195–96), and Chandler commented scornfully on the similar situation in analytic detective fiction: "There may be one somewhere that would really stand up under close scrutiny. It would be fun to read it, even if I did have to go back to page 47 and refresh my memory about exactly what time the second gardener potted the prize-winning tearose begonia" (1944, 393). Is detective fiction such a confusing mixture of the relevant, irrelevant, and misleading that one cannot read it at all? Critics and apologists alike agree that detective fiction directly counters the perversities of modernist literature, yet what Chandler scorned is precisely the model of reading proposed for T. S. Eliot's poetry and James Joyce's fiction. The fact that Jake Barnes wears a Princeton polo shirt is mentioned only twice in *The Sun Also Rises* (pages 45 and 194 of the Scribner edition) but it carries a major meaning in that work.

At the end of Arthur Conan Doyle's *Hound of the Baskervilles*, Sherlock Holmes reenters the fiction after a long absence and proceeds to throw it away in a manner that is common in detective fiction. He tells Watson that he has in fact been present all the while, as "an unknown factor," making his own observations and deductions, constructing his own, unreported fictions. Watson cries, "Then my reports have all been wasted"—but those reports are the text we have been reading. As a last moment in that work, Holmes condemns detective fiction to instant erasure in another way: "So each of my cases displaces the last, and Mlle. Carère has blurred my recollection of Baskerville Hall. Tomorrow some other little problem . . . will in turn dispossess [it]."[3]

W. H. Auden began his essay on detective fiction as the personal confession of an addict:

> For me, as for many others, the reading of detective stories is an addiction like tobacco or alcohol. The symptoms of this are: firstly, the intensity of the craving—if I have any work to do, I must be careful not to get hold of a detective story for, once I begin one, I cannot work or sleep till I have finished it. Second, its specificity—the story must conform to certain formulas (I find it very difficult, for example, to read one that is not set in rural England). And, thirdly, its immediacy. I forget the story as soon as I have finished it, and have no wish to read it again. If, as sometimes happens, I start reading one and find after a few pages that I have read it before, I cannot go on. (400)

To take Auden at his word would account for many of the features of such reading: the compulsion to read, the demand for similarity, the disappointment and, afterward, shame.

Addiction was a pervasive metaphor in commentary on detective fiction: Stern wrote that "[the readers] take their daily dose of murder with the frenzied enthusiasm of a drug addict" (531–32); Wilson complained of a fan letter that it "has made my blood run cold: so the opium smoker tells the novice not to mind if the first pipe makes him sick. . . . The addict reads not to find anything out but merely to get the mild stimulation . . . of the suspense itself of *looking forward* to learning a sensational secret" (1945, 396); and Blake answered his own question, Why do we write detective stories? "Because the drug addict (and nearly every detection-writer is an omnivorous reader of crime fiction) always wants to introduce other people to the habit" (398). The works themselves can be read as narcotic, inside and out— "The notable amounts of tobacco and other drugs consumed by the great detectives assist in glamorizing a reading that is itself drugged and addictive: able to account for its pleasure only in terms of sheer compulsiveness ('I couldn't put it down,' 'I had to finish it'). From the distractedness which is the language of the text, we are in turn distracted, by the promise of the 'fix' which is fixed meaning" (Miller 1979, 101). If, like food or drugs, literature can also be used to control strong feelings or anxiety, this would help to explain one of the more singular facts about detective fiction: that it is narrative without affect.[4]

Grand addictions called "manias" arose at explosive moments in the history of popular fiction, notably the intense cultlike activities surrounding the figures of Holmes, Mike Hammer, and Bond. The image and exploits of each hero detached from the texts and stimulated devotion or dependency in many readers. The primary symptom was the delusion that a fictional character was real: "a lot of people believe in Mike Hammer—they write letters to him, asking his advice about certain things, giving him tips and so on" (Southern 76). Allen Dulles talked with Fleming about new tools and gadgets, and he put his "people in [the] CIA to work on [a Bond gadget] . . . as a serious project, but they came up with the answer that it had too many bugs in it" (Tornabuoni 18). Groups of devotees banded together in fan[atic] clubs and studied the texts with scriptural intensity; addictive reading involves not only a hunger for the end but an obsessive attention to detail. "Bond fans seize at once on any little contradiction, any mistake: when Fleming wrote that the Orient Express had hydraulic brakes instead of compressed air . . . when he allowed Bond to order asparagus in *bearnaise* sauce instead of *mousseline*, hundreds upon hundreds of letters arrived to point it out and put him right" (Tornabuoni 14–15).

The adored object at the center of this frenzy is not merely an exemplary hero, he is also an addict; that is what gives him his edge. Holmes is a cocaine addict, and his drug use is written into his tales. Bond is an alcoholic: "When he has no action to occupy him and he is restricted to everyday office routine Bond becomes restless, irritable, nervous, smokes too much, drinks to excess: so much so that his chief, M, had to send him to a clinic in Sussex for a health cure" (Tornabuoni 25). The rhythms of detection belong to larger rhythms of manic-depression featured most prominently in the texts of Sherlock Holmes: depressed between cases, he feels alive only when he is working (Roth 167). One of Holmes's predecessors, William Legrand, is also "subject to perverse moods of alternate enthusiasm and melancholy" (Poe 1902, 5:96). The task the detective accepts, the extraordinary case or mission, brings him to life: "He was concerned with more important things. He was *working*. He was in effect once more O'Mara" (DI 48). Of course this is a literary tautology—the hero of a story only has an identity when the story is being told—but it is also an addictive structure.

Like the reader of detective fictions, Holmes is addicted to cases. Investigating crime gives him a high. In Wilkie Collins's *Moonstone*, detection is a fever: "If there is such a thing known at the doctor's shop as a *detective-fever*, that disease had now got fast hold of your humble servant" (Collins 1966, 160); and, in the presence of a crime, Lord Peter Wimsey "rampages off . . . like the jolly old war-horse sniffing the T.N.T" (SP 18). The kind of work our heroes and our readers engage in produces a special kind of excitement.

As a characteristic of his reading addiction, Auden mentioned inability to defer the excitement, the need to finish the book that night. William Ernest Henley, reviewing H. Rider Haggard in 1887, made the same point: "*She* had to be read 'in a gasp.' 'For my part I couldn't put it down until I had finished it'" (quoted in Cohen 102). The hero of *Caleb Williams*, a book frequently described as part of the narrative trajectory leading up to detective fiction, had "an invincible attachment to books of narrative and romance": "I panted for the unravelling of an adventure, with an anxiety perhaps almost equal to that of the man whose future happiness or misery depended on its issue. I read, I devoured compositions of this sort. They took possession of my soul" (Godwin 4).[5]

Another symptom of the reading addiction is the need for repetition: the readers, Stern wrote, "know all the tricks; they have followed all the detectives, erudite, dumb, exotically Oriental, depressingly homespun; they are familiar with all the ways a human being can be put to death . . . there is nothing new to them under the sun, and they complain continually that mysteries get worse and worse. Yet Heaven help the writer who tries to give them anything but the old familiar brand" (532). The notion of the formula now refers to an interface, like the combination to a safe, a set of circumstances that matches or keys the shape of desire. In his essay "The Analysis of a Detective Story," Charles Rycroft repeated Geraldine Pederson-Krag's parallel "between the voyeur's inability ever to be satisfied with his peeping and the detective story addict's compulsion to read endless variations of the same basic mystery tale" (115).

Auden indexed a specific craving, the need to read stories that are set in rural England, and details of this kind make all the difference to desire. Mystery and detective fiction consists of a narrow range of stories, yet a given reader will receive pleasure from only a few of these and may not even be able to read the others. Somerset Maugham went on record as liking detective fiction and disliking another kind of thriller, the "shocker." He read "shockers only by accident, when I have been misled by the title or by the wrapper into believing that I was about to embark on a story of crime" (46). The specific contours of the formula are easily communicated by code words and images: a cover picture, a squib, a summary, or a short extract on the inside page. A phrase like "in the tradition of Ambler" means something very different from "in the tradition of Fleming." While the addiction lasts the reader will insist on reading these two or three stories on some relatively fixed frequency, although the titles must be different and the dates of publication must be current.

The detective novel ends in disappointment; its solutions do not fulfil the promise of ratiocination held out by the form. This is the last of the points in Wilson's indictment: "It is only when I get to the end that I feel my old crime-story depression descending upon me again—because here again, as is so often the case, the explanation of the mysteries, when it comes, is neither interesting nor plausible enough. It fails to justify the excitement produced by the picturesque and sinister happenings, and I cannot help feeling cheated" (1945, 395). Northrop Frye suggested that the logic of the solution must be weak; that an inadequate solution is actually a defining feature of the genre. The case against the criminal is "only plausibly manipulated. If it were really inevitable, we should have tragic irony, as in *Crime and Punishment* . . . [where] there can be no question of any 'whodunit' mystery" (46–47). But in a review of *Barnaby Rudge*, Poe announced that the explanations of all narrative enigmas or puzzles fail to satisfy the reader, that disappointment is inevitable in all explained forms (1902, 11: 58–59).

Short of taking on a detective novel and arguing with its solution, there is no advancing this proposition. Marcello Truzzi made a perfectly matter-of-fact observation when he wrote, "the simple fact is that the vast majority of Holmes's inferences just do not stand up to logical examination. He concludes correctly simply because the author of the stories allows it so" (70). Commentators apologized for the clumsy logic of Poe, Conan Doyle, Christie, etc., but hastened to add that this was understandable since they were pioneers in the form.[6] This makes no sense; logic is not subject to development; and it suggests that readers of detective fiction have only been dreaming under a spell of logic. Solutions that do account for everything—like those to certain fantastic tales discussed by Todorov—tend to be elaborate and to satisfy only a compulsion to explain. Todorov, echoing Sir Walter Scott, notes a curious inversion whereby an adequately explained tale becomes more fantastic than the corresponding miraculous one would have been (Scott 1966, 11; Todorov 1973, 46).

Other symptoms of our addictive relationship to popular narrative are that the reading is done in a trance state and followed by feelings of shame. Leslie Fiedler described the experience of watching television—"sitting half asleep in our chairs, or lying in our beds somewhere between dreaming and waking"—as the "fulfillment of all to which the popular arts have aspired from the start" (203). Detective fiction has, for much of its career, been written and read under a ban of shame, which it shares with other forms of popular fiction. George Elliott wondered "whether Chandler will ever be elected into literary history [because] he is known and enjoyed by those who have the power to vote him in—critics, writers, scholars, literary historians." The argument continued: "And even so it begins to look as though his nomination for membership may not be seconded. . . . Ashamed of their pleasure . . . [they] would deny it any literary value" (354–55). Elliott concluded that shame is a shame. When Wilson's derogatory articles on detective fiction provoked a rush of angry letters, he decided that "detective-story readers feel guilty, they are habitually on the defensive, and all their talk about 'well-written' mysteries is simply an excuse for their vice, like the reasons that the alcoholic can always produce for a drink" (1945, 395).

If the reading of detective fiction is a compulsive and highly ritualized activity, then perhaps Auden's is the most successful definition. He may have been making a personal confession, but he also defined detective fiction by ticking off its salient rituals. Poe also made a distinction between popular and art fiction that provided the beginning of a checklist of differences: "After perusal of the one class, we think solely of the book—after reading the other, chiefly of the author. The former class leads to popularity—the latter to fame. In the former case, the books sometimes live, while the authors usually die; in the latter, even when the works perish, the man survives" (1902, 11: 206). Fiction, according to Leslie Fiedler, "is intended to be bought and taken home, where one of two things can happen to it. It can be used or played with and then thrown away, like Kleenex or a child's toy; or it can, for reasons hard to identify at least *a priori*, be kept and treasured, like a diamond or a grand piano" (198).

2 ∎ Borderlines and Boundaries

IF I INSIST AT THE BEGINNING OF THIS STUDY THAT DETECTIVE fiction is not about crime, corpses, detectives, police forces, and security agencies, I will be claiming no more than many mystery writers have confessed: "I find no cause to regret my conclusions that crime drama owes virtually nothing to the real-life criminal; that it cannot usefully employ such knowledge of him as is available; that all it really takes from crime is an idiom for the expression of an idea that is not concerned with the actuality of crime" (Vickers 191). "The detective story is no more a picture of real life than *Hamlet* is a picture of how people really talked and behaved at the court of Denmark in the Middle Ages. Murders have been committed from time immemorial and their perpetrators discovered and punished, but *never* in the way that detective writers represent" (Hare 62). Geoffrey Hartman claims that he doesn't "believe for a moment that Chandler and Macdonald tell it like it is" (219), and Bruce Merry introduces his study of spy thrillers by insisting "at every point that the thriller writer is not *mimetic:* the narrative image rarely corresponds to the known and ascertainable facts about real-life spy networks and intelligence operations" (1).[1]

The generic self-consciousness of detective fiction is primarily devoted to this eccentricity. Works of detective fiction regularly consider the problem of realism and acknowledge a great divide between the actual investigation of crime and the investigation of crime in detective fiction. The narrator of Philip Macdonald's *Rasp*, for example, observes that Boyd "showed none of the chagrin commonly attributed to police detectives when faced with the amateur who is to prove them fools at every turn" (R 17–18). A given work will usually conclude that its depictions have little in common with detective fiction, because detective fiction, as everyone knows, is artificial and unrealistic; as Joel Black stated, "Detective fiction is the most inauthentic and artificial of all the varieties of crime literature" (45). This separation ceremony is a ritual, and it is no more to be credited than Defoe's insistence, in the preface to *Robinson Crusoe*, that "the Editor believes the thing to be a just History of Fact; neither is there any Appearance of Fiction in it" (3). Although this tendency to expose the genre from within is quite superficial, it nevertheless points to a flagrant absence of realism.

In *The Billion Dollar Brain*, Len Deighton has his hero dismiss the contours of the spy thriller: "Every senior-grade Russian intelligence man knows that I came into town on the train last night. They know who I am just as I know who they are. No one puts on false hair-pieces and pebbles in one shoe and sketches the fortifications any more" (quoted in Merry 49). Deighton blows the cover story of cover stories: they are not strategies of operation and survival, but games that fiction plays. Deighton has not, however, dispensed with the conventional paraphernalia of spy fiction; he is self-consciously recharging them for another round of play. On the other hand, the text can just as easily confuse the distinctness of fiction and fact, and that also calls the adequacy of the representation into question. In Robert Merle's *Day of the Dolphin*, a scientist apologizes for the flurry of clandestine activity disrupting his laboratory: "I know, it sounds like a grade-B spy movie, a Flint or a James Bond. Unfortunately, Arlette dear, it's true. James Bondism is becoming the air we breathe" (quoted in Merry 159).

During detective fiction's classical period, it was complemented by a literature of parody. Yet it is hard to read the pieces by P. G. Wodehouse, James Thurber, or S. J. Perelman as outside voices because there is such a harmony of tones across this border. Detective fiction featured self-parody: "I have an ulterior motive, said he, throwing off his side-whiskers and disclosing the well-known hollow jaws of Mr. Sherlock Holmes" (UD 27). " 'Go on,' he continued acidly. 'Say it. "You have the facts, Bathgate. You know my methods, Bathgate. What of the little gray cells, Bathgate?" Sling in a quotation; add: "Oh, my dear chap," and vanish in a fog of composite fiction' " (OD 198–99). "I've never liked this scene. . . . Detective confronts murderer. Murderer produces gun, points same at detective. Murderer tells detective the whole sad story, with the idea of shooting him at the end of it. Thus wasting a lot of valuable time. . . . Only murderer never does. Something always happens to prevent it. The gods don't like this scene either. They always manage to spoil it" (LL 170).

The passage of time, however, reveals parody where none was intended. By 1945 analytic detective fiction seemed "manifestly ridiculous" to one writer: "If we were to judge from most murder stories, murders are most prevalent among the middle and upper classes and as often as not are solved, not by the police, but by private individuals possessed of bulging brains and a vast assortment of strange knowledges" (Russell 124). What is really at issue here is not just the discrepancy between representation and fact, but the scandalous face of representation itself, for the conventions of detective fiction are in themselves absurd violations of the obvious. In 1944 Chandler attacked analytic detective fiction on behalf of a new detective literature of the real. His essay "The Simple Art of Murder" was a response to Sayers's defense of detective fiction in her *Omnibus of Crime.* Chandler claimed that Sayers herself realized "that her kind of detective story was an arid formula which could not even satisfy its own implications. . . . It was second-grade literature because it was not about the things that could make first-grade literature. If it started out to be about real people . . . they must very soon do unreal things in order to form the artificial pattern demanded by the plot. . . . They became puppets and cardboard lovers and papier-mâché villains and detectives of exquisite and impossible gentility" (1944, 394–95). Chandler exposes analytic detective fiction, and twenty-two years later Chandler's formula is exposed by Ross Macdonald, who wants realism in detective fiction to start with himself: Chandler "invested the sun-blinded streets of Los Angeles with a romantic presence. While trying to preserve the fantastic lights and shadows of the actual Los Angeles, I gradually siphoned off the aura of romance and made room for a more complete social realism."[2]

For detective fiction, genre is life, and it is as if instructions regularly go out along the line of development to say anything you have to say to protect the survival of the genre. This is an old story even within the domain of literary realism, but it will be useful to expose its delusions once again. For Chandler, realistic detective fiction began with Dashiell Hammett: "The realist in murder writes of a world in which gangsters can rule nations and almost rule cities. . . . Where no man can walk down a dark street in safety because law and order are things we talk about but refrain from practising; a world where you may witness a hold-up in broad daylight and see who did it, but you will fade quickly back into the crowd rather than tell anyone, because the hold-up men may have friends with long guns, or the police may not like your testimony" (1944, 397–98). This passage has been quoted often before, authorized so often to bear the meaning of hard-boiled detective fiction. It is simply not so. Chandler describes a territory very different from the one his readers travel (see Knight 77). Chandler and his commentators have *forgotten* the contents of Chandler's and (with two early exceptions) Hammett's fiction. Eddie Mars in *The Big Sleep* may be identified as a "mobster," but he has no criminal connections and no field of operations. His role is thoroughly private: he is a cuckolded husband who works up a blackmail scheme; he is one of three blackmailers in the book. Chandler has a habit of including a "notorious" gangster in each of his novels as a peg on which to hang cynical comments on corruption in America. The characters who play the game of *The Maltese Falcon* move through a nominal San Francisco without ever touching any familiar aspect of the city. Whether written by Hammett, Chandler, or Macdonald, hard-boiled detective fiction is as private in its characters and concerns and as confined in its social implications as a country-house murder story.[3]

One branch of detective fiction, the spy thriller, insists on political currency. This condition can be satisfied by quite irrelevant set pieces like the lecture on German concentration camps in Ambler's *Epitaph for a Spy*. His *Background to Danger* opens with a dissertation on the complex interrelationships between the worlds of industrial capitalism and political intrigue, but the tale quickly settles down into an isolated contest between Kenton and two Russian agents, on the one hand, and a special villain, Colonel Robinson, on the other. We very soon forget, because we do not need to remember, that what is in contention here are photographs that would implicate the Pan-Eurasian Petroleum Company in the internal policies of Rumania, as the photographs move back and forth from one side to the other until Robinson is killed and Kenton can go home again. There is no Rumania in this tale, no hostile borders, no armies waiting to be mobilized. The political density of Graham Greene's *Confidential Agent* is more sustained, but eventually that story also becomes a very private affair. The details are not important here, but the political dilemma is resolved by a rival lover who hires men to impersonate the police. These games are played in the spirit of Stevenson's confessional preface to *The Dynamiter:* "Horror is due to ourselves, in that we have so long coquetted with political crime; not seriously weighing, not acutely following it from cause to consequence; but with a generous unfounded heat of sentiment, like a schoolboy with the penny tale, applauding what was specious" (Stevenson iii).

At the threshold of analytic detective fiction, social and political history was put under a ban by a generic boundary line, which hard-boiled detective fiction and the spy thriller would also respect. As Holmes, Gregson, and Lestrade examine the room in which murder was committed in *A Study in Scarlet*, Lestrade announces "in a pompous and self-satisfied manner" that he has just made a "discovery of the highest importance." He points to a dark corner of the room where the word *rache* [revenge] is scrawled in blood-red letters. Holmes ignores this and turns back to his tape measure and magnifying glass. He tells Watson later that this "was simply a blind intended to put the police upon a wrong track, by suggesting Socialism and secret societies. . . . Simply a ruse to divert inquiry into a wrong channel" (SSt 30, 33). The wrong channel is social reality. In "The Bruce-Partington Plans," Holmes asks Watson if there is anything of interest in the papers and Watson records his awareness that "by anything of interest, Holmes meant anything of criminal interest. There was the news of a revolution, of a possible war, and of an impending change of government; but these did not come within the horizon of my companion" (HLB 913).

In *The Maltese Falcon* the district attorney wants to investigate Floyd Thursby's murder as a gangster killing, but Spade ridicules such a notion. Later he tells his lawyer that Bryan is "nursing a gambler's-war pipe-dream" (MF 133, 135). The realism of Chandler's commentary is already scorned as the stuff not of realism, but of wilder fiction: the pipe dreams referred to are Hammett's own early baroque fantasies, *Nightmare Town* and *Red Harvest*. The ruling out of politics in the spy thriller is worked through other conventions: for example, the old boys of Buchan's club world fall from grace if they talk as if they have accurate knowledge of the political intrigue in which they engage; they treat it as if it were a school cricket match. The ban on political realism may also be announced through a structural figure stipulating that the hero both is and is not a member of the security service—that is, both is and is not a historical agent—since the agency, if called to account, will deny any knowledge of him.

A certain lack of realism has long been acknowledged as a matter of proportion: the detective form will usually not venture beyond the point where the crime is explained and the criminal identified. This is another formulation of the boundary between fiction and history: "Neither the murder nor the trial nor the punishment is portrayed in classic detective literature" (Kaemmel 59). "The murderer, once detected, is positively rushed off-stage at the end" (Brophy 30). Detective fiction avoids arrests, trials, imprisonments, and executions, and it stops at the point where the fiction would have to go public and engage the machinery of the state. Parody has been quick to seize upon this disjunction: "Don't be afraid to hang the criminal at the end. . . . We want him *hanged*; don't let him fall into the sea out of his aeroplane. . . . Hold him tight by the pants, till you get him to the gallows. And *don't* let your criminal get ill in prison, or get so badly wounded or so heavily poisoned that he never gets tried because he is 'summoned to a higher court'" (Leacock 1942, 218–19). "The criminal, robust though he seemed only a chapter ago when he jumped through a three-story window after throttling Sub-Inspector Juggins half to death, is a dying man. He has got

one of those terrible diseases known to fiction as a 'mortal complaint' "
(Leacock 1938, 335). Here, as always, the artificiality of the form is
expressive: by refusing to hand the criminal over to the legal system, it
denies referentiality.

Authors give various reasons for the premature closure of detective
fiction. An interesting one, found in articles with titles like "A Lawyer Looks at Detective Fiction," is that the much-vaunted solutions
(upon which the constitution of analytic detective fiction rests) would
not hold up in court. This damaging fact is also represented within the
work when the detective knows who the criminal is but has no real
evidence—"I have all the threads—or rather, all the threads which
lead inexorably to the murderer of Mrs. French. They don't make solid
proof, such as is demanded by our venerable courts of law and our
prosecuting system" (FPM 219).

Another reason given is that the mechanics of arrest and trial are
anticlimactic, but this is not necessarily the case; what is true is that
the exciting mechanics of arrest and trial belongs to another popular
genre. A surprising amount of detective fiction (and its commentary)
is taken up by *boundary statements*, which reassert generic or modal
boundaries; in this case, a separation between detective fiction and
an older branch of popular fiction that provides gratification through
the conduct of a trial and execution.[4] Detective fiction lies about the
shape of crime, detection, and the legal system, but these lies signify.
The artificial, even absurd, conventions are insisting "look, I am a detective story, I am not the story of a famous crime; I am an analytic
detective story, not a thriller with professional spies," and so on. So
many of the signs in these texts refer, as Jean Baudrillard puts it, to
"the reticulation of their networks" (quoted in Linker 46). The generic
self-consciousness of detective fiction may be the most telling act of
signification in popular fiction.

The apologists for analytic detective fiction discussed in chapter 1
have granted that it lacks realist appeal. In its defense, they have often
allowed the genre to be understood as a purely formal structure, like
a puzzle or game, an affair of rules governed by an aesthetic of which
the crucial, and probably the only, principle is *playing fair*. The presence of articulated rules governing fair play is a unique feature of

analytic detective fiction, and, if nothing else, attests to the artificiality of the form. Bogan has made the exciting suggestion that the same impulse that drove the genre to insist on outside rules acts within the form as a concern for narrow boundaries—"within its closed universe, Poe further limits its locale by inventing the convention of the locked room" (476)—and most detective fiction does take place in strictly confined space.

These lists of rules—S. S. Van Dine provides twenty, whereas Ronald Knox gives only ten—are extremely redundant, repeating a few articles of concern so that what is communicated is not principle but prayer, a litany for getting it right. The rules seem to collapse as follows: there must be a single detective who solves the crime openly and methodically (Van Dine, nos. 1, 2, 4, 5, 6, 9, 14, 15; Knox, nos. 2, 6, 7, 8, 9). There must be a single criminal, a private and relatively prominent individual (Van Dine, nos. 10, 11, 12, 13, 17, 19; Knox, nos. 1, 5). The crime must be murder (Van Dine, no. 20; Knox, nos. 3, 4, 10). There must not be a love story, and there should be no literary style (Van Dine, nos. 3 and 20).

These constraints are designed to make sure authors play fair with their readers: "If the tale is to meet the definition of . . . 'a challenge to the use of one's wits,' it follows that the solution must be one which the reader could reasonably arrive at for himself. And this requirement is nowadays, quite rightly in my view, interpreted with great strictness. The author must play fair with the reader" (Hare 59–60). This ethic is almost as old as the form, as a remark from Owen Wister's *Virginian* indicates, "If I'd knowed that one was a detective story, I'd have got yu' to try something else on me. Can you guess the murderer, or is the author too smart for yu'? That's all they amount to" (139). But the aesthetic of playing fair just doesn't hold. As stated or practiced, it is confused and illogical, belonging to a notion of reading as "getting it right," and that is, in another place, one of the constitutive acts of literature.

The model of fair play is in conflict with another equally active one, which adds up to getting it wrong. According to the first, the reader is expected to be a peer of Holmes, not Watson. Yet the inevitable explanation for the Watson figure is that he represents the reader's level of understanding. According to this second model, readers are expected to be overwhelmed by the detective's brilliant deductions and inferences. Are we subordinates or equals in this contract?

This model is a bluff by admission: what the detective novelist really must do is play fair *and* mislead. Cyril Hare explained what he meant by fair play: "inducing [the reader] . . . to disbelieve or overlook what is under his nose all the time. . . . Basically, when you strip a detective plot to its bones, I think you will usually find that it is by misleading you over [an essential factor], that the detective has succeeded" (72–74). The would-be writer is provided with "rules" for playing fair and hoodwinking the reader at the same time: the writer "may use the old conjuring technique, and immediately after presentation of the clue introduce a bit of action so exciting and important that the reader forgets all about the casual mention of the clue that went just before"; or "the author may bury the clue among a number of equally casual things which have no great significance"; or "the clue and its application are separated by fifty or a hundred pages; put together, the two are significant, but if the reader has forgotten the first one, the second one will mean nothing to him" (Rodell 271–72). The writer must do exactly what the criminal has done: "every clever crime is founded ultimately on some one quite simple fact—some fact that is not itself mysterious. The mystification comes in covering it up, in leading men's thoughts from it" (IFB 72).

The rule that the crime must be murder has no obvious connection with the myth of fair play, yet writers insist it is indispensable: "Where there is no murder," H. Douglas Thompson wrote, "it almost seems like wasting the detective's valuable time" (135). Archie Goodwin asserts that only the Nero Wolfe cases that involve murder get written up (RB 2). The reasons behind this requirement are specious—as the most serious crime it proceeds from the most serious motive—and circular—murder is popular; it sells books. Maugham simply made it a brute element of appeal: "Theft and fraud are crimes, too, and they may give rise to some very pretty work in detection, but they arouse in me an interest that is no more than languid" (46).

The expanded convention is even more curious: the crime must be murder, but there should be only one: "the writer should be chary of his murders. One is the perfect murder; two are permissible, especially when the second is a consequence of the first" (Maugham 47). This completes a triad in the genre: one detective, one criminal, one murder. In fact, the rule has less to do with murder than with marking the difference between English and American, analytic and hard-boiled detective fiction. As Harrison Steeves wrote, "That is the fault of the American authors of crime stories; they can never be satisfied with one or even two murders; they shoot, poison, or blackjack en masse; they turn their pages into a shambles and, by surrendering thrill to sensationalism, hold their reader in a grip that he resents" (520).

The demand for a single murder is reflected in the murder itself, which is always a "clean kill." The killer must also be clean or at least cool. As one detective argues, cool killers are the only ones that cool detectives can catch: "The thug who smashes the skull of a pal in a dark alley with a bludgeon, or gives him dope, is the obscure one. He usually goes free. Logic and deduction can't find him. . . . [But] take the other kind of criminal—the cool, calculating amateur, the man of intellect, who seeks retribution, and who covers his crime with the chain of circumstance. He is the man we catch. The one dominating peculiarity of this kind of criminal is his egotism. Sherlock Holmes can catch him. Why? Because he doesn't kill on the impulse of the moment. He meditates. He premeditates. He schemes" ("UM" 95).

One murder is thrilling; more than one is sensational. There is a difference being marked here, and it has to do with more than numbers. Something is being prohibited in detective fiction, obviously not crime, but crime made too much of. According to R. Austin Freeman, "the true detective fan is impatient or disgusted if too much is made of the morbid sensations of crime and crime-hunting" (10). This crime surplus is then projected onto hard-boiled detective fiction, although it is almost as aseptic a form. What is being forbidden is affect. "There is no murderer in detective fiction so foul as the author," O'Faolain wrote, because he has killed emotion and sympathy (242). The detective story is "notoriously fatal to any real emotion" (Bishop 345). The goal of the one permissible murder is "excitement without anxiety, suspense without fear, violence without pain and horror without disgust" (Watson 79).

Nicolson is quite shameless about this:

"I dreamed all night of people lying in pools of blood," declared my unsympathetic friend. . . . "How *can* you read those things and go to sleep at all?" And she will never believe me quite a human being again because . . . I can put out the light and sleep like a child . . . the reason being that where she has seen, with horrible distinctness, an old man lying in a pool of his own blood, I had seen—a diagram. . . . We seek our chamber of horrors with no adolescent or morbid desire to be shocked, startled, horrified. We handle the instruments of crime with scientific detachment. It is for us an enthralling game, which must be played with skill and science, in which the pieces possess no more real personality than do the knights and bishops and pawns of chess. . . . But those who seek to read character and emotion into our pieces . . . miss the essence of this most entrancing game. (118–19)[5]

Alvarez, who thinks that analytic and hard-boiled detective fiction are worlds apart, nonetheless finds an "air of moral lobotomy" in Hammett's novels (169). Detective fiction is self-conscious about this feature as well and often internalizes the discrepancy between the event and affect: "And suddenly Appleby found himself shocked at the quality of pure intellectual pleasure that he himself could get from this wretched business" (SS 90).

The absence of affect in detective fiction proves nothing, it has been argued, except the fiction's lack of worth: "yet the fact remains that most of these stories seem to flourish in an emotional vacuum, and that fact would seem at the very outset to come perilously close to barring them from the realm of art" (Steeves 517). On the other hand, one might account for this singular fact in a nonjudgmental way, by looking for a contemporary body of writing that tells a comparable story, but that is all affect and has been equally condemned in the name of art. Such writing is easy to find in a ragged stretch of forms called Gothic or horror fiction. It is usually listed among the historical antecedents because of the obvious resemblances between explained or rationalized Gothic and detective fiction.

One strand of Gothic fiction, the haunted house story, was mass-produced in England and America from the 1860s through the first two decades of the twentieth century: haunted house stories and detective stories are roughly contemporary literary events. Between them are a remarkable structural similarity and a remarkable semantic difference. At the turn of the century, a corpse found in an old room belonged not to crime but, more often, to spectral influences; it belonged to the past of that room as supernatural ambience. Todorov sees an obvious kind of equivalence between the two forms: "It has often been remarked, moreover, that for the reading public, detective stories have in our time replaced ghost stories."[6] He finds the relationship valid "only for a certain type of detective story (the 'sealed room') and a certain type of uncanny narrative (the 'supernatural explained')," but all detective fiction is of the locked-room type, that's what the rules imply (1973: 49–50).

The resemblances between a typical haunted house story and Poe's "Murders in the Rue Morgue," for example, are structurally precise. There is a room in which incredible and terrifying events have taken place, and their influence still infects that space but does not go outside. Into these rooms, a disbeliever in the supernatural will dare to go—a rationalist, a materialist, and a skeptic. In the older form, he runs out screaming, marked with some emphatic sign of profanation, white hair or madness. In the later form, he exorcises or neutralizes a place that had been dominated by old anxieties.

In a mediating work like Bulwer-Lytton's "Haunted and the Haunters," the hero is a man who likes to sleep in haunted houses; he responds to the challenge of a good ghost, and, like the detective, is irreverent in his attitude toward the supernatural. The first strange sign that he sees is, appropriately enough, a footprint, and, like the detective, he reads the ground: reads a story in the shape and placement of that footprint. The work is a mix of both forms; the hero-narrator describes everything as if to show that he is withholding nothing, but is attempting to play fair with the reader. He is driven out of the room in terror and solves the mystery by locating the source of the strange effects, which, the text claims, are not supernatural, although they come from a superior order of human power.

The relationship between detective fiction and the tale of terror is the major feature of the Poe canon. His tales of terror are all affect; they are told by a narrator who can barely contain the hysterical energy that threatens to overwhelm the self and the narrative line. On the other hand, the tales of ratiocination are narrated in a level tone of voice that describes, analyzes, quantifies, and explains. And yet, in "The Murders in the Rue Morgue" the room in its wild disorder—the corpse of one woman jammed up a narrow chimney aperture and, outside, the older woman with her throat so entirely cut that her head falls off as the men attempt to raise her—is clearly the territory of the sensation tale. Dupin, however, only reads and thinks that scene. The excited crowd that rushes up in response to the cries from behind the locked door is organized as a matrix of linguistic possibilities (each speaking certain languages and understanding certain others), and Dupin contacts the frenzied orangutan through a classified ad.

In his study of the fantastic tale, Todorov identifies the two tendencies of literary Gothic—"that of the supernatural explained . . . as it appears in the novels of Clara Reeves and Ann Radcliffe; and that of the supernatural accepted . . . which is characteristic of the works of Horace Walpole, M. G. Lewis, and Maturin"—with two genre categories, the "uncanny" and the "marvelous" (1973, 41–42). He identifies the fantastic itself with the uncertainty felt by the reader and the central character about which of two orders of effect the experience belongs to: "The fantastic occupies the duration of this uncertainty. Once we choose one answer or the other, we leave the fantastic for a neighboring genre. . . . The fantastic is that hesitation experienced by a person who knows only the laws of nature confronting an apparently supernatural event" (1973, 25). The affect appropriate to the fantastic dissipates as soon as we are offered a solution. In detective fiction, Gothic emotion disappears with the appearance of the detective, and it remains in abeyance as long as he is on the scene. That is one reason why he is almost constantly present. In *The Hound of the Baskervilles*, however, Watson is left alone for much of the fiction, and, as a result, the modality immediately reverts to Gothic.

The ability of the detective to conquer space or dominate circumstances is not in question in analytic detective fiction. The detective is in control even when he is not in control: in *The Sign of Four*, as Holmes lowers his lamp to find some traces of the criminal, "a startled, suprised look come[s] over his face" when he sees a wall thickly covered with naked footprints, barely half adult size; but he "had recovered his self-possession in an instant. . . . 'I was staggered for the moment,' he said, 'but the thing is quite natural. My memory failed me, or I should have been able to foretell it' " (SF 112).

Within this context, analytic detective fiction can be understood as a repudiation of Gothic, a fictional ghost-chasing. An early detective series by William Hope Hodgson was devoted to the investigations of Carnacki, the Ghost-Finder (CGF), who only accepts cases where the certainty of a supernatural presence is high. Detective fiction is also opposed to science fiction, which obscures the distinction between natural and supernatural. This genre rationalizes all phenomena; any Gothic trope—demonic beings, metamorphosis, dematerialization—is asserted to be within the limits of an expanded universe of explanation. The invisibility of the protagonist of Wells's *Invisible Man*, for example, is repeatedly acknowledged to be "marvelous," but the reader is not able to know whether it is marvelous as the supernatural is or marvelous as the imagined effects of a contemporary or a futuristic science are, and the distinction really doesn't matter.

All of the forms of mystery fiction dealt with here are incompatible with Gothic, but only analytic detective fiction quotes it as an originating moment. The statement that detective fiction lacks affect is imprecise; these works often begin in a highly sensational manner. The detective novels of Christie, John Dickson Carr, and Margery Allingham open as full-fledged works of Gothic fiction. This is generally the case with the only works that gripped Auden, stories set in an English countryside. The atmosphere, however, is far from pastoral, it is ghost-ridden: "the underlying horror which seems always to lurk somewhere beneath the flamboyant loveliness of a lonely English countryside in the height of summer, a presence of that mysterious dread, which the ancients called panic, had become startlingly apparent" (GCM 111). One of the functions of the Watson is to evoke the Gothic that must be remembered in order for it to be dispelled again; it is a function familiar enough to be subject to parody: "There's something terrible going on here. Can't you feel it? In this lonely old mansion—poor thing!—polluted with a miasma of corrupt and rotting ambitions, black hatreds, hideous impulses, rheumatism, catarrh, coughs, colds, and indigestion" ("Veendam" 324).

Detectives do not solve crimes. The "affairs" they investigate are special events—the spy of fiction is only sent on special missions. They are described as events of rare occurrence and embedded in elaborate frames; they can be called crimes only by virtue of a transcendentaliz-ing modifier. They are "remarkable" crimes or "extraordinary" crimes: "We are, I feel convinced, in [the] presence of one of those mysterious crimes the causes of which are beyond the reach of human sagacity" (MLq 51); "It's the most damned complicated, incomprehensible busi-ness I ever want to come up against" (OD 137). The crime in analytic detective fiction is actually a *miracle* and is so termed by the police or the Watson: "We are faced," Arsene Lupin claims, "by mysteries which are, so to speak, absolute and compact, which offer no gap through which the keenest eye can see and which it is useless to hope to clear up by ordinary methods" ("LH" 229). The crimes of "The Murders in the Rue Morgue" and "The Purloined Letter" are literally miracles. The two events—the murder of a woman and her daughter and the concealment of a letter—have certainly occurred and yet it can be dem-onstrated that neither of them could have taken place: the room of the first could neither be entered nor left, and the letter of the second was not in the room that contained it. The purpose of the frequent maps and timetables is to define the crime as an impossibility within the known space and time of this private corner of the universe.

Chesterton's Father Brown solves crime in the service of his God be-cause his theology does not admit of supernatural interference. But first he must prove that so-called miracles are actually crimes. In many tales, the context of the miracle is a new religion that challenges Brown's Christianity either by asserting the supernatural or by denying sin. The first predecessor tale cited by Sayers in her *Omnibus of Crime*, a biblical anecdote about Daniel, exhibits this balance between a true rationalism and a false supernaturalism. The detective (Daniel) and the criminals (the priests of Bel) are locked in a narrative trap. Each day Bel consumes "twelve great measures of fine flour, and forty sheep, and six vessels of wine"; if Daniel can explain how the food and drink disappear the priests will die, but if the priests can prove that Bel is a hungry god then it is Daniel who is up for it (1929: 51). Here, the reality of the supernatural would mean the death of the detective.

The crimes that fictional detectives solve, moreover, are miracles in a box (in Poe's "Thou Art the Man" and Freeman Will Crofts's *Cask* the corpses are literally sealed into wine cases). This is the internal equivalent of the outside rules; the locked room mystery is the pure detective story. Chesterton insisted that the "good detective story . . . is concerned with an enclosure, a plan or a problem set within certain defined limits" (1921, 27). The fiction is further sealed off by tropes of scandal and suicide: the first is an arbitrary horizon invoked as a reason for not letting any word of the crime get out; the second seals the crime at the other end.

Analytic detective fiction is notorious for its extreme and ornate framing, murders committed during the performance of an opera or play, for example. The enclosure can be the Orient Express roaring through the countryside, sealed off by its very mobility, and, within that, the Calais Coach sealed off from the rest of the train. Or the crime may be contained within a textual frame: in a Father Brown story, a suicide note is reread as a statement of murder after Brown notices that the paper is the wrong shape. When he is told that the slice cut from one edge was not big enough to include other words, he asks, "What about quotation marks?" (AA 58). And the genre is equally constricting with regard to time: early on, watches and clocks tended to stop at the precise moment of the murder. Analytic detective fiction usually takes place within a very short compass, and there is a corresponding convention that no time is to be lost in solving the crime, because clues quickly go stale or evaporate.

In the suspense novel and the spy thriller, these constraints are intensified by the pressure of a deadline, a moment when the book must stop. The hero is often given an impossible task to perform—to save a friend from execution or Western civilization from annihilation—and then given an impossibly short period of time in which to perform it. This is the timing of sports, as Buchan attests: "then it [a journey] becomes a 'sporting event,' a race; and the interest which makes millions read of the Derby is the same in a grosser form as that with which we follow an expedition straining to relieve a beleaguered fort, or a man fleeing to sanctuary with the avenger behind him" (vi).

However differently they may read, Hammett's and Ellery Queen's novels have much in common. Like *The French Powder Mystery* (most like Poe's "Masque of the Red Death"), *The Maltese Falcon* moves through a succession of close interiors without the representation of an outside. A notable feature of the spy thriller is a penultimate episode where the hero is imprisoned in a box that is designed to inflict torture, very much like the dungeon in Poe's "Pit and the Pendulum." Escape from this box is impossible—and yet the hero escapes. This structure also belongs to the showman escape artist, to Houdini: a man is hand-cuffed and gagged, wrapped in chains, sealed in a bag, sealed in a box with metal bands; the box is wrapped in chains, lowered into the East River, and, before a minute has passed, a head bobs in the water. The equivalent structure in hard-boiled detective fiction would be the small bedroom in which Beaumont is imprisoned in Hammett's *Glass Key*, guarded by an "apish man" who plays with him like a punching bag or yo-yo. Every time Beaumont comes to, he painfully pulls himself up and staggers to the door where the apish man sits, waiting with sadistic amusement for just the proper moment of imbalance to send Beaumont reeling back again (GK 83–84).

In Ian Fleming's *Doctor No*, starting in a room of which the "walls were entirely naked except for . . . [an electrified ventilation grille] just below the ceiling," Bond must move through a set of "boxes." Next to this room is a circular shaft of polished metal "about four inches wider than Bond's shoulders," which he must climb, and this leads to a section of red-hot tunnel filled with giant tarantulas (DN 154–55). In another spy thriller, Desmond Bagley's *Freedom Trap* (FT), the hero meets his control, Mackintosh, in an office in a dingy building reached through a maze of streets in London. He is told that he must cosh a postman in another office building and steal from him a yellow box of Kodachromes that contain diamonds. He must do this in order to be brought into court and sentenced to an impregnable maximum security prison. He must get into this prison, from which there is no breaking out, so that he may do just that. Once inside, he will con-tact a ubiquitous gang of criminals called the Scarperers who engineer impossible escapes. Eventually, he escapes by means of a large cherry-picker, which is moved over the wall, extending before it a platform of steel.

The miracle box of analytic detective fiction and the death-and-torture box of hard-boiled detective fiction and the spy thriller have been identified as adult and juvenile substitutes: "Show [Sexton Blake] . . . a sheet of writing in which the fist is alternately regular and irregular, and he will be unable to tell you, from the incidence of the palsied patches, that it was written in a train travelling between Norwood and London Bridge. But nail him down in a crate and throw him off the bridge at Westminster and while you are still dusting your hands and saying 'That's that' he will be right there behind you. Only an adult will accept a *tour de force* like the first. Only an adult will sneer at a *tour de force* like the second" (Turner 127).[7] An opposition that once constituted the difference between adult and juvenile thrillers now aligns analytic with the two other branches of detective fiction. Such categorical swings are not uncommon. And the boxes of detective fiction are themselves special forms of earlier enclosures common to romance: the underground cave in which Robinson Crusoe hides himself from cannibals; the closet from which Clara Wieland hears two aggressive male voices threatening to alternately stab or strangle her to death; the cave in which Tom Sawyer and Becky Thatcher are trapped; the archaic stone trap in which Allan Quatermain is locked at the end of *King Solomon's Mines.*

Because of the apparently supernatural character of the crime, the analytic detective may himself be identified as a wonder worker: "you must be a wizard to have guessed"; "I can't at present see the faintest possible loop-hole . . . but you always were a marvel" (MAS 111, 89). "How in the name of all that is wonderful did you get these facts" (SF 93). "Why, that's true, sir . . . though how you come to know it, Heaven only knows" (SSt 35). And the detective is not above deliberate mystification; in the tradition of other imperialist heroes such as Herman Melville's Ahab or Mark Twain's Hank Morgan, he exploits the rhetoric of supernaturalism as a cover for his power trip. His mystifications are usually codified in linguistic forms that could be called the *oracle* or *enigma:*

"But she was alone," objected the detective.

"She was murdered when she was all alone," answered the priest. (AA 75)

The *prophecy:*

"It's jolly difficult to know how to treat him."

"That difficulty will not exist long," pronounced Poirot quietly.

John looked puzzled, not quite understanding the portent of this cryptic saying. (MAS 33)

Or an alternate form of the miracle itself, the *bombshell:*

That wonderful observer will pick up the umbrella the murderer has dropped in the death chamber, glance at it for an instant, and nonchalantly remark that he is five feet eleven, with a stoop in his shoulders and a scar below his left armpit; that he spent three years in America when a boy, and dissipated his estate before he was twenty-five; that his third wife is buried in a Scotch kirkyard, and that his aunt on the spindle side makes admirable gooseberry wine; that he speaks modern Greek with a Cockney accent, lost his favourite pyjamas in the wash, and is fond of . . . melodrama, which he invariably witnesses from the third row of the pit. (Zangwill 268)

Despite the detective's collaboration with the Gothic—"My hobby, one of my hobbies, is investigating ancient superstitions. High and low magic; occultism, necromancy, divinations, all the mumbo-jumbo of literally raising the devil. It fascinates me like a toy" (RWM 91)—he is a realist and a rationalizer of miracles. He demonstrates endlessly that there are no supernatural interventions into the affairs of this world: "Are we to give serious attention to such things? The agency stands flat-footed upon the ground, and there it must remain. The world is big enough for us. No ghosts need apply" (CBSH 1034). The detective draws a new and true map of the world, one in which space and time are consecutive and inclusive. He acts as a representative of empirical philosophy and bourgeois capitalism, and yet the space in which he does so is bounded and empty.

3

The Constant Character

APOLOGISTS AND CRITICS ALIKE HAVE DISCUSSED HOW DEFICIENT detective fiction is in its characterization, and yet the power of the form is surely character, not, perhaps, as depth or variety, but as singular character or character type. Detective fiction displays this character, and to a large extent it must be his thoughts, speech, and gestures that lure readers back to the stories. The motive for serialization, which is stronger here than in any other form of popular fiction, must be a desire to visit him regularly and repeat the pleasure of being introduced to notations of idiosyncrasy and decor that await readers at the threshold of another Holmes or Hercule Poirot story.

There is, nevertheless, a disparity between that golden word *character* and the power of personality that rides on the exchanges of the text. For the detective himself, it has been asserted, is not really an exception to the absence of character in detective fiction: he too is flat and thin, a bundle of functions without adequate subjectivity. Blake approved of this conception of character and imagined an ideal hero "who shall be as undistinguished as a piece of blotting paper, absorbing the reactions of his subjects; a shallow mirror, in which we see reflected every feature of the crime; a pure camera-eye" (404). Most commentary, however, regards this lack of subjective density as a fault. What Fausto Antonini wrote of James Bond could certainly be said of the majority of detectives: "He has no intimate psychological dimensions, has no emotive or rational depth" (104).

What, then, are the contents of his powerful draw? And if he has no contents, no depth or inside, why are certain forms of superficial inscription so attractive? What metaphorics of character are put into play? For one basic type of analytic hero the easy answer is, he is a thinking machine: "he is not a complete human being; he is an incarnate analytical intellect, and little more" (Hare 66). One of the early detectives was given the epithet, the Thinking Machine.[1]

The image of the machine connotes logic and thus reinforces the definition of the genre as a puzzle, and it connotes science, which adds a dimension of contemporary relevance to the genre. It also excuses the indifference of the heroes to the misery of their fellow characters. Finally, the image of the machine is self-reflexive: it codifies what we already know about the hero from the outside: that he is a fixed, undeveloping character type whose performance is an attractive redundancy.

The other distinctive protagonists, the hard-boiled detective and the amateur spy, may be likened to another kind of machine, an engine: the "iron horse" of early Westerns or, better yet, the "little engine that could." "To John Buchan, I think, can be credited the prototype," Michael Gilbert wrote, "the normal, decent, muddle-headed, obstinate man; a little stronger in the leg . . . a little cleverer than you and me, but not much. It's his obstinacy that gets him through. He refuses to recognize defeat" (114). A better word than "obstinacy" might be *perseverance*, which, according to Samuel Smiles, a mid-nineteenth-century British author of self-help books and industrial biographies, was the motto of George Stephenson, the railway pioneer. A name like Bulldog Drummond expresses perseverence and tenacity, the ability to move ahead undeflected by time or circumstances. This trait is shared with the heroes of adventure fiction by Haggard, Edgar Rice Burroughs, and Jack London, where it is framed as survival rather than investigation. In either case, perseverance is also rationalized as the ethical imperative of *duty*, the first requirement of imperialist enterprise.

When Holmes makes his first appearance, in *A Study in Scarlet*, he is a version of the engineer-hero of Wells and Dreiser; when he appears in *The Sign of Four*, he has been recast as a Bohemian and aesthete. Helmut Heissenbüttel has written of a strong pressure in the form to disguise the detective. The disguises he refers to, however, are not assumed faces, although they were used by early detectives, for example, Eugène Sue's Narcisse Borel—this man "had his skin stained . . . and face completely shaved, so as to be able to assume the different disguises necessary to his dangerous expeditions; for it was often necessary for him to unite the sudden transformations of a comedian with the energy and courage of a soldier." The disguises are, instead, distracting traits: "Sherlock Holmes is a Persian slipper with shag tobacco in it . . . a keen face; a deer-stalker hat; a love of music and of his own violin" (Heissenbüttel 89; "D" 439; Hare 66). To this may be added the disguise of distracting roles, because the detective has too many characteristics; he is "simultaneously a clairvoyant and a scientist, a ghost and a student of human character, a master of disguises and the ultimately honest man" (Schwartz 446).

The engine is disguised as an Edwardian dandy, yet the ornamentation (if that is what it is) is work of some intensity and holds much of the charm of these texts. The ornamentation, moreover, is expressive and resonant, whereas the essential structure is mechanical and usually unfulfilled.

Which is the disguise? Why was the detective so persistently displayed as a dandy, fop, silly ass, glutton, gourmand, anal compulsive, cynic, *ennuyé*—characterizations that might seem to undermine the logic and method that the genre claims as its justification? These questions refer only to the analytic detective, although the answers have implications for the other protagonists as well. Why does Chesterton tell us so often that Brown is insignificant-looking? Why is Poirot anal-compulsive—dust on the mantelpiece or a tilted picture sets his nerves quivering. Why is Gideon Fell an antiquarian? Why is Nero Wolfe so reluctant to leave his apartment; why does he collect orchids? Why are Lord Peter Wimsey and Albert Campion aristocrats who pass themselves off as dim-witted fops and speak in silly school-boy banter? The answers to these questions occupy chapters 4 and 5.

Mark Twain was fascinated by detective fiction as a fable of social manipulation, and he expressed this as crude parody. In such works as "The Double-barreled Detective Story" and *Tom Sawyer Detective*, he gave the detective role to a boy, in *Pudd'nhead Wilson* to a permanently arrested adolescent: he chose a radical and reductive base for the character type, and it functioned as an unmasking. In Arnold Bennett's *Grand Babylon Hotel*, an American millionaire reflects on why he is involved in detecting and spying; he decides he has been influenced "by a natural spirit of adventure" and "a mere childish, obstinate desire to carry this one through" (155). With Twain, I identify an adolescent core in the detective character: at a moment of insight in *The Schirmer Inheritance*, the hero realizes that the "talented, ambitious, pretentious Mr. Carey, with his smug, smiling family . . . and his Princeton and Harvard degrees, *liked* playing detectives. . . . The elaborate defenses of his youth, the pompous fantasies of big office chairs . . . were beginning to crumble, and . . . the pimply adolescent was belatedly emerging into the light" (SI 138–39). For James Bond, however, the word "adolescent" is redemptive and makes most of the difference between wrong and right action: "It struck Bond that Colombo had made a good life for himself. . . . It was a criminal life—a running fight with the currency laws, the State tobacco monopoly, the Customs, the police—but there was a whiff of adolescent rascality in the air which changed the color of the crime from black to white—or at least to grey" (Fleming quoted in Amis 80).

One of the differences between art and popular fiction is that the latter often consists of two parallel tracks, adult and juvenile. The differences between them are obvious: the juveniles are rougher and simpler and have an adolescent detective. Eddie Parks, the "Newsboy Detective" of George Ade's parody, has "an open countenance, a flashing eye and a determined look. Such is the youth who at the age of nine has made himself a most celebrated detective in the great city of Chicago, the terror of all criminals" (18–19).

Twain's "Double-barreled Detective Story" even dramatizes a conscious antagonism between the juvenile and the adult detectives—they are also opposed as backwoodsman and urban detective, as well as representatives of American and British culture. Vacationing in the American West, Sherlock Holmes is confronted by a youthful counterpart, Archy Stillman. The criminal, Fetlock Jones, is also an adolescent: he is Sherlock's nephew, and he has nothing but contempt for his uncle. When committing a crime, it is safest to have Holmes at one's side; Fetlock knows that "he can't detect a crime except where he plans it all out beforehand and arranges the clues and hires some fellow to commit it according to instructions" (1958, 451). Stillman exposes Holmes's solution to the crime as wrong in every detail and offers a triumphant solution in exchange. Soon after, Holmes is hanged in San Bernardino, mistaken for another man.

The pioneers of detective fiction wrote on both tracks: Conan Doyle wrote boys' books; Max Pemberton edited a boys' magazine, *Chums*; and Arthur Morrison wrote a child's adventure, *Hole in the Wall*. Later writers of mystery and detective fiction also wrote fiction for boys: for example, Stevenson, Buchan, Edgar Wallace, Geoffrey Household, Ambler, and Leslie Charteris. In a collection for juveniles entitled *Spies and More Spies* are pieces by Symons, Carr, Gilbert, and Ambler (Turner 15–16).

Other works of masculine adventure—books like *Treasure Island, Kim, King Solomon's Mines, The Time Machine*, and *War of the Worlds* —collapse such a distinction; they are subject to a law of literary gravity that, after a critical period, moves them from an adult to a juvenile library. Not only do certain books cross the border, but their rhetoric indicates that the transference had already been written into the text. Charles Dickens's *Oliver Twist* takes us to the London underworld, the site of vast criminal networks; but what we are shown are gangs of *boys*. This discrepancy can be read as a fulfillment of the book's linguistic logic, for the opening presented a simple substitution code in which "boy" means "thief"—looking at a boy, adults intuitively know that this is someone who was born to be hanged. Male popular fiction betrays the operation of this code. In works like *Tarzan, Stranger in a Strange Land*, and *Superman* comics, the narrative unfolds the prowess and achievements of the infant, the adolescent, and the adult male as a continuous and coordinated sequence.

Reading "boy" as "hero" may well explain the relationship between juvenile and adult adventure, mystery, and detective fiction. The transfer between them operates through the dialectic that Leo Braudy posits for generic development itself: "Genre films essentially ask the audience, 'Do you still want to believe this?' Popularity is the audience answering, 'Yes.' Change in genre occurs when the audience says, 'That's too infantile a form of what we believe. Show us something more complicated' " (179). If detective fiction were adolescent fantasy, the one discrepant rule of detective fiction—that there may be no love interest—would make sense, and we would not need the alibi that it is forbidden as a distraction to method. As Sigmund Freud stated, "anyone who knows anything of the mental life of human beings is aware that hardly anything is more difficult to them than to give up a pleasure they have tasted. Really we never can relinquish anything; we only exchange one thing for something else. When we appear to give something up, all we really do is to adopt a substitute" (1920, 46).

If adult popular fiction is a replacement for adolescent fantasy, it works through a process of extrapolation. Where the child is powerless and vulnerable in an adult world, the fantasy denies this and substitutes extravagant counterformations: "Chandler was always dreaming. He dreamed of being more attractive than he was, taller than he was, less trammelled than he was, braver than he was" (James 1979, 137). The invariable features of extrapolation would be the invulnerability and invincibility of the hero.[2]

One could almost grade the various forms of popular fiction on how nakedly they extrapolate from the infantile will to power: Westerns and jungle adventures are inhibited from making their heroes Supermen, Living Torches, or Fantastic Hulks, but they can and do posit extraordinary strength and agility: they suggest invincibility in their language and arrange for invincibility in their construction. Works of science fiction play a double game by presenting vulnerable heroes who possess transcendentally powerful weapons. Detective fiction substitutes one form of power for another, uncanny intelligence for extraordinary strength. On the other hand, the intelligence of detective fiction is generally misunderstood to be superhuman; and the hero of prowess often has this quality in reserve: brought to new life by the scream of Jane Porter, Tarzan packs the history of detective fiction into his instinctive moves—"For a moment he scrutinized the ground below and the trees above, until the ape that was in him by virtue of training and environment, combined with the intelligence that was his by right of birth, told his wondrous woodcraft the whole story as plainly as though he had seen the thing happen with his own eyes" (Burroughs 154).

Surely one of the functions of the silly-ass disguises of Wimsey and Campion is to bring dialogue and behavior back into confused proximity with juvenile modes. In the opening of Sayers's *Murder Must Advertise*, Wimsey appears (in disguise), "chucking pennies over the parapet to that brass band. I got the bombardon twice. The penny goes down with a tremendous whack, you know, and they look up all over the place to see where it comes from and you dodge down behind the parapet" (MMA 41). In the opening of *The Gyrth Chalice Mystery*, Campion is introduced as a "tall thin young man with a pale inoffensive face, and vague eyes behind enormous horn-rimmed spectacles. . . . He was carefully, not to say fastidiously, dressed in evening clothes, but the correctness of his appearance was somewhat marred by the fact that in his hand he held a string to which was attached a child's balloon of a particularly vituperant pink" (GCM 19). The murder in Ngaio Marsh's *Overture to Death* has been committed by a gun inside a piano, which is rigged to go off when the soft pedal is played. One of the policeman says disgustedly that "It's like one of those affairs in books." When Roderick Alleyn asks what sort of book would have inspired something like this, the policeman says "one of the fourpenny boy's yarns in paper covers like you buy at the store in Chipping. I used to buy them myself as a youngster. There's always a fat lad and a comic lad and the comical chap plays off the fat one. Puts lighted crackers in his pants and all that" (OD 101).

Many detectives show themselves most splendidly in the company of children, with whom they have an instant rapport: In Carter Dickson's *Night at the Mocking Widow*, a group of children are on the street when Sir Henry Merrivale arrives, and "an electric shock seemed to spark and quiver through the group." The object of their admiration is Sir Henry's large suitcase on wheels, and "conscious of eyes upon him—he did not note the fifteen pairs of adult eyes behind the window-curtains—H.M. guided the suitcase casually, with one finger, as though leading in a Derby winner. . . . Children and dogs poured across the street." Merrivale proposes a race between the suitcase and a dog, and young Wyatt is "overcome by the stranger's brilliance." The suitcase accidentally starts rolling and it rolls down the high street and bumps into Colonel Bailey, who will later be identified as the murderer and a demented writer of poison pen letters (NMW 17–19, 36–38).

The name for the Imperial Secret Service in Rudyard Kipling's *Kim* is "The Great Game." Kim looks forward to the time when he can engage in this colorful and exciting life, but he is told that he is too young and must wait till he is older. The text provides equations that are made to be reversed: you must grow up before you can play the game; you have to grow up before you can be a child. Many statements in adventure fiction are constructed to be read this way: the narrator of Erskine Childers's *Riddle of the Sands*, for example, is told an incredible story of German conspiracy by Davies. He resists being lured into adventure, and he looks at Davies "trying to see the man through the boy, to distinguish sober judgement from the hot-headed vagaries of youth." On the contrary, readers of male popular fiction want to see *the boy through the man*, and if given a compacted formula—seeing the boy through the man through the boy—so much the better. The narrator wants to see in Davies a figure of both juvenile and adult power, one who will manfully authenticate a tale that only a boy would believe and lead him through it triumphantly. Davies is that "man," although the data to support this claim are often conveyed in clauses like, "once set on the road he gripped his purpose with child-like faith and tenacity" (RS 99).

It is a rare detective tale that does not transform its chosen men into boys: "I actually felt light-hearted. I might have been a boy out for a spring holiday tramp, instead of a man of thirty-seven, very much wanted by the police" (TS 31). The metaphoric register is regularly used to key the fiction in obvious ways, so that Brown has a "high and almost childish voice" and Campion wears "an expression of almost childlike discomfort" (AA 19; GCM 156).

The striking aquiline face of Sherlock Holmes, reinforced by the screen image of Basil Rathbone, has provided a profile for the amateur detective, but the faces in the work of contemporary and later writers are far different. They are images of infantilism and adolescence that reflect, through a fictitious young manhood or middle age, the original and enduring fantast. Among the detectives who have achieved popularity, there is little adult physiognomy, little muscular manhood; instead, we have a large group of wispy-haired, pale-eyed young men and fat eccentrics: Brown, with a face "as round and dull as a Norfolk dumpling" (AA 7); Reggie Fortune, who, "in spite of . . . middle age," looks "a rather plump twenty-five. . . . An irreverent damsel christened him 'Cherub,' and the name has stuck. . . . His blue eyes have still . . . a wistful childlike surprise at this wonderful world" (MMF 2); Fell, whose "face was large and round and ruddy, and had a twitching smile somewhere above several chins. But what you noticed there was the twinkle in his eye" (HN 12); and many others. They are clumsy—Brown "had several brown paper parcels, which he was quite incapable of collecting. . . . He had a large shabby umbrella, which constantly fell on the floor" (AA 7); they are compulsively oral—great eaters and drinkers, fussy eaters and messy eaters; and they are all extremely self-indulgent: many, like Wolfe and Poirot, sulk and throw tantrums. "I don't believe we're ever going to catch the Sparrow." "The sparrow?" "Yes. Don't you remember 'Who Killed Cock Robin?' It must have been the first detective story you ever read. You know it was the Sparrow who did the dirty work" (R 84).

Sown with regressive signals, mystery and detective stories share the framing fictions of the *adventure* and the *game* with the master-genre of romance (analytic detective fiction preempts this understanding by claiming that it is already like another game, the crossword puzzle). Early in its history detective fiction identified itself as adventure through its titles, although "adventures" soon coexisted with appeals to Gothic (the "mystery"), the professions of law and medicine (the "case"), and the sociopolitical realm (the "crime" or the "affair"). When Holmes asks Watson to accompany him to Baskerville Hall, Watson registers the fact that the "promise of adventure had always a fascination for me" (HB 695); and in Buchan's *Thirty-Nine Steps*, Richard Hannay says to a "literary" innkeeper, "You're looking for adventure. . . . Well, you've found it here. The devils are after me, and the police are after them. It's a race that I mean to win" (TS 39).

The adventure is fundamentally a wish: Lt. Gulliver Jones, the protagonist of a Martian romance, exclaims, "Yes, yes . . . anything were better than this, any enterprise however wild, any adventure however desperate. Oh, I wish I were anywhere but here, anywhere out of this red-tape-ridden world of ours! *I wish I were in the planet Mars!*" The place of adventure is a distinct realm, away from "here," and the other side of the adventure is guilt (the internal equivalent of the reader's shame): "what would they all think of me? Would they brand me as a deserter, a poltroon, and a thief?" (Arnold 16, 49–50). Here is the same sequence from a proper boy's book, *Through Russian Snows* by G. A. Henty:

> One incredible day Julian Wyatt found himself aboard a French lugger being taken a prisoner from his native England by a crew of smugglers. It was incredible because only a few hours earlier he had no thought that anything like that could happen to him—in fact . . . he had been out, shot-gun under his arm, quite happily intent on shooting some rabbits for the pot. . . . That was an incredible change in his fortunes. But even more bewildering was the knowledge that back in England his abrupt disappearance would be regarded as admission of guilt in a crime far more serious than smuggling. Julian, in fact, would be wanted for murder. (5)

Here, the wish is suppressed and replaced by a symptomization of the primary helplessness: Julian has no desire to go toward the adventure; he is taken against his will and his wish.

At a certain point in his adventure in *Kidnapped,* David Balfour is troubled by doubts and feels a pull to disengage and return to a state of adult responsibility; he is troubled by doubts as to "why I was going to join myself with an outlaw . . . whether I should not be acting more like a man of sense to tramp back to the south country direct . . . and what Mr. Campbell or even Mr. Henderland would think of me if they should ever learn my folly and presumption." He immediately meets "a great, red-headed gentleman, of an imperious and flushed face," the Red Fox, who *is* a man of adult responsibility—"I have power here. . . .

I am King's Factor upon several of these estates"—and David feels an instinctive revulsion for him: "I had no sooner seen these people coming than I made up my mind (for no reason that I can tell) to go through with my adventure." There is a shot, and the Red Fox falls dead. David immediately leads the chase up the hill, but when he calls back to the others to follow, he sees that he is being pointed at and accused of complicity in the crime. He claims to be amazed. Soldiers spread out and run after him, and a voice close by tells him to duck in among the trees. The voice belongs to the outlaw, Alan Breck, who was the cause of David's authoritarian concern at the beginning of the passage (Stevenson n.d. [1886], 149–55).

Although the metaphorics (and the fact) of physical adventure tend to fall by the wayside, the pursuit of crime remains a game, fun, a lark— "O, Shades of Doyle! What a game!" says Anthony Gethryn (R 39). Philip Trent thinks that turning to detection "would be rather a lark" (TLC 40). Lord Peter Wimsey arranges to have the murder trial of Harriet Vane reopened because "I wouldn't lose the fun of all this for the world. Sort of case I fairly wallow in" (but a few pages later Wimsey acknowledges that murderers also murder for fun) (SP 38, 41). Raffles tells Bunny that it is all a game to him—"and the one game he knew that was always exciting, always full of danger and of drama. I could just then have found it in my heart to try the game myself" (E.W. Hornung quoted in Mierow 15). Leithan, the hero of Buchan's *Power House*, has never "been farther from home than Monte Carlo, but he liked hearing about the ends of the earth." His chum, Tommy, an explorer and international traveler, tells him: "Poor old beggar! . . . To spend your days on such work when the world is chock-full of amusing things. Life goes roaring by and you only hear the echo in your stuffy rooms." Leithan then reverses these values: "I once played the chief part in a rather exciting business without ever once budging from London. And the joke of it was that the man who went out to look for adventure only saw a bit of the game, and I who sat in my chambers saw it all and pulled the strings" (PW viii–ix, 12).

"Adolescents are excessively egoistic," Anna Freud wrote, "regarding themselves as the center of the universe and the sole object of interest and yet at no time in later life are they capable of so much self sacrifice and devotion" (137). It would take very few reminders to implicate the detective hero in unbridled egotism such as that which is thematized in Émile Gaboriau's *Monsieur Lecoq:* "This night would undoubtedly decide his future as a detective, so he swore that if he could not conquer his vanity, he would, at least, compel himself to conceal it" (MLq 41). (The text contains proverbs such as, "By hiding one's self on well-chosen occasions, one gains greater notoriety when one emerges from the shade" [MLq 44].) In the first Poirot novel, Hastings marvels at the "colossal cheek of the little man" (MAS 181), and Watson, in *The Sign of Four,* confesses that he was "irritated by the egotism which seemed to demand that every line of my pamphlet should be devoted to his own special doings" (SF 90). In the more juvenile forms of popular fiction like the Western, the jungle adventure, or the super-hero comic strips, it is the male body that is exhibited, its nakedness highlighted by theatrical costume.

Detective fiction is all about a man who enthralls because he performs a miracle of accomplishment. As if this were not glorious enough, he and his agents inside and outside the text are continually manipulating our attention so as to draw out and intensify this display. While the hard-boiled detective and the thriller hero have more latitude for moments of display—Hannay assures Sir Harry, " 'My nerves are good enough.' I took down a hunting knife from a stand on the wall, and did the old Mashona trick of tossing it and catching it in my lips" (TS 56)— the exhibitionism of the analytic detective usually takes a theatrical form, although the detective can sometimes be demonstrative in older ways as well: after Dr. Grimsby Roylott bent a poker "into a curve with his huge brown hands," Holmes "picked up the steel poker and, with a sudden effort, straightened it out again" (ASH 265). Detective fiction must be subtle enough to prevent confusion with the exhibitionism and theatricality that is also the proper mark of the villain. What else than a supreme act of exhibitionism is the crime?

Three analytic conventions claim immediate attention in this regard: the bombshell solution, the withholding of information, and the assembling of the community at the time of the solution. The bombshells that cap the opening of a Holmes tale are microcosms of the overall narrative. Unabashedly theatrical, they were certainly the flashiest displays found in early detective fiction—so flashy that they were overexposed by Conan Doyle, and almost no one who followed could use them earnestly. They are offered as a kind of intellectual muscle flexing, a gratuitous demonstration of Holmes's acute observation and his ability to draw inferences from details.

In the first Holmes novel, Gregson and Lestrade ask for his help, and Holmes replies with "a world of sarcasm," that it "would be robbing you of the credit of the case if I were to presume to help you." He turns to leave, but, before he does, turns back and says—"I'll tell you one thing which may help you in the case. . . . The murderer was more than six feet high, was in the prime of life, had small feet for his height, wore coarse, square-toed boots, and smoked a Trichinopoly cigar. He came here with his victim in a four-wheeled cab, which was drawn by a horse with three old shoes and one new one on his off fore-leg. In all probability the murderer had a florid face, and the fingernails of his right hand were remarkably long. These are only a few indications, but they may assist you" (SSt 31–32). Such displays of acumen prompt Watson to say something like, "By George, Holmes, that's amazing" and allow Holmes to round off the game with the never-spoken but insistently implied "Elementary, my dear Watson."

When the topic was fair play, the withholding of information was the great authorial sin; nevertheless, the detective invariably withholds information. A range of reasons are given for this move: "You see, my friend, you have . . . a countenance so transparent, that—*enfin*, to conceal your feelings is impossible" (MAS 170). "It is simplicity itself . . . so absurdly simple that an explanation is superfluous" (SF 91). Holmes even insists that his withholding of explanations is in the interests of fair play; it gives Watson a chance to solve the mystery himself. At the end of this range, however, the reasons unkey the conventions: "I'm not going to tell you much more of the case, Doctor. You know a conjurer gets no credit when once he has explained his trick" (SSt 33). When Campion is asked to explain why he has kept his secret so long, he says, "Just low cunning. . . . A foolish desire to impress" (GCM 95). "You do love being mysterious, don't you?" "*Touché!* I believe I do, you know. I've been discovering a lot of youthful traits lately very ill in accord with my age" (R 99).

Wolfe "loved to stage a good scene and get an audience sitting on the edge of their chairs" (RBx 47). In *The Mysterious Affair at Styles*, Inspector Japp, on instructions from Poirot, assembles the household in the living room; Poirot politely sets chairs for everyone. This event is a double staging, because it is a performance that will convict Alfred Inglethorpe of murder in order to free him from that charge. Poirot begins: " 'Mesdames and messieurs' . . . bowing as though he were a celebrity about to deliver a lecture." When he accuses Inglethorpe, a "little gasp ran round the circle." When Inglethorpe refuses to speak, Poirot approaches and stands over him: " 'Speak,' he cried menacingly. . . . Mesdames and messieurs! I speak! Listen! I, Hercule Poirot'" (MAS 96, 97). In *Overture to Death*, Roderick Alleyn assembles the members of an amateur theatrical production on the stage where the murder occurred. On a round table are laid various enigmatic objects, the clues; eight chairs are set out; and Alleyn mutters: "Shock tactics. . . . Damn, I hate 'em. So infernally unfair, and they look like pure exhibitionism on the part of the police. Oh, well, can't be helped" (OD 287).

The ultimate exhibitionistic fantasy is the staging of one's death and resurrection. Holmes did it (and so did Tom Sawyer). Since Holmes's death, Watson has been attempting "with indifferent success" to play the game of sleuthing alone. One night, he walks against "an elderly, deformed man," knocking several books out of his hand. He tries to apologize but the man turns away with "a snarl of contempt." Later, a visitor is announced, and it is the old man. Watson turns his head for a moment, and when he looks again, "Sherlock Holmes was standing smiling at me." Watson faints for the first time in his life. Holmes is taken aback, and says, "I had no idea that you would be so affected. . . . I have given you a serious shock by my unnecessarily dramatic reappearance." I do not believe Holmes and suggest that that "snarl of contempt" expresses a layer of feeling for the doctor that is usually dissembled (RSH 483–86).

Holmes is no Tom Sawyer who times his resurrection to coincide with the peak of the funeral laments, but he isn't bad. Twain's fiction, by the way, is a subtext for this chapter, particularly the characters Tom Sawyer and Huck Finn, who keep suggesting themselves as uncoded versions not only of the detective and his Watson but also of the analytic and the hard-boiled detective. Twain's work is devoted to the staging of exhibitionistic fantasy, particularly *Tom Sawyer; A Connecticut Yankee*—where Hank Morgan states, "I never care to do a thing in a quiet way; it's got to be theatrical or I don't take any interest in it" (249); and *Pudd'nhead Wilson*, which is a long slow setup for the hero's scene of triumph and self-display as a forensic detective.

Jacques Futrelle's "Problem of Cell 13" tells the story of a Houdini-like escape from prison. Futrelle's detective, Augustus S. F. X. Van Dusen, Ph.D., L.L.D., F.R.S., M.D., is called "The Thinking Machine." At a dinner with two other scientists, he advances a theory that one of his guests, Dr. Charles Ransome, "emphatically" declares to be impossible. Stung by this rejoinder, the Thinking Machine responds that "nothing is impossible. . . . The mind is master of all things." Dr. Ransome laughs "tolerantly" at this, and he is "slightly amused" when the Thinking Machine petulantly declares that any man, by applying his brains and ingenuity, can leave a high security prison cell whatever the conditions imposed on his incarceration might be. The brag is translated into a challenge because Ransome is now caught up in the game: the other's tone "nettled him, and he resolved to see the experiment to the end; it would be a stinging reproof to egotism" (BTM 2, 5).

In appearance and behavior, the Thinking Machine is a barely disguised child. While he is being searched, Ransome notes "the pitiful, childlike physical weakness of the man." When he asserted the power of mind over all things, his tone had been petulant because "He always spoke petulantly." The tale does not detail the steps actually taken to escape; these, we are told, had been worked out by his second day in prison, and, when related, they are both banal and overingenious. What is acted out is a series of theatrical gestures that have nothing to do with the actual escape; they are designed to bait, frustrate, and eventually humiliate the warden of the prison who is entrusted with enforcing Ransome's parental edict. The Thinking Machine must not only win the bet, but he must win it easily and adorn it with the trappings of omnipotence. As he leaves home, he tells the cook, "One week from to-night, at half-past nine, these gentlemen . . . will take supper

with me here." On the night of the escape, the warden receives a special delivery letter inviting him to supper as well. A guard who is sent
to check the cell reports that the prisoner is still there, but a minute
later the Thinking Machine walks into the warden's office (BTM 4, 2,
23–24).

Like Ransome, the warden accepts the brag as a personal challenge:
"If that man escapes from that cell I'll—hang it—I'll resign." The warden is successor to a long line of parents, schoolmasters, and preachers
driven to distraction by the "bad boys" of juvenile fiction, but he is even
more vulnerable than they, for he is given extraordinary authority to
enforce his regime. Within the prison, every statement made by those
in authority is an order, and every order must be instantly obeyed. In
the story, this authority is shaken through a tantalizing play: the Thinking Machine's first exhibitionistic taunt is to throw a piece of linen
with a written message out the window; the message is "This isn't the
way I intend to escape" written backward. Although the warden cannot
decipher this simple code, he chuckles and exclaims, "Plan of escape
number one has gone wrong." The guard does wonder where the prisoner got the pen and ink. The warden confiscates the prisoner's white
linen shirt, but, two days later, a guard finds another piece of white
linen with the message "Only three days more" (BTM 12, 11, 17).

Like Melville's "Bartleby," the tale consists of a series of assaults
upon the grounds of the warden's authority, not merely the physical
constraints, but assumptions about containment and finitude—specifically, the notion that the sum of the parts is always equal to the whole,
a proposition that another thinking machine, C. Auguste Dupin, also
perversely denied (Poe 1902, 7: 44–45). At the time of his imprisonment, the Thinking Machine asked for one five- and two ten-dollar
bills, which surprised Ransome and the warden, as the amount fell far
short of bribe money. The five-dollar bill was attached to the coded
message. A few days later another five flutters to the ground. When the
prisoner is searched, five one-dollar bills are found in his pocket. The
warden "felt—he knew—that this man was making a fool of him." On
the fifth day, the warden wears a hunted look; he knows that the prisoner is amusing himself at his expense. In confirmation, another linen
note flutters to the ground, followed by a half dollar (BTM 1–33).

The devout, quiet, apparently humorless Father Brown also has aspects of a child who drives adults crazy. At one point in an investigation, Brown proposes to resolve a dilemma quickly and efficiently. The quickest way to convince them all of the truth, he says, is to have the doctor repeat the five questions he asked that morning, and he, Brown, will answer them:

"You know how all the garden was sealed up like an air-tight chamber," went on the doctor. "Well, how did the strange man get into the garden?"

Without turning round, the little priest answered: "There never was any strange man in the garden."

There was a silence, and then a sudden cackle of almost childish laughter relieved the strain. The absurdity of Brown's remark moved Ivan to open taunts.

"Oh!" he cried; "then we didn't lug a great fat corpse on to the sofa last night? He hadn't got into the garden, I suppose?"

"Got into the garden?" repeated Brown reflectively. "No, not entirely."

"Hang it all," cried Simon, "a man gets into a garden, or he doesn't."

"Not necessarily," said the priest, with a faint smile. "What is the next question, doctor?"

"I fancy you're ill. . . . How did Brayne get out of the garden?"

"He didn't get out of the garden," said the priest, still looking out of the window.

"Didn't get out of the garden?" exploded Simon.

"Not completely," said Father Brown.

Simon shook his fists in a frenzy. . . . "A man gets out of a garden, or he doesn't . . ."

"Not always," said Father Brown. (IFB 49–50)

The conversational byplay between the Holmes and his Watson that makes up much of the matter and much of the charm of the form is single-mindedly devoted to the humiliation of the latter. If Watson says "This is all an insoluble mystery to me. . . . It grows darker instead of clearer," Holmes answers, "On the contrary . . . it clears every instant" (SF 109). If Hastings exclaims "But this is childish," Poirot counters, "No, it is very momentous" (MAS 72–73). In *The Sign of*

Four, Watson asks Holmes if he would think him impertinent were he to test Holmes's proficiency. Watson gives Holmes a watch to read "with some slight feeling of amusement in my heart, for the test was, as I thought, an impossible one." Holmes understands the challenge and manipulates Watson's desire to triumph over him. He examines the watch for a long time, so that Watson can "hardly keep from smiling at his crestfallen face" (SF 92).

He finally hands it back, complaining that the watch has just been cleaned, there is hardly anything to be read on it. He has, however, made a few inferences: that the watch belonged to Watson's eldest brother who inherited it from his father, that he was a man of untidy habits, that he "was left with good prospects, but he threw away his chances, lived for some time in poverty, with occasional short intervals of prosperity, and finally, taking to drink, he died. That is all I can gather." The waters are very muddy now, for what Watson had offered up as his stake in the game are his family secrets. He springs from his chair, reproaches Holmes with acting unworthily: he has spied on Watson, made inquiries about his "unhappy brother," and then pretended to deduce it all from the watch. Holmes apologizes ingenuously: "Viewing the matter as an abstract problem. I had forgotten how personal and painful a thing it might be to you" (SF 92–93). Although he has collaborated in the insult, Watson's feeling that he has been violated in the exchange is right on the mark.

Heroes of masculine forms of popular fiction often possess a legendary renown or kerygma: "There was to come a time when the mere mention of the Saint was sufficient to fill the most unimaginative malefactor with uneasy fears, when a man returning home late one night to find the sign of the Saint—a childish sketch of a little man with . . . an absurd halo over his round blank head—chalked upon his door, would be sent instinctively spinning round with his back to the nearest wall . . . and an icy tingle of dread prickling up his spine" (FSO 3).

> "The Newsboy Detective wishes to see you."
> The great official gave a sudden start.
> "The very one!" he exclaimed.
> The next instant he was clasping the hand of Eddie Parks. (Ade 18)

This communal magic is a form of fascination; in Conan Doyle's *Uncle Bernac,* the hero is told: "You have only been in France a few days, Monsieur de Laval . . . but it seems to me that all the affairs of the Empire are already revolving round you" (Doyle 98). In an earlier form, it is a property of the *darling* of romance literature—Edward Waverley, Tom Sawyer, Huck Finn, Jim Hawkins, Jamie, Master of Ballantrae, Kim. Actually, the darling is suspended between adoring and baleful glances, and the resolution of that ambivalence constitutes his plot or destiny.

The structural equivalent to the kerygmatic "one and only" is "only me," another formula for the narrative hero. In the naive heyday of analytic detective fiction, the detective is the only one who can solve the crime: "When Molly Lauck was poisoned, a week ago today, it looked phony from the beginning. By Wednesday, two days later, it was plain that the cops were running around in circles, and I came to you. I know about you. I know you're the one and only. . . . I doubt if *anyone* could crack it but you" (RBx 8–9). Sometimes we are allowed to see this glory less as a virtue than an adolescent refusal to share the limelight: in *The Rasp,* the policeman Boyd offers a solution to the crime, and Gethryn says that it doesn't sound at all right to him. Boyd tells him they know that Deacon is the criminal because his fingerprints are on the murder weapon. "'Are they now?' said Anthony irritably. 'How d'you know? What did you compare 'em with?'" He asks if they have found anything like a motive, and Boyd answers that they have. "Anthony ground his heel savagely into the gravel" (R 55–56). And Lew Archer thinks: "rough stuff . . . would put me in the wrong. I wanted them to be in the wrong, falling on their faces with foolishness" (GC 28).

Popular fiction tells stories in which the extrapolated adolescent becomes master of time and space, master of circumstances, or master of a community of adults, and the structure always has an emphatic retrospective component that I call adolescent revenge. Detective fiction can be defined as the story of a hero who counters transgressions against law and authority while repeatedly engaging in acts of transgression against law and authority.

All detective fiction begins as Hannay's adventures do: "I had started my new life in an atmosphere of protest against authority" (TS 28).

In another key, *The Ipcress File* opens with an interview between the nameless hero and a government minister in a flat that looked "like Oliver Messel did it for Oscar Wilde": "The Minister said, 'Quite,' a couple of times, and I let a quarter inch of ash away towards the blue Kashan rug" (IF 7). This, however, is a double game, for detective fiction slavishly upholds authority both outside and inside the form: it preserves the lost authority of narrative in a chaotic modernist culture; it deifies the authority of reason or the imagination (it exhausts its data in the solution, so its story goes, and closes with a terminal authority). Finally, it authorizes authoritarianism for the individual, for society, and for the bourgeois state—"The game of detection, then, produces a representational model for the fictional production of presence, authority, power" (Riddel 138).

Adolescent revenge appears in mystery and detective fiction through one of the most artificial conventions in the form, the police paradox. This stipulates that there is no possibility that representatives of the official police can contribute to the solution of a crime, mystery, or espionage scheme. In analytic detective fiction, the police paradox is conveyed through the fiction of a stupid or incompetent constabulary. The police are baffled or bewildered by the crime, or, conversely, mistakenly confident; they overlook clues; they arrest the wrong man. When Rollo Martins identifies the narrator of *The Third Man* as a policeman, he tells him, "I've always hated policemen. They are always either crooked or stupid" (ThM 178). This is not a fact of experience but a convention of the Western novels that Martins writes for a living.

After the 1950s it became hard to sustain the police paradox in anything like the outrageous form it had assumed in Conan Doyle or Christie. Although it has to be regularly modified and recoded, it remains one of the unconditional conventions of the genre. The same convention rules that the detective must be an amateur. This resonant word takes on many meanings, but here it signifies that the hero must be the sole recipient of celebration and applause. The hero triumphs over and humiliates his companion, the official representatives of the law, and the criminal.

The desire to insult and humiliate the police exerts such strong pressure in the form that it is often written backward, so that the police are made to mock and laugh at the detective: they label his oracular pronouncements ridiculous, and they are contemptuous of his trivial and undignified activities, for example, his kneeling on the ground and taking minute measurements. In *A Study in Scarlet*, for twenty minutes Holmes measured the distance between marks "entirely invisible" to Watson while "Gregson and Lestrade . . . watched the manoeuvres of their amateur companion with considerable curiosity and some contempt" (SSt 31). This convention was already deeply embedded in the detective tales of Poe. The prefect of police in "The Murders in the Rue Morgue" and "The Purloined Letter" has "a fashion of calling every thing 'odd' that was beyond his comprehension, and thus lived amid an absolute legion of 'oddities,' " and he laughs heartily and long at Dupin's suggestion that the whereabouts of the missing letter might be "*too* self-evident" (1902, 6: 29–30).

The police paradox operates even when the detective is a policeman. A contemptuous distance between detective and police can be worked in a variety of ways, for example, the policeman on vacation or the policeman's last case before retirement. On vacation, Charlie Chan's attitude (couched in typically racist diction) toward authority is that of the amateur: "Pretty quick I go home, lifelong yearning for travel forever quenched. Keep in mind, much better police do not find who killed Louie Wong. If they do, our fruit may be picked when not yet ripe. We should handle case. Officers of law must be encouraged off of ranch at earliest possible time" (CP 121). It can be worked out through competition between city and country police or through the police hierarchy, where, for example, the detective-policeman is hampered by a grandiose and incompetent superior like the police commissioner in the Ellery Queen mysteries. While Maigret occupies an important official position and can call on a large apparatus to help him, "this does not make him into a representative of the power of the state; instead, he finds himself in a permanent state of guerilla warfare against its deputies" (Heissenbüttel 89). In *The Moonstone*, the paradox operates between two policemen, and Sergeant Cuff finds that "Superintendent Seegrave has been proved wrong, up to this time, in all his conclusions" (Collins 1966, 176).

Outside the form, the police paradox becomes the object of ridicule and contempt. Several of the most effective jeers were delivered by Hammett and Chandler in the name of another kind of detective fiction: "To supply this genius with a field for his operations the author has to treat his policemen abominably. He doesn't let them ask any questions that aren't wholly irrelevant. They can't make inquiries of any one who might know anything" (Hammett 383). And yet the police paradox is totally operative in hard-boiled detective fiction as well. Its presence there is not characterological as in analytic detective fiction but structural; the police are deliberately excluded from participation in the investigation:

> "We've got to call the police," Spencer said grittily.
> "Why?"
> "Oh my God, Marlowe—we have to."
> "Tomorrow . . ."
> "We've got to call the police. There is such a thing as law."
> "We don't have to do anything of the sort. We don't have enough evidence to swat a fly with. Let the law enforcement people do their own dirty work." (LG 259)

Clever or stupid, enthusiastic or cynical, policemen cannot succeed in *The Maltese Falcon* because they do not know what crime has been committed—they were never told. Spade arranges a meeting in his apartment between Brigid and Joel Cairo. Lieutenant Dundy appears while it is going on. Spade stands in the doorway blocking Dundy and his men, and when Dundy demands that he let them in, Spade says, "You're not coming in. What do you want to do about it? Try to get in? Or do your talking here? Or go to hell?" The episode is self-reflexive; the room (the box) to which the police are denied access is the fiction itself. After a few minutes there is a scream for help from inside. Dundy announces "I guess we're going in," and Spade agrees. They find Brigid cowering in a chair and Cairo standing over her with a pistol. Various strands of involvement begin to emerge incoherently as they scream at one another, and Dundy proposes to move them all to his space—to take them down to headquarters. But Spade is able to exclude him again, by inventing a scenario that also expresses the meaning of the police paradox: Spade's "grin was a taunt. . . . 'I dare you to take us in, Dundy. . . . We'll laugh at you in every newspaper in San Francisco. . . . Wake up. You've been kidded. When the bell rang I said to Miss O'Shaughnessy and Cairo: "It's those damned bulls again. They're getting to be nuisances. Let's play a joke on them. When you hear them going one of you scream, and then we'll see how far we can string them along before they tumble" ' " (MF 63–70). Only "bulls" would try to force their way in to the room of mystery and detection. They are a nuisance, and both the detective and the criminals collaborate in a fantasy designed to involve and then humiliate them. Spade threatens them with the opposite of what is true for the fiction; he implies that if they believe the sinister implications of the scene, they will become a laughing stock.

Sometimes the police exclude themselves. Cynical and weary, Nulty, the policeman in *Farewell, My Lovely*, wants no problems to cross his desk. The exclusion of the police is often a product of political corruption—"There's a hush on part of this. . . . This Grayle packs a lot of dough in his pants. And law is where you buy it in this town. Look at the funny way the cops are acting. No build-up, no newspaper handout. . . . Nothing but silence and warnings to me to lay off" (FML 116)—and, after Orson Welles's *Touch of Evil* (1958), corruption could be no more than an image: "Under a wide-brimmed white hat, his face was flushed. Veins squirmed like purple worms under the skin of his nose. His eyes held the confident vacancy that comes from the exercise of other people's power" (D 31).

In *A Study in Scarlet*, Holmes is deceived by an actor impersonating an old woman, and his first thought is of the police: "I wouldn't have the Scotland Yarders know it for the world. . . . I have chaffed them so much that they would never have let me hear the end of it" (SSt 40). An angry and sweating Archer performs "vaudeville" for the deputies that are searching him: "I'm Captain Nemo. . . . I just came ashore from a hostile submarine" (GC 28). The contest between the detective and the police often takes the form of resentment and implacable anger; Spade and Philip Marlowe are cop-haters. Dundy tells Spade, "It'd pay you to play along with us a little, Spade. You've got away with this and you've got away with that, but you can't keep it up forever." Spade replies arrogantly, "Stop me when you can" (MF 63). Randall accuses Marlowe of lying to the police, and Marlowe answers, "It was a pleasure" (FML 86). Marlowe has a lengthy speech in *The Long Goodbye* on the difference between detectives and policemen in which he lists the defeats and humiliations he suffers as part of his job, and he ends it by saying, "But I can always tell a cop to go to hell. Go to hell, Bernie" (LG 230).

The professional spy thriller has a number of structures that express the police paradox and the hero's amateur status. The spy is isolated from the others in his organization because of his reputation and renown, his superior ruthlessness, his special talents or more sentimental traits of character: for example, he is the last active agent in a field dominated by university-trained bureaucrats. The spy is specially chosen for a mission that does not go through official channels— "I'm a sort of policeman," says Bond, they "send me out from London when there's something odd going on somewhere in the world that isn't anybody else's business" (DN 94). Duplicating this, he is told that should his involvement become known, he will be disowned by the organization to which he belongs: "Don't contact me if anything goes wrong, because I won't know what the hell you are talking about" (IF 18). The spy thriller also found hard-boiled detective fiction ready to hand for adaptation and soon began to produce heroes like Deighton's Harry Palmer and Ross Thomas's Mac McCorkle who, like Spade and Marlowe, were insubordinate and sulky boys.

Given the labyrinthine ground of the thriller and the shading and multiplication of motives, allegiances, and identities, the hero often cannot trust his own organization. The most gratifying resolution is to have the agent's superior turn out to be the criminal. In fictions of this kind, amateurism is no longer a premise, but a condition that is achieved at the cost of some pain. It is a scandal, either a disgrace or a crime: in Noel Behn's *Kremlin Letter*, the transfer of Charles Rone from his regular service to a special spy unit, surely an easy authoritative gesture, is framed as a disgrace to the uniform and a defection from naval intelligence.

The exclusion of the police takes its most revealing form in the amateur thriller, of which *The Thirty-Nine Steps* is a prototype. An ordinary man stumbles upon a secret of tremendous implication: the existence of a covert, conspiratorial organization devoted to the subversion or destruction of his civilization. The threat posed by thrillers is vast (it shares this territory with science fiction), and the enemy is all-powerful and ever-present. The hero—he will tell us this himself many times—is woefully inadequate to the task of meeting this crisis. Yet this is exactly what he does. A more sensible response would be to turn it over to institutions that are designed to counter conspiracies, to relieve himself of the heavy responsibility not only of doing it himself but also of keeping it to himself. The hero will usually tell us that he wants to turn it over, but, for one reason or another, circumstances prevent his doing so.

In hard-boiled detective fiction, the hero desires to exclude the police; here he desires to include the police, and it is the same story. Hannay cannot go to the police for three reasons. First of all, he has no time. The enemy knows of his involvement from the moment he makes his discovery, and he is kept on the run. He cannot go to the police because he is wanted by the police: he is identified by them as the murderer of Scudder. Finally, he cannot go to the police because they would mock and scorn him; they would not believe the story he has to tell; it is too fantastic to be believed. Hannay dredges up every reason he can think of not to go to the police:

> Supposing I went out now and called in the police. . . . What kind of story was I to tell about Scudder. I had lied to Paddock about him, and the whole thing looked desperately fishy. If I made a clean breast of it and told the police everything he had told me, they would simply laugh at me. The odds were a thousand to one that I would be charged with the murder, and the circumstantial evidence was strong enough to hang me. Few people knew me in England; I had no real pal who could . . . swear to my character. . . . Besides, if I told the whole story and by any miracle was believed I would be playing their game. Karolides would stay at home, which was what they wanted." (TS 22)

In addition (according to Scudder), the police would be ineffective even if convinced and alert: "No good. They might stuff your city with plainclothes detectives and double the police, and Constantine would still be a doomed man" (TS 12).

When a thriller's hero does go to the police, his expectations are realized. Paternal authority looks at him derisively or sadly and suggests that he go home, have a cup of tea, a hot bath, and get some sleep. Vadassy, in *Epitaph for a Spy,* decides that "Beghin was a fool and I was in his hands. . . . If I had to trust myself to Beghin and the Department of Naval Intelligence in Toulon my chances of getting to Paris on Monday were remote. No, I would do my own thinking. . . . I must do the unmasking" (ES 50–51).

The police paradox is nonsense in all its forms; police are aware that espionage exists and that it may take secretive and convoluted forms. The laughter visited upon Hannay and Holmes in such different contexts is a trace from outside the form—a trace of the repudiation that accompanies investment in fantasy. The function of the police paradox is to allow the protagonist to do it all by himself, but what he is doing is valorizing fantasy. In opposition to adult authority, he will redeem a scenario in which the fantasy turns out to be the great truth with crucial implications for the lives of the others who smugly denied that there was a story to tell in the first place.

In *Dead Cert,* Inspector Lodge tells Alan York, "In view of the verdict at the inquest, your story is considered, on the whole, to be the product of a youthful and overheated imagination" (DC 68). As Greene's confidential agent is telling his story to the police, he thinks that it "was of course an incredible story. . . . There was a pause; nobody said anything; the detective didn't even trouble to make a note. His companion pursed his lips and stared mildly round as if he were no longer interested in the tales criminals told" (CA 85). Hannay concludes, "It was so big that I didn't blame Scudder for . . . wanting to play a lone hand. . . . The real thing was so immortally big that he, the man who had found it out, wanted it all for himself. I didn't blame him. It was risks after all that he was chiefly greedy about" (TS 46). The fable of the "Boy Who Cried Wolf" is usually read against the boy, but in mystery and detective fiction it is endlessly rewritten as a celebratory fable. Either way, it is a tale of adolescent fantasy in conflict with a world of adult values. In its classic form, the boy is punished for lying; in its popular forms, the adults are punished for disbelieving in the potency of the word, for demanding that a fiction be identifiably real or imaginary in a world where the imaginary is colored with shame.

4 | The Seal of Subjectivity

CASPER GUTMAN GUFFAWS AT SAM SPADE, TELLING HIM "BY GAD, sir, you are a character!"; but that, according to outside commentary, is precisely what Spade is not (MF 165). If the absence of character is the great flaw in detective fiction, it is work at which the detective collaborates: postures of mystification and evasion occupy him as much as the solving of crimes. In one of Marlowe's frequent gestures of self-dismissal, he tells Bernie Ohls, "Ten years from now you might pass me on the street and wonder where the hell you had seen me before." Ohls's reply indicates a surplus of "self" in Marlowe: "You self-sufficient, self-satisfied, self-confident, untouchable bastard" (LG 298).

Many adjectives seal off that self. The most prominent, perhaps, is "tough," a word that expresses the core value of American hard-boiled fiction and its hero. Images and structures for inaccessible selfhood, however, are distributed with uncommon insistence over a wide range of detective heroes: analytic detectives such as Holmes, Brown, Campion, Wimsey, Poirot, and Wolfe; hard-boiled detectives like Spade, Marlowe, and Archer; and the protagonists of Greene and John Le Carré, those disillusioned men who claim to have lost the capacity to feel. Only a certain type of spy, such as Hannay, Ambler's bumbling heroes, or Bond is presented as open to inspection.

The face of the hard-boiled detective, when it is not hidden behind the mask of first-person narrative, is readily identified. Spade's face, enhanced by the screen image of Humphrey Bogart, is more than a mask of cool self-control; it is an extreme representation of the dead-pan, the American death mask.

Misanthropic retirement as a detective characteristic was first designed by Poe. The Chevalier C. Auguste Dupin lives with a companion in a "retired and desolate portion of the Faubourg St. Germain. . . . We admitted no visitors. Indeed the locality of our retirement had been carefully kept a secret from my own former associates; and it had been many years since Dupin had ceased to know or be known in Paris. We existed with ourselves alone" (4:151). In "The Mystery of Marie Rogêt," while the prefect recounts the details of the case, Dupin is hidden behind spectacles of green glass, behind which he appears to be asleep (5:8). He consults with no one, solving the case from the newspaper accounts that the unnamed narrator brings him.

Baroness Orczy's detective is known as the Old Man in the Corner, a grotesque "old scarecrow" who sips coffee in the A.B.C. Restaurant, knotting bits of string into a ball and solving crimes that are brought to him, and when Miss Jane Marple is introduced she sits placidly knitting at "an informal club of village friends . . . attempting to stump one another with curious outcomes to curious tales" ("MDUR" 206; Slung 65). Holmes, "who loathed every form of society with his whole Bohemian soul"—in the "Five Orange Pips," he tells Watson that he has no friends and does not encourage visitors—is the very image of the Old Man as Watson wonders how, without leaving his room, he can "unravel some knot which other men can make nothing of" (ASH 218, 161). Nero Wolfe, that image of "massive misanthropy and misogyny," is reluctant to leave his house, "convinced that outdoor air was apt to clog the lungs" (Grella 411; RBx 7). The "amateurism" or "privacy" of the detective, which is a condition of these forms, is also a sign of this separateness. He works by and for himself, even though he may have a nominal employer or may even be a member of an organization.

The hard-boiled detective is also an isolated figure. Marlowe lives alone and spends his evenings alone: cooking for himself, listening to classical music, or working out chess games. From time to time old friends will wonder why they haven't seen him for a long time, press invitations upon him that will never be followed up. Marlowe tells a potential client, "I'm a native son, born in Santa Rosa, both parents dead, no brothers or sisters, and when I get knocked off in a dark alley sometime . . . nobody will feel that the bottom has dropped out of his or her life" (LG 74). Of Archer, the "only personal detail we learn . . . is that his wife has left him" (Hartman 214). Ross Macdonald's *Doomsters* opens with a "dream about a hairless ape who lived in a cage by himself. His trouble was that people were always trying to get in. It kept the ape in a state of nervous tension. I came out of sleep sweating, aware that somebody was at the door," and in his *Galton Case* Archer identifies himself to two policemen as that monumental misanthrope, Captain Nemo (D 3; GC 28).

The most extreme images of misanthropy are found in the thriller, because its greater social and physical latitude often lends it a freedom that verges on fantasy. *The Thirty-Nine Steps* opens with Hannay a stranger in London and, within a few days, he finds himself in solitary flight through the moors and mountains of Scotland. The unnamed protagonist of *Rogue Male* may have a "tendency to agoraphobia" beforehand, but the plot of the novel which has him relentlessly pursued by a German secret service unit determines that any social contact is fatal and, further, that he must go to ground in the English countryside (RM 30).

The thriller begins out in the cold, with misanthropy and alienation as its nominal topics, if one accepts Stevenson's *Pavilion on the Links* and Conan Doyle's *Surgeon of Gaster Fell* as the inaugurating works of this type of mystery story. In both of them, a young man drops out of the human race and takes himself to a remote part of England where he becomes the unwilling witness of an adventure; he is drawn into heroic action and social participation through curiosity and then love. This structure was set in early thrillers like William Le Queux's *Mysterious Mr. Miller* where the hero is a recluse who has lost all interest

in life since the failure of his one great love affair, and he has to be
brought back to life by the excitement of adventure.

Dick Francis is fond of this pattern: in *Odds Against* Sid Halley is a
former steeplechase jockey who suffered a fall that crippled his hand,
followed by a painful divorce. He was given a job in a detective agency
(as a gesture of pity, he assumes) and for several years has been going
through his paces, indifferent to his present life and future prospects.
Shot by a petty thief, he lies wounded on the floor and becomes interested enough in the case to want to pursue it, as if it has taken all of
this to arouse a flicker of interest in him. The head of the agency asks
if Halley has ever seen a zombie wake up, and says, "Good God. At
last. . . . And it took a bullet to do it" (OA 64–65).

At his most colorful, the analytic detective is an overdetermined
character, built out of various masks and roles that are conventionally
associated with misanthropic isolation: the mask of the scientist, the
dandy or aesthete, and the aristocrat. The scientism of the early detectives is actually used to provide a context for their seeming indifference
to the fear and pain that accompany mystery and crime: "Detection,"
says Holmes, "is, or ought to be, an exact science and should be treated
in the same cold and unemotional manner" (SF 90). The lack of affect
identified earlier as a quality of the genre is also a characteristic of the
protagonist: "You take it cool, Mr. Fortune. . . ." "No use feelin' feelings," Reggie drawled. "We have to go on. We want the truth" (MMF
239). And Wolfe lectures a client: "You are quick on the trigger to re-
sent it if I do not show tenderness and consideration for your cousin's
remorse and grief. I know none because I have none. If I offer anything
for sale in this office . . . it certainly is not a warm heart and maudlin
sympathy for the distress of spoiled obtuse children" (RBx 97).

The appropriation of the fin de siècle dandy and aesthete is more in
the nature of a recovery, because Poe's original detective was himself
an adaptation of the dandy of Benjamin Disraeli and Bulwer-Lytton.
This type is easily fed back into detective fiction as, for example, Ben
Hecht's Prince Julien de Medici: "In the firelight . . . [his] face . . . appeared like a gray and scarlet mask of ennui. Now after twelve years, he
had matured into a nervously brilliant man, engagingly cynical, egotis-

tic as a child and subtle-minded as a Jesuit. . . . His name, his manner, his genius combined with his wealth attired him in an unassailable superiority" (FD 17).

Between the first and second adventures of Sherlock Holmes, Conan Doyle's detective was recast as a Bohemian. When Watson first meets Holmes in a laboratory, his fingers are stained by chemicals; he is an applied scientist, the new technocrat and Spencerian engineer of the naturalistic novel and science fiction: like Ames in Dreiser's *Sister Carrie*, the technical revolutionary in Wells's *The Shape of Things to Come*, or the chief attendant in Wells's "Lord of the Dynamos"—"a heavy red-headed brute with irregular teeth. He doubted the existence of the Deity but accepted Carnot's cycle, and he had read Shakespeare and found him weak in chemistry" (1960, 7).

The second Holmes takes cocaine, reads "old black-letter" volumes, loves opera, plays the violin masterfully—Mendelssohn lieder—and composes music. Holmes, who was a cultural illiterate in *A Study in Scarlet*, now quotes Goethe and Jean Paul and speaks in quick succession of miracle plays, medieval pottery, Stradivarius violins, and Ceylon Buddhism (SF 89, 128, 115, 121, 134). Poirot is a "quaint dandyfied little man" (MAS 17). Wimsey is also a great dandy, but his pose is acknowledged to be the symptom of a deeper alienation. At Balliol in 1909, he had "acquired affectations, an exaggerated Oxford manner and a monocle"; but it was after a "bad nervous breakdown," as a consequence of being "blown up and buried in a shell-hole near Caudry" in 1918, that he "adopted an impenetrable frivolity of manner and a dilettante pose, and became, in fact, the complete comedian" (UD viii–x).

The aristocracy of the amateur detective is partly an inheritance from the sensation novels of Collins, Mrs. Henry Wood, and Elizabeth Braddon, and partly a Darwinian-imperialist trace (Edwards 1971, 19; see Phillips). Burroughs's *Tarzan of the Apes* argues that aristocratic privilege, which appears to be a degenerative system protecting a class of feebleminded idlers, is still evolutionarily intact and only needs the proper setting to show itself as heroic action. Peter Wimsey is the second son of the fifteenth Duke of Denver (UD vi); Col. Anthony Ruthven Gethryn is the "son of a hunting country gentleman of the old type"

(R 8); and Sir Henry Merrivale "holds one of the oldest baronetcies in England" (NMW 39). More appropriately, perhaps, Alleyn "looks like one of those swells in the English flicks" (VM 57).

In America many of the early detectives were descendants of the New York Dutch: Van Dusen Ormsberry, Ellery Queen, and, through an acronymic twist, "Average" Jones, so called because his parents had christened him Adrian Van Reypen Egerton Jones (AJ 1–3). Philo Vance represents the mingled scientific, aristocratic, and aesthetic pose of the early analytic detective:

> Vance was what many would call a dilettante. . . . An aristocrat by birth and instinct, he held himself severely aloof from the common world of men. . . . The great majority of those with whom he came in contact regarded him as a snob. Yet there was in his condescension and disdain no trace of spuriousness. His snobbishness was intellectual as well as social. . . . Perhaps he may best be described as a bored and supercilious, but highly conscious and penetrating spectator of life. He was keenly interested in all human reactions; but it was the interest of the scientist, not the humanitarian. (BMC 9–10)

The biographical detachment of the detective is doubled by the "impenetrable reserve" of his face. The "Great Detective's" face, Leacock wrote, is more important for detection than his body: "His face has to be 'inscrutable.' Look at it though you will, you can never read it. Contrast it, for example, with the face of Inspector Higginbottam. . . . Here is a face that can look 'surprised' or 'relieved,' or, with great ease, 'completely baffled' " (1946, 30). This face is a product of energetic repression: "Mr. Georges La Touche was commonly regarded as the smartest private detective in London. . . . He was not much in appearance. Small, sallow, and slightly stooped, he would have looked insignificant only for the strength of the clear-cut features and the intelligence of the dark, flashing eyes. Years of training had enabled him to alter his expression and veil these tell-tale signs of power, and he had frequently found the weak and insipid impression thus produced, an asset in allaying the suspicions of his adversaries" (C 249).

Brown's face is blank and empty: he is "a drab and insignificant little man" with "a face of wood" (AA 153, 89). Campion's face is notorious for its inanity rather than its blankness; it is a "pale, smiling, and ineffably inane" face, often verging on "apparent imbecility." But this is exposed as a mask (although the exposure is a remasking): at rare moments his eyes go hard and the vacuity leaves his face (GCM 150, 69). Also, the eyes of analytic detectives are ordinarily inaccessible. Brown has "eyes as empty as the North Sea" (AA 7). Campion's face is "half-hidden by enormous glasses," and his eyes are "vague and foolish behind his spectacles" (GCM 52, 62); and Gethryn's "greenish eyes" are "veiled by their lids" (R 19). The extreme example of this tendency is the blind detective, such as Ernest Bramah's Max Carrados.

Surprising or startling others, the detective cannot himself be surprised; reading and interpreting character and situation, the detective cannot be read. Even volatile individuals like Poirot possess this opacity. Accidentally provided with a crucial piece of information, Poirot's face remains calm, and Hastings marvels at his "astonishing" self-control (MAS 49). Women detectives also possess this self-control: "Save for an almost imperceptible indrawing of her breath, she gave me no hint of the shock which must have stunned her as it did me. I was staring with mouth agape. But, then, I presume you have discovered by this time that I was not designed for a detective!" ("MNL" 149). Chan also tells us that this is a convention: "I observe you have ignorance concerning detective customs. Surprised detective might as well put on iron collar and leap from dock. He is finished. Mr. Madden's appearance staggering blow for me, but I am not letting rival policeman know it, thank you" (CP 244). And the convention was still active in the thriller in 1965: "It caught me like a blow in the face and I began sweating immediately because years of training had kept my eyes and mouth and hands expressionless as the shock of the words hit me, and the body, denied instinctive reaction, has to do something at a time like this; so I sat facing him with calm eyes and a quiet mouth and motionless hands, and felt the sweat coming" (QM 12).

The detective's speech is also under tight control. If he is hard-boiled, he says little, often insultingly little. The Continental Op almost never speaks; the "silent treatment" makes people nervous (FP 17). The hard-boiled detective's voice ordinarily lacks inflection; it is set at a level of weary cynicism. Yet he is not completely unfeeling. His speech is often unaccountably harsh. Although he talks through tight lips, his voice can be described as a spitting, growling, or snarling. If the detective is analytic, he chatters. Either way little pertinent information gets out.

The speech patterns of these two types of detective—the drawling, bantering style of the analytic and the wisecracking style of the hard-boiled—are formally distinct but structurally identical. Wilson has complained of the "awful whimsical patter of Lord Peter" (1945, 392), and Wodehouse has parodied the language of what he calls the "Effervescent Detective" (who knows it better?): this detective is "so delightfully flippant with it all. . . . Viewing the body brings out all that is gayest and sprightliest in him. . . . So this is the jolly old corpse, is it inspector? Well, well, well! Bean bashed in and a bit of no-good done to the merry old jugular, what? Tut, tut, mother won't like this at all" (242). The real thing is not all that different: "Sleuth, you surpass yourself. . . . Minister murdered by Bathing Belle—only not at the seaside. Cock Robin's murderer not Sparrow as at first believed, but one W. Wagtail! Gethryn, you're fatuous. Take to crochet" (R 40).

The obvious purpose of the detective's banter is to screen character and feeling, but through its evocations of the nursery and the public school, it is also a weapon of adolescent revenge. Such language feeds the mocking and baiting relationship between the detective and the Watson. Alleyn explains a previous occurrence to a colleague: "Miss Gaynes came in and reported the loss of her money. When I offered to cast the eye at her ravished suit-case she was unflatteringly tepid and melted away." The constable is bewildered, so Alleyn translates: "I phrased it badly. . . . I offered to examine Miss Gaynes's leather folder. She declined, and shortly afterwards withdrew" (VM 70–71).

If the flip talk of the analytic detective echoes the patter of P. G. Wodehouse, the wisecracking of the hard-boiled detective reflects the compulsive quipping of Groucho Marx, whose well-known two-way rejection—"I wouldn't belong to a club that would have me as a member"—hints at the self-pity that underlies such talk. Because wisecracking substitutes anger and disgust for withheld feelings, the hard-boiled detective always seems angry or depressed. Wisecracking tarnishes whatever in American experience it derisively points to, while it hides the subject behind screens of smug disapproval and the secure dismissals of comedy. I do not agree with George Grella, who feels that the "insults and wisecracks are the badge of their courage" (415); I sympathize with Lieutenant Randall, who asks Marlowe, "If I drink some [coffee], will you talk to me decently . . . without wise-cracking?" (FML 165).

Marlowe's wisecracking is gratuitously indecent, both racially and sexually. Having found three marijuana cigarettes in a "Chinese or Japanese silk cigarette case," he spins a scenario of "a trade article that might have cost thirty-five to seventy-five cents in any Oriental store, Hooey Phooey Sing—Long Sing Tung, that kind of place, where a nice-mannered Jap hisses at you, laughing heartily when you say that the Moon of Arabia incense smells like the girls in Frisco Sadie's back parlor" (FML 85). Sometimes the weary detective exposes the mechanism of his compulsion by reproducing it as a tic that could go on until he ran out of energy: "An hour crawled by like a sick cockroach. I was a grain of sand on the desert of oblivion. I was a two-gun cowpoke fresh out of bullets" (LG 111).

Through his wisecracks, the hard-boiled detective expresses a deep compulsion to retort and turn exchanges into challenges. During Marlowe's first visit with Mrs. Grayle, she decides to look in on her husband, but Marlowe says, "Let him wait." She remarks that there is "such a thing as being just a little too frank," and Marlowe replies, "Not in my business. Describe the evening. Or have me thrown out on my ear. One or the other. Make your lovely mind up" (FML 109). The tough detective draws a metaphoric line on the ground, particularly with the police: "You're not ready to pinch me yet, are you Dundy? . . . [Then] there's no particular reason why I should give a damn what you think, is there, Dundy?" (MF 20).

According to Hartman, the "basic flaw" in the novels of Chandler and Macdonald is a flaw of character, quite different from the basic flaw of character O'Faolain charges to the form: "the only person," Hartman wrote, "whose motives remain somewhat mysterious, or exempt from this relentless reduction to overt and vulnerable gestures, is the detective" (216). A great moment of mystery occurs at the beginning of each work as a narrative proceeds from an absence of motive; the mystery is why the detective takes the case in the first place. The analytic detective's explanation is simple: the case interests him as a problem. The hard-boiled detective says only that it's his job, although he must often be coaxed or threatened into taking a case he claims he doesn't want. Yet the rhythms of involvement are neither smooth nor coherent. The rhythms often resemble those of seduction: the detective insists that he does not want to get involved, will not get involved, is not going to get involved, as he moves closer to the criminal fault. This resembles Jake Barnes's sequence of weakening refusals to introduce Brett to Pedro Romero in *The Sun Also Rises*.

Hammett's *Thin Man* is forced to begin as a novel of manners because Nick Charles refuses to get involved in the Wynant case. However, everybody continues to offer him the case (nobody seems to hear his denials), until he seems to suffer identity confusion and not know whether he is working the case or not, or even how one comes to refuse a case: "To be honest with you, I don't know. If people keep on pushing me into it. I don't know how far they'll carry me" (TM 623). At other times the space of the motive is brutally foreclosed. "I'm just sitting here because I don't have any place to go. I don't want to work. I don't want anything," Marlowe tells Orfamay Quest just before he takes her case (LS 4).

Marlowe's involvement in the search for Velma in *Farewell, My Lovely* is a good example of the hard-boiled detective's helpless drift. He happens to be in a black ghetto looking for a missing barber and notices Moose Molloy outside the barbershop as he is leaving. Molloy is a giant of a man and Marlowe stops to watch him. Molloy walks into a saloon, and before the doors have stopped swinging, a young black man comes sailing out and lands in the gutter. As Marlowe walks to the saloon doors, a seemingly detached sound track plays: "They were motionless now. It wasn't any of my business. So I pushed them open and looked in." Marlowe does it because it is none of his business, but he is also saying that why he did it is none of our business. Upstairs, Molloy notices Marlowe and asks the obvious question, "Who the hell asked you to stick your face in?" Before Molloy tears up the saloon, Marlowe says to the bartender who believes that the two are together,

"I couldn't help myself. . . . [He] dragged me up. I never saw him before." He later tells Lieutenant Nulty, "I just happened to be there" (FML 1–9, 13).

Marlowe tries to hand the case to Nulty: he can only let go of what is none of his business if he can find somebody else to take it. Nulty doesn't want any cases either; he wants Marlowe to "take a gander around for this dame." Marlowe asks him three times why he should do it: "What's in it for me?" "What good is it going to do me?" "Is this for love—or are you paying anything in money?" All that Nulty can suggest is that Marlowe might get into a jam someday and need a pal. And Marlowe agrees to take the case: "Nothing made it my business except curiosity. But strictly speaking, I hadn't had any business in a month. Even a no-charge job was a change" (FML 13–15).

Marlowe follows Molloy because it is none of his business, and he takes the case because, what the hell, he hasn't anything better to do. This pattern is repeated in Marlowe's next offer of employment, which appears to be unrelated to Molloy and the search for Velma. Lindsay Marriott, a gay man, wants Marlowe to act as his bodyguard in an exchange of jewels. The fiction this time is of a job that feels bad and, for that reason, should not be taken up, and again Marlowe says no three times: "You want a bodyguard, but he can't wear a gun. You want a helper, but he isn't supposed to know what he's supposed to do. You want me to risk my neck without knowing why or what for or what the risk is." The most appropriate refusal, however, can never find expression; it is as if what is really attractive about these jobs are their sucker terms (FML 42).

Marlowe says later, "I ought to walk away from this job, Marriott. I really ought." But he never walks away from a case: he cannot be warned off by police or threatened off by gangsters; he cannot even be fired by his clients. The cover story for this tenacity is remarkably empty: he does it because it's his job to do it. And yet, when the hard-boiled detective talks about this job, it is made to seem squalid. Although this private detective does not victimize striking workers or peep for images of sexual abandon, the oppressive aspects of the profession are brought in to flavor his "smelly business" (FML 46, 106).

This erosion of resistance, the seductive vortex of involvement takes a verbal form in hard-boiled detective fiction, but it tends to be structural in the spy thriller. Like Alice, Buchan's heroes "stumble into" their adventures, and that act of stumbling initiates events that entangle them further. The hard-boiled detective "falls for" or "gets hooked on" a case; the amateur spy is "sucked" into it. Ambler protagonists like Latimer or Kenton declare that these adventures are ridiculous, that they will get on the next plane to London and resume their ordinary lives, but they are forcibly prevented from withdrawing.

Both the hard-boiled detective and professional spy are in it for the money, and yet they take wry pride in telling us that they don't get any money, or, sometimes, that they don't even want the money. In the film version of *A Funeral in Berlin*, Colonel Stok, a dedicated Bolshevik, tells Harry Palmer,

> "You're good at your job. You need only one thing."
> "What's that?" asks Palmer.
> "A reason for doing it."

Palmer flatly states, "thirty a week," and it is clear that money is not his reason for staying on the job. Money is also alleged to be the motive in *The Maltese Falcon:* Joel Cairo tells Spade that he "made somewhat extensive inquiries about you before taking any action . . . and was assured that you were far too reasonable to allow other considerations to interfere with profitable business relations." Money is the only remaining signifier of value in that world, and Spade tells Brigid that it is an adequate substitute for narrative: "We didn't exactly believe your story. . . . We believed your two hundred dollars" (MF 44, 29). But this money isn't there: the falcon turns out to be lead, and what little money there is goes on a crazy circuit: it is given by Gutman to Spade, who gives it to Brigid. When Spade returns it to Gutman it is one thousand dollars short. Gutman accuses Brigid of secreting it under her dress, but it is he who has palmed it. He is made to return the bill; the money is again taken from Spade at gunpoint, but not before Spade removes a bill for his expenses (MF 156–80).

In *The Long Goodbye*, on the other hand, Marlowe says he doesn't make a dime out of it, but when he is reproached for his behavior, he cracks, "I just did it for the money." The money in this story consists of frozen assets that may not circulate for sacramental reasons: he keeps the bill that Terry Lennox gave him as a retainer in a coffee can in the freezer (LG 230, 133). According to Hartman, "What Marlowe says to a beautiful woman who offers him money is puzzlingly accurate: 'You don't owe me anything. I'm paid off.' Puzzling because it is unclear where his real satisfaction comes from. . . . What is there in it for him? . . . We don't ever learn who is paying off the inner Marlowe or Archer. Their motives are virtually the only things in these stories that are not visible" (217).

The dialectic of involvement and indifference that characterizes hard-boiled detective fiction is patterned in *The Maltese Falcon* through Spade's alternation between his office, in which relationships are opened, to his apartment, in which they are closed. He allies himself initially with Brigid in his office, but it is from his apartment that he calls the police to turn her in. After turning Iva away at his hotel door, he receives her again in his office, making an insincere commitment to her. He meets Joel Cairo and accepts money from him in his office and betrays him twice in his apartment. Whenever he leaves the relative safety of the office or the apartment, his self-control lapses. It is in Gutman's hotel room that he is given knockout drops; in Brigid's hotel room, he rages at his helplessness as she manipulates him sexually. His two great outbursts of rage take place in Brigid's hotel room and the DA's office.

The book opens and closes with Spade alone. The intervening narrative moves out to touch groups of people who circulate around Spade, people whose interests he has taken on. He dismisses no one, he enters into a nominal contract with everyone he meets; yet, at the end, Spade has eliminated every threatening character from the book. The pattern is a schizoid one: a passive, withdrawn, and isolated hero who fears involvement is launched upon a project where he is deeply involved in a more than ordinary tangle of greed, fear, hatred, and love. He claims throughout that he is not really touched by any of this, and he persists until the end when he is again alone, outside all involvement.

The most famous cluster of markers for the inaccessibility of the detective hero is celebrated as "tough." While toughness probably crystallized around the figure of the hobo at the turn of the century, it became prominent in the fiction and film of the 1920s and 1930s and was distributed over a wide range of heroic male types: the street tough, the criminal, the private detective, the newspaper reporter, the shyster lawyer, and, most remarkably, the middle-class rural protagonists of Ernest Hemingway (see Widmer). The term is passionately overdetermined, and as a cult quality closely associated with the mystical meaning of America, it is reproduced with deep fascination in the narrative forms of the twentieth century. The hard-boiled detective protagonist is written over ground prepared by Kipling and Joseph Conrad and amplified by Hemingway and William Faulkner.

Mike Hammer brags, "I lived to kill because my soul was a hardened thing. . . . I lived because I could laugh it off and others couldn't" (OLN 149). Toughness may be, for all the text reveals to the contrary, only hardness: "the Op's toughness is not merely a carapace within which feelings of tenderness and humanity can be nourished and preserved. The toughness is toughness through and through, and as the Op continues his career . . . he tends to become more callous and less and less able to feel" (Marcus 22). In his untouchability and his radical isolation, the hard-boiled detective resembles the psychopathic personality. Alvarez observed that Spade and Nick Charles, "in their controlled, cynical, alcoholic ways, both qualify as psychopaths" (169).

The conventional description of a detective from a novel of 1880 affirms this emotional monstrosity: "Mr. Taggett has a heart of steel; without it he would be unable to do his distressing work. The cold impartiality with which he sifts and heaps up circumstances involving the doom of a fellow-creature appears almost inhuman; but it is his business" (Aldrich 246). The detective's indifference is glaring because he is always seen in juxtaposition to the aggravated desire or fear of others. And this is intensified by the intimacy of his exposure to others' lives; as Eudora Welty said of Archer, he finds his way "through their lies and fears, into other people's obsessions and dreams" (1). His work forces him to intrude into the most secret corners of the lives of those he investigates, yet he expresses neither sympathy nor repugnance.

We know from Twain of the intimate relationship between the deadpan and the triumph of the ego—of tough and cool as conquest. In *Funeral*

in Berlin, the protagonist is sent into an embattled East Berlin to contact a defecting Red Army colonel. He doesn't like the situation, but he
goes. Once inside, he is swept up by the police, but he doesn't protest
or even try to use his cover story. It turns out that this was the flamboyant method chosen by Colonel Stok to arrange for the interview. The
reader has to be surprised by this narrative collapse, but the protagonist acts as if he is not, and yet his interior narrative is hidden from us:
whether he knew that this was Stok's ploy, guessed it was but wasn't
sure, experienced some doubtful and uneasy moments, or was terrified
throughout. Sitting in the police office, he thinks cynically, "I knew
there must be a way out. None of those young fellows on late-night TV
would find it any sort of dilemma." Yet, when Stok asks him "Have I
caused you great inconvenience?" he answers, "Not unless you count
being scared half to death"; whereupon Stok laughs, and the reader
has no idea (or two incompatible ideas) of what the hero has been feeling (FB 32–33). Detective fiction is played out through a challenge to
the reader that operates quite differently from the official challenge
issued by writers like Ellery Queen: a challenge to guess and not know
the relationship between language and feeling, between toughness and
subjectivity. When Leamas's control suggests that toughness is an act,
a survival mechanism—"We act it to one another, all this hardness; but
we aren't like that really. I mean . . . one can't be out in the cold all the
time; one has to come in from the cold . . . do you see what I mean?"—
Leamas says numbly: "I can't talk like this, Control" (SC 23).

Toughness or tightness is a surface text written over the space of
repression. With Hammett, hard-boiled detective fiction shifted to first-
person narrative. This allowed it to shut out or distort an outside perspective, and it used first-person narrative so as to shut out or distort
any inside perspective. The Old Man tells the Op, "You'll know how
to handle it," and what fills the space of the subject is the information,
"I pretended I agreed with him" ("FP" 7). This teases us with access
but offers only false currency. In a scene between Archer and Lawson,
a hospital pathologist, in *The Doomsters*, Archer is sufficiently present
to notice that "Lawson stiffened perceptibly, as if he realized that he'd
been talking very freely." Archer also "notices" that Lawson notices
that Archer has disappeared from the scene: "He noticed that I wasn't

listening, and peered into my face with professional solicitude. 'What's the trouble, fellow? You got a cramp?' " The trace of the subject here is an enigmatic expression that is diverted through the body, and if we read it as a diver's cramp, we can surmise that Archer is returning from a great distance. Even when the space of the subject is completely open to the reader, nothing proper to it is there: "Felt from inside, like a rubber Halloween mask, my smile was a stiff grimace. Jerry Hallman relieved my embarrassment, if that is what I was feeling" (D 66, 42).

Not only is there a ban on feeling, even extreme physical sensations are dissembled. When Marlowe first meets Molloy, a hand fastened on his shoulder "and squashed it to a pulp. . . . The big man stared at me solemnly and went on wrecking my shoulder with his hand" (FML 2). Yet once in every hard-boiled novel all the withheld pain is assembled for a grand extravaganza in a long, liminal passage describing, for example, the hero's recovering consciousness after being knocked out or drugged.

Tough, then, has nothing to be but style, and one of the celebrated features of hard-boiled detective fiction is the presentation of a style that refers indistinguishably to a character and to a text. It is written, according to Alvarez, in "a prose in which the most grotesque or shocking details are handled as though they were matters of routine, part of the job" (170). Hard-boiled style will not register the anxiety of experience or even participate in its organization: it is a prose that refuses to get involved or to acknowledge what its involvement is. Appealing instead to a "dead" or catatonic model of perception, it strings together moments of ease and tension, as in this passage from Hammett's "Fly Paper": "Babe liked Sue. Vassos liked Sue. Sue liked Babe. Vassos didn't like that. Jealousy spoiled the Greek's judgment. He kept the speakeasy door locked one night when Babe wanted to come in. Babe came in, bringing pieces of the door with him. Vassos got his gun out, but couldn't shake Sue off his arm. He stopped trying when Babe hit him with the part of the door that had the brass knob on it. Babe and Sue went away from Vassos' together" ("FP" 6). The narrator pretends to be ignorant of the rhythms of love and jealousy, of loss and reward. He also doesn't seem to know that certain kinds of coming in can be described as crashing through or breaking into. His perception is also a beat behind, still stuck with Babe wanting when Babe has crashed through the door, with Sue holding on when the door has sent Vassos sprawling.

Chandler takes this complex one step further by keeping the dynamics of shock but suppressing the human register (not only in the service of hard-boiled style but of an ugly racism as well): "The doors swung back outwards and almost settled to a stop. Before they had entirely stopped moving they opened again, violently, outwards. Something sailed across the sidewalk and landed in the gutter between two parked cars. It landed on its hands and knees and made a high keening noise like a cornered rat. It got up slowly, retrieved a hat and stepped back onto the sidewalk. It was a thin, narrow-shouldered brown youth. . . . It had slick black hair. It kept its mouth open and whined for a moment. People stared at it vaguely" (FML 2). Clearly the vaguest starer is Marlowe/Chandler himself.

Another strategy for tightening the narrative line, familiar in Hemingway as well, is to suspend subjectivity under a cover of surface details. In the following passage, Spade has just received the call telling him of Miles Archer's death:

> Spade's thick fingers made a cigarette with deliberate care, sifting a measured quantity of tan flakes down into curved paper, spreading the flakes so that they lay equal at the ends with a slight depression in the middle, thumbs rolling the paper's inner edge down. . . . [He] began to dress. He put on a thin white union-suit, grey socks, black garters and dark brown shoes. When he had fastened his shoes he picked up the telephone, called Graystone 4500 and ordered a taxicab. He put on a green-striped white shirt, a soft white collar, a green necktie, the grey suit he had worn that day, a loose tweed overcoat, and a dark grey hat. The street-door-bell rang as he stuffed tobacco, keys and money into his pockets (MF 10–11).

Prose that doggedly refuses to leave space for grief and shock is prose that is itself in a state of shock. But the grotesque investment in detail, particularly sartorial detail, also signifies this prose knows its survival depends on style. Spade will solve the murder of Miles Archer merely by knowing Archer died with his overcoat buttoned.

The triumphs of this style are its cracks, its wisecracks, extravagantly praised as artistic gold in Chandler and profundity in Macdonald. The compulsive and autonomous activity of wisecracking sparks Marlowe's internal narrative as much as his conversation. When the "nice girl" in *Farewell, My Lovely*, Anne Riordan, pleads with him to be serious and drop his "bunch of gag lines," Marlowe simply cracks wise, but so silently that she can't hear it: "I stopped fooling around and got my battle-scarred frown back on my face" (FML 79). As language in a state of shock, wisecracking betrays a fear of implication: the similes for which Chandler is praised could be described as frozen connotation. In an adjacent cultural context, they are the brazen and pathetic gag mechanisms of Groucho Marx or W. C. Fields.

Wisecracking is an urgent activity; it treats all phases of subjectivity as if they were equally perilous. Marlowe refuses (or is unable) to treat a moment of sensibility as if it were casual: he cannot even say "I parked my car," but cracks instead, "I drove past and gave the sidewalk cafe my business to the extent of using its parking space" (FML 38). The wise-cracks are supposed to prove that the subject has no cracks, but we read it otherwise. The hard-boiled detective cracks because he is afraid of cracking, and the fear of opening up is dramatized in Chandler through Marlowe's repeated encounters with "false" psychoanalysts. Before he has even met Jules Amthor, Marlowe is sneering at the imagined claim that he can normalize sexual attitudes, but the fear expressed is that Amthor can and will dissolve toughness: "Men would sneak in on him too, big strong guys that roared like lions around their offices and were all cold mush under their vests" (FML 87).

The hard-boiled detective has been described as soft almost as often as he has been called tough: he is "really" a sentimentalist, a romantic idealist. I map a part of that story again, with the understanding that the fiction of the depths is as much a cliché as the carapace of tough-ness. He possesses an ethical core that dictates sacrificial involvement in the lives of others, so that his underlying character is actually of pas-sionate dedication and concern; he is a knight or crusader, Christ, Ivan Karamazov, or Miss Lonelyhearts. This ethical humanism bleeds into the texts themselves: both Marlowe and Lew Archer express passion at detached moments, although it is literally repudiated by the fictions in which it is embedded—"I'm a romantic, Bernie. I hear voices crying in the night and I go see what's the matter. You don't make a dime that way. You got sense, you shut your windows and turn up more sound on the TV set. . . . Stay out of other people's troubles. All it can get you is the smear" (LG 229). "The problem was to love people, try to serve them, without wanting anything from them. I was a long way from solving that one" (BC 119).

Even telling it like it is, Marlowe gets it wrong. If you can't resist a plea for help and you happen also to be a private detective, you should stand to make many dimes. Marlowe also dissembles the structure of his employment: private detectives respond to pleas during the day, not at night. If the voices of the day shadow your nights with guilt, you should not be a private detective, and all of this suggests that Marlowe has chosen an occupation that guarantees to fill his life with pain. But the dramatization of Marlowe's days asserts the opposite, because Marlowe listens to those voices with weary cynicism or anger.

Behind the dead eyes and the tight voice of the hard-boiled detective is self-disgust and rage; behind these, tears; and behind this, tenderness and a desire to trust. It is a model of abused innocence, a familiar version of maleness in so much twentieth-century literature. The point of these stories is the strenuously impacted cover-up: on the convoluted edge of tough, hard is already soft, toughness is already caring too deeply. Sentiment infiltrates hard-boiled fiction as its opposite, as sneering at sentiment or quoting sentiment—quotations that are often on the point of crumbling. After the homosexual Marriott is killed, Marlowe refuses to turn the investigation over to the police, giving as his reason that "the poor guy paid me a hundred bucks to take care of him—and I didn't. Makes me feel guilty. Makes me want to cry. Shall I cry?" (FML 110). But the cynicism is also in quotation marks, because he honors this commitment.

Marlowe is defensive about his sentimentalism. At the end of *Farewell, My Lovely*, he suggests that Velma should allow herself to be shot by a cop to spare her husband, an "old man who loved not wisely, but too well." The policeman, Randall, tells him sharply, "That's just sentimental," and Marlowe shuts off the conversation: "Sure. It sounded like that when I said it. Probably all a mistake anyway. So long." When the wisecracking stops, the language becomes mawkish, the similes wet: her fingers "touched mine and I held them for a moment and then let them go slowly as you let go of a dream when you wake with the sun in your face and have been in an enchanted valley" (FML 158, 249). This passage and others like it reflect the "real" Marlowe—and the "real" Chandler because Chandler is "really" a bad writer or one of the best writers in a genre that writes badly. Bad writing, rather than being a failing of the genre, is actually a characteristic of it, emerging from its center.

Alvarez said that "such toughness makes them seem impregnable, but it is also a burden. At moments, fatigue and distaste for themselves come over them like a sickness" (169). For the hard-boiled detective and the professional spy, self-disgust is pervasive, but displaced as a function of the job. The social semantics of peeping, snooping, manipulating, grilling, abusing are always available to justify it. After getting Mrs. Florian drunk in order to pump her, Marlowe thinks: "A lovely old woman. I liked being with her. I liked getting her drunk for my own sordid purposes. I was a swell guy. I enjoyed being me. You find almost anything under your hand in my business, but I was beginning to be a little sick at my stomach" (FML 26).

The last alibi behind the detective's behavior is a fear of being dependent and vulnerable: the fear of being played for a sap or a sucker, of being a fall guy, as in Sam Spade's mythopoeic speech at the end of *The Maltese Falcon*. This is seen as a victimization and death. Such a fear of being used or written upon keeps them tight, wary, tough; it keeps them defensive and permanently angry; it keeps them always on the edge of self-pity and tears, begging to be played for a sap.

5

The Pleasures
of Being Merely Male

SOON AFTER HARD-BOILED DETECTIVE FICTION WAS ESTABLISHED
as a genre in the late 1920s, its excesses were reflected in the lens of
parody and identified as a masochistic fantasy: "The hero is usually
captured by the big, bad villains, given a shot of morphine, awakens in
an isolated house with a huge gorilla sitting in the room, methodically
chewing gum. The hero asks questions, makes wisecracks, and from
time to time the gorilla calmly gets up, walks over to the bed and beats
up on the hero. After that, three or four other villains come in and start
exercising. The hero is beaten into unconsciousness two or three times,
but eventually manages to slug his way into the clear" (Gardner 206).
The amateur thriller is also a masochistic fantasy: its protagonist is pro-
pelled on a dark journey of flight and evasion, constant setbacks, and
catastrophic turnings. In chapter 2, I argued for strong historical and
structural connections between detective fiction and a pure literature
of suffering, the haunted house tale, or an even more dynamic predecessor, the sensation tale of Poe, such as "Buried Alive" or "The Pit
and the Pendulum," which features a succession of the most fiendish
tortures that the Spanish Inquisition can design. Analytic detective fiction, which is not masochistic, begins with the rewriting of these stories

so as to distance the element of suffering, to recast it in a mode of omnipotence and control; the scene of suffering in "Murders in the Rue Morgue" is filtered to the reader from behind locked doors and through the testimony of many bewildered auditors, and we encounter it directly only after it is frozen in death.

A word such as *masochism* is always under sentence of erasure. Its presence in detective fiction can be easily masked by its general prominence in fiction as a source of pleasure in structures that, on the one hand, necessarily work through delay and deferral and, on the other, dwell inordinately on frustration, pain, and defeat. Even so, the word is still felt to diminish or dirty pleasure, as if a right word for pleasure destroyed it. Kingsley Amis's shifty dismissal of the term, however, is a pretty accurate description of the erotic center of the spy thriller: "*Masochism* is more appropriate at first sight, but is impaired by the difficulty that the masochist enjoys being knocked about. Bond gives no sign of pleasure. . . . But I suppose he might really be enjoying himself all the time, sort of without knowing it. I look forward to being told by some learned puritan that, since there are 'really' no accidents in life, Bond is 'secretly' a glutton for punishment in some sense approaching the literal, and seeks capture 'deliberately' in order to land himself a treat" (22).

Freud, Karen Horney, and Theodor Reik argue for a generalized personality disorder, a moral masochism widespread in art culture. Reik isolates two peculiar features of this complex that align it very closely with popular fiction: the "special significance of phantasy" ("phantasy is its source," not a pathway along which it pursues its goal) and "suspense" (two "qualities of this peculiar element of tension are demonstrably different from anything in normal sexuality: the preponderance of the anxiety factor and the tendency to prolong the suspense") (Reik 1957, 206–7, 222; see Freud 1953 [1924], 255–68 and Horney 260, 267).

Masochism flourishes in hard-boiled detective fiction particularly. In *Farewell, My Lovely* the pain is regularly totted up: "You're so marvellous. . . . So brave, so determined and you work for so little money. Everybody bats you over the head and chokes you and smacks your jaw and fills you with morphine, but you just keep right on hitting between tackle and end until they're all worn out" (FML 246). Though Amis declares that fictional suffering is fully explained by fictional circumstances, the pain and suffering of the hard-boiled detective are gratuitous in their intensity and extent:

> "God in heaven!" she exclaimed involuntarily, "What hap—" then caught herself.
>
> "A hoodlum threw a glass of acid in my face." He shrugged. "Occupational hazard, Aunt Mamie. I'm a cop. I take my chances." (CK 6)

Hard-boiled detective fiction savors the possibility of pain: "He was holding himself very still. He was going to slug me and we both knew it" (LG 30). "I dropped and did a frogleap sideways and the swish of the blackjack was a long spent sigh in the quiet air" (FML 222).

And it is a pleasure: masochism is reproduced as tough talk, the peculiar wit of hard-boiled fiction. The ban against "literary" writing is suspended once or twice in a novel to render the extravagance of physical pain, although, ironically, it can only take the form of an even more egregious example of bad writing: "He clenched his teeth again. He felt as if his head was raw, his neck torn. Jagged pain struck at him when he lowered his head, and he hadn't the strength to move it up again quickly. Go slow. Go *slow*. Right hand against the floor, right knee over the left leg, right knee on the floor. Over, gradually, take the strain on right hand and knee. Pain was pulling at his head, ugly, jagged, ripping claws. And his head and face burned with a strange heat. He was getting up, mustn't fall back, once he was up it would be better. Up—up—*up!*" (SIW 83).

Reading Amis against himself, I do believe that the hero of popular fiction seeks out his punishment:

> "Say that again," he said softly.
> I said it again.
> He hit me across the face with his open hand. . . .
> "Say it again," he said softly.
> I said it again. His hand swept and knocked my head to one side again.
> "Say it again."
> "Nope. Third time lucky. You might miss." (LL 123–24)

Asking for pain is the point of the detective's dares and challenges and his wisecracks: When Lew Archer is asked his name by a man who has just beaten him up, he quips, "Sacher-Masoch" ("FW" 238). He may even do it responsibly, in which case it gets absorbed into the craft of professionalism: "The quick way was to reverse the order of things. To find one man among three and a half million I must let him find me. . . . Then try to finish him off before he finished me" (QM 24).

After Marlowe has "faced down" Moose Molloy, the latter says to him, "You take some awful chances, brother," and indeed he does (FML 234).[1] In confrontations, Marlowe needlessly provokes a violence that claims him as its object:

> "Somebody bump into your arm, cheapie?"
> "I tripped over an enchilada."
> Negligently, not quite looking at me even, he slashed me across the
> face with the gun barrel. (LG 284)

When the situation explodes, Marlowe will often act surprised. The writing also pretends to be unaware of its provocations. There is an extravagant masochistic setup in the George Stevens film *Gunga Din* that indicates the lengths to which the denial of masochism can go. The soldiers three stumble upon a temple filled with frenzied thugs being worked up into bloodlust against the British. Douglas Fairbanks leaves to get help and tells a dim-witted Cary Grant to hold them there until he gets back. Grant thinks about it for a moment and marches out of hiding singing a soldier song. He steps onto the platform and tells the momentarily stunned mob that they are under arrest.

Spade is knocked out by Joel Cairo after Spade refuses to let him search his office. Later, Cairo expresses amazement: the black bird was not there, so "why should you have risked serious injury to prevent my searching for it?" (MF 43). Marlowe's lawyer is bewildered by his refusal to talk to the police, which results in three days in jail: "If you had had a grain of sense you'd have told the police you hadn't seen Lennox for a week. . . . There's no law against lying to the cops. They expect it. . . . [But you] had to play the big scene. . . . How ingenuous can a man get, Marlowe. A man like you who is supposed to know his way around" (LG 44–45). Characters around the detective claim to be puzzled by his behavior, which is often read as an indication of the extraordinary purity of his motives; this lawyer, however, associates it indirectly with exhibitionism.

A strong connection between masochism and exhibitionism can be clearly seen in works like Kafka's "In the Penal Colony" or "The Hunger Artist." This is the third distinctive feature of masochism, what Reik calls "the demonstrative" ("it is meant to stress that in no case of masochism can the fact be overlooked that the suffering, discomfort, humiliation and disgrace are being shown and, so to speak, put on display" [1957, 235]). Tom Sawyer's fantasy of his own death is highly theatrical: at the height of the grieving and wailing, Tom will appear and receive in person the tribute of love and praise made available for his eulogies. The Connecticut Yankee becomes boss of England at the center of an assembled multitude, tied to a stake awaiting death by burning.[2]

Hard-boiled detective fiction and the spy thriller often include a masochistic set-piece (a punishment structure), usually a scene of imprisonment or torture, for example, the orchestrated beating of Ned Beaumont by an "apish man" in a small locked room (a version of the Gardner monomyth). Punishment structures often open the spy thriller, as in the double imprisonment in *The Freedom Trap*, or the more ordinary opening of *Epitaph for a Spy*, where a tourist is caught up by the police and told there is conclusive proof that he is a spy. In the opening of *The Spy Who Came In from the Cold*, Leamas acts out a slow and humiliating process of deterioration. We learn later he is really acting in order to convince his colleagues in the Circus that he is "going to seed"; this will make him attractive to the enemy as a double agent, and he is soon "transformed from a man honorably put aside to a resentful drunken wreck." He leaves the service under suspicion of embezzlement and haunts the streets in grubby clothes, unshaven and drunk. He provokes a fight in a grocery store and beats the grocer brutally, so that, like the Thinking Machine, Marlowe, and others, he can maneuver himself into prison (SC 29, 33, 50). The alibi for this painstaking performance is that it is the only way to accomplish the mission, but the fiction is one of self-degradation.

Dick Francis is particularly bold in exploiting masochistic situations.

As a former steeplechase jockey, he is well qualified to write of pain. Many of his heroes are jockeys themselves, small men who fall repeatedly and live with bruised flesh and broken bones; their experiences of enduring pain sustain the episodes of domestic torture that climax the novels. In *Odds Against*, Sid Halley has had his hand crushed in a fall from a horse. His wealthy father-in-law has decided to investigate a series of racecourse accidents, and his plan of action consists of inviting Halley to a country weekend and exposing him to the sadistic behavior of the assembled suspects.

The James Bond novels are centered on episodes of torture:

> Bond has a physical endurance that is really outstanding and which has allowed him to endure ordeals of exceptional severity. In *Casino Royale* he was bound naked to a chair without a seat and was beaten about the testicles with a carpet beater for about an hour. In *The Moonraker* he was buried under a landslide. . . . In *Thunderball* he was almost quartered by an apparatus for vertebral traction while under treatment in a clinic. In *Live and Let Die* . . . he escaped from a mortal struggle with an octopus. A barracuda wrenched away a piece of his shoulder. At the end he was tied naked to a girl (also naked) and attached to the cable of a paravane of a yacht, then dragged across a coral reef. (Tornabuoni 25)

Bond's mission in *Doctor No* is to move through an obstacle course—a set of mechanisms designed by a sadist—that seems to have been waiting to inflict pain on Bond alone.

From the perspective of masochism and torture, the paradigmatic thriller is Household's *Rogue Male* where an anonymous protagonist spends almost the entire book trying to avoid capture by a group of foreign agents in England. He has no information they want; he has seen nothing that is a danger to them; they are motivated only by a desire to punish him. The novel begins with the capture of the hero as he is about to assassinate the leader of a foreign country—Hitler, it is suggested. His motives are kept obscure: "Like most Englishmen, I am not accustomed to inquire very deeply into motives. . . . I remember asking myself when I packed the telescopic sight what the devil I wanted it for; but I just felt that it might come in handy" (RM 12).[3] The hero claims he is indifferent to politics and rather admires the dictator.

His cover story is a rich one, the story of a basic form of adventure fiction as well as the motive for analytic detective fiction: he had proposed this feat for himself as an intellectual challenge governed by the principle of fair play. He wanted to see if a lone hunter could penetrate the security system and get within shooting range. He denies any murderous intent; the challenge only extended to getting the dictator within his sights.

The pain that follows his capture is harrowing. He is tortured by the security forces and left hanging at the edge of a cliff in order to stage an accidental death. After his fall, it feels to him "as if the back of my thighs and rump had been shorn off. . . . I travelled on my belly, using my elbows for legs and leaving a track behind me like that of a wounded crocodile, all slime and blood. . . . For all I knew, my bowels were only held in by mud." The English are trained to suffer pain, that is part of their glory, but this man is more extensively trained than most—he had been through an initiation ceremony on the Rio Javary because it was the only way to persuade the tribesmen to teach him how to exercise muscular control over hemorrhage—"My friends have sometimes accused me of taking pride in the maceration of my flesh. They are right. But I did not know that I could persuade myself to such agony as that climb" (RM 6, 8, 9).

Rogue Male shifts into a mode of intense masochism after betraying the possibility of its opposite, a sadistic act of assassination. In this fiction as elsewhere masochism and sadism are caught up in a quick exchange, each a cover for the deeper reality of the other (see Reik 1957, 254). The forms of detective fiction distribute themselves across this territory: analytic detective fiction is sadistic fantasy, whereas the other forms exploit masochism to a greater or lesser degree, but they are always capable (as in the scandalous instance of Mickey Spillane) of inverting their cover.

These sadomasochistic rhythms are featured in certain historical fantasies such as Baroness Orczy's *Scarlet Pimpernel* and Johnson McCulley's *Mark of Zorro*. In both works, the protagonist appears as two characters (a Clark Kent and a Superman), radically separated as masochist and sadist, effete dandy and aggressive brute: "The mask of the inane fop had been a good one, and the part consummately well played. No wonder that Chauvelin's spies had failed to detect, in the apparently brainless nincompoop, the man whose reckless daring and resourceful ingenuity had baffled the keenest French spies." Those who are not in on the secret cannot conceive of bringing the two together. As fop, Sir Percy courts rejection: "in repose one might have admired so fine a specimen of English manhood, until the foppish ways, the affected movements, the perpetual inane laugh, brought one's admiration of Sir Percy Blakeney to an abrupt close." Most painful is the fact that his disguise disgusts the woman he loves, the woman who would love him if he were not a despicable fop and coward but who cannot be served or saved unless he remains so: "she did not heed her husband's voice or his inane laugh, her thoughts had gone wandering in search of the mysterious hero" (Orczy 132, 43, 61).[4]

Sir Percy is a twin of detectives like Wimsey and Campion. In fact most analytic detectives pass through a transformation from Sir Percy to Pimpernel: "But Anthony was listening no longer. He was, in fact, no longer there to listen. He had suddenly turned about and sprung into the hall. As Mrs. Poole said later in the servants' hall, 'I'd never of believed such a lazy-looking gentleman could of moved so quick. Like the leap of a cat, it was' " (R 139). "The social intimates of the exquisite Van Dusen Ormsberry would never have recognized him in this alert, hard-mouthed man. . . . And yet it was here, if ever, that the real man could be seen, the man that lurked, alert and forceful, shrewd, vigorous, possessed of unfathomable energy, behind the suave veneered surface with which it amused him to mask his true countenance" (MKF 67). These cycles of masochism and sadism are implicit in the emotional rhythms of Sherlock Holmes's life: he is manic-depressive, depressed between cases and manic when he is on the job.

The appeal of the masochistic cover is so great that it invades a sadistic form like the Western. In detective fiction, agents who possess an overabundance of aggression are known as "cowboys": when Coffin Ed Jackson and Grave Digger Jones first appear in Chester Himes's *Crazy Kill*, a policeman exclaims, "Jesus Christ! Now we've got those damned Wild West gunmen here to mess up everything" (CK 28). Jack Shafer has his hero Shane walk into a barroom full of bullies and order a glass of soda pop; this is a setup for a later scene of singular masculine bravado in the same setting: the earlier masochism is an excuse for the sadistic behavior. For much of Max Brand's *Destry Rides Again,* the hero appears as a relentless destroyer. Following Destry's release from jail, however, there is an episode that has only a tenuous connection with his oath of revenge. He pretends to be "a whipped cur"; he cringes before the twelve jurors who convicted him; and he enrages his sweetheart by his cowardly behavior. In the film of this title, the hero is a sheriff who will not wear guns, and, although there is no source in the written text for this, it is an equivalent masochistic setup.

George Grella wrote that Spillane "represents the perversion [the hard-boiled tradition] . . . has undergone in the hands of the inept and the unthinking" (414). The perversion is sadism, and it agitates almost every page of Spillane's stories. Hammer is a casual sadist: he greets an elevator operator of whom he is fond, with "an easy jab in the short ribs" (IJ 17). There were, however, more sophisticated examples of sadistic mystery fiction even within the time frame considered in this book, for example, Richard Stark's Parker, and the Coffin Ed Jackson and Gravedigger Jones novels. Spillane expresses perversion as regression. The crudeness and rough cast of his fictions represent a reversion to the origin of hard-boiled detective fiction, which from the early days of *The Black Mask* through the novels of Ross Macdonald had been steadily transforming itself from a sadistic to a masochistic fiction.

Spillane can be read as a final moment of the hard-boiled, the moment when its cover is blown: at the end of Hammett's first novel, *Red Harvest,* the Op expresses anxiety about behavior that he is forced to recognize as sadistic: "Poisonville is right. It's poisoned me. . . . I've arranged a killing or two in my time, when they were necessary. But this is the first time I've ever got the fever. . . . This getting a rear out of planning deaths is not natural to me" (RH 160, 163). Commentary illuminates this connection: in one of the defenses of detective fiction discussed in chapter 1, sadism is held up as the artistic redemption of the genre as it evolves (back) into the crime novel. In an early version of this argument Sean O'Faolain charts this movement through his title "Give Us Back Bill Sikes," pointing, surely, to one of the greatest sadists in literature.

It is conventional for the villains of mystery fiction (when they are visible) to be sadistic. Spillane neatly illustrates a forthcoming topic: the mutual distribution of features between hero and villain—" 'Damn,' I spat out, 'he's kill crazy! Dumdums in the gut, head and heart. Pat, I'm going to enjoy putting a bullet in that crazy son of a bitch more than I enjoy eating. I'd sooner work him over with a knife first' " (IJ 95). Hero and villain function as one engaged unit in the erotics of violence; Fausto Antonini likened their relationship to a " 'strip-tease' of the instinct of death" and identified the dialectical equation between them as *vita tua mors mea, mors tua vita mea* (your life is my death, your death my life) (112, 107). Only the villain, however, is allowed to justify cruelty philosophically.

Analytic detective fiction is the most uniformly sadistic of the detective forms: "Sherlock Holmes was transformed when he was hot upon such a scent as this. Men who had only known the quiet thinker . . . would have failed to recognize him. His face flushed and darkened . . . his eyes shone out . . . with a steely glitter" (ASH 211). Another reason the detective must be an amateur is to carry the resonance of the erotic (or the lover) contained in that term: "On the morning when the murder was made known in London, there was the fullest meeting of amateurs that I have ever known since the days of Williams; old bedridden connoisseurs, who had got into a peevish way of sneering and complaining 'that there was nothing doing,' now hobbled down to our club-room: such hilarity, such benign expression of general satisfaction, I have rarely witnessed" (Thomas De Quincey, quoted in Altick 24).

Because of the analytic detective's detachment and thorough control of the investigation, his cruelty is mostly verbal. Holmes and Wolfe are great bullies, and Wolfe and other detectives pounce upon slips of the tongue, hammer at discrepancies, and torture their victims through a process called "grilling" (aggressive questioning is shared by the hero as investigator and the enemy as interrogator and torturer). Ellery Queen, for example, enjoys browbeating witnesses: he "looked curiously at each person in the room—curiously and slowly, as if he enjoyed the scrutiny" (FPM 34). Under the guise of necessity, Poirot can be extremely cruel:

He turned to Megan Barnard. The girl's face was very pale. She was breathing hard as though braced for an ordeal. Poirot's voice came out like the crack of a whiplash. . . .

"I visualize the scene on the beach thus. The man admires her belt. She takes it off, he passes it playfully round her neck—says, perhaps, 'I shall strangle you.' It is all very playful. She giggles—and he pulls—"

Donald Fraser sprang up. He was livid. "M. Poirot—for God's sake." Poirot made a gesture.

"It is finished, I say no more. It is over." (ABC 195, 208)

Neither Fraser nor Barnard, by the way, is the murderer.

Sadism in analytic detective fiction is not wholly verbal; it is also present as sins of omission and indifference. There is a convention of gentlemanly execution, whereby the detective allows a member of his class to commit suicide to spare him the disgrace of a public trial. In several of the Wimsey books, the detective is responsible for the conventional second death (in novels that are forbidden to have more than one), which is caused by the elaborate detours of his investigation. In hard-boiled detective fiction of course, the disregard for human life is pervasive; it becomes the form's great claim to social realism. All Hammett's heroes, Alvarez wrote, "are indifferent to murder, all are marginally corrupt"; the genius of Hammett "lies in his ability to make corruption seem normal without ever quite endorsing it" (169).

Cornell Woolrich's *Phantom Lady* is a suspense novel, a merger of analytic and thriller. In it, the sweetheart of the accused man dedicates herself to clearing her lover and, to that end, persecutes a bartender she believes to have suppressed important evidence. She shows up at the bar every night and sits there silently, looking at him. She follows him home after work and stands in front of his house, looking up at his window. When the strain becomes unbearable, he rushes out of the house into the path of a car. There is no authorial comment.

When asked what he would call a public school, Wimsey answers, Eton, then magnanimously adds Harrow. To the suggestion of Rugby, he protests, "No, no . . . that's a railway junction" (MMA 125). It is also the site of *Tom Brown's Schooldays*, and Wimsey was educated there along with most of the English gentlemen sleuths. In 1857 Thomas Hughes defined a type of exemplary male distinctly different from any that had appeared or would appear in adult fiction until Kipling and Conrad. The "manly boy" as he emerges from the work of Hughes resembles the masochistic hero described in the first part of this chapter. Hughes's novel is almost a celebration of masochism: "[Riding in coaches] you knew what cold was, and what it was to be without legs, for not a bit of feeling had you in them after the first half-hour. But it had its pleasures, the old dark ride. First there was the consciousness of silent endurance, so dear to every Englishman,—of standing out against something, and not giving in" (Hughes 54). Sitting in his car in the rain, waiting for something to develop, Marlowe notes that a "pool of water formed on the floorboards for me to keep my feet in" (BS 18).

The manly boy is defined by an eagerness to seek out pain—"Wherever hard knocks of any kind, visible or invisible, are going, there the Brown who is nearest must shove in his carcase"—and to remain obstinately involved in issues: "And the most provoking thing is, that no failures knock them up, or make them hold their hands." When successful, they neither seek nor accept praise. Thomas Arnold's sermon to the school in the novel defines a new type of Christian martyr: "The true sort of captain too for a boys' army, one who had no misgivings and gave no uncertain word of command, and, let who would yield or make truce, would fight the fight out . . . to the last gasp and the last drop of blood" (Hughes 2, 3, 105).[5]

Hughes's schoolboy fills the pages of school and sports stories in England and America and detective fiction of both the adolescent and adult variety. One of the conventional situations in detective stories, for example, was morally illuminating contact between the boy and that great, good, shadowy adult, the headmaster. Martin Green sees this figure as mediating the paradox at the center of Kipling's *Stalky and Co.*, whereby the saving message of the school is obedience and yet the boys' real education occurs as a series of rebellious acts against certain lower orders of authority (275). The two heroes of *Murder at the Keyhole* spend most of the book frustrating representatives of Scotland Yard, but eventually they are confronted by a senior officer: "We protested against many of his statements and some of his inferences. But a lecture it was, such as a schoolmaster, speaking more in sorrow than in anger, might have given two delinquent schoolboys. We were, according to this account, very decent but very foolish fellows" (MK 197).

The headmaster in *The Thirty-Nine Steps* is Sir Walter, who appears first as a fisherman: "a huge man in untidy old flannels and a wide-brimmed hat. . . . I thought I had never seen a shrewder or better-tempered face. . . . I stood up and looked at him, at his square cleft jaw and broad, lined brow and the firm folds of cheek, and began to think that here at last was an ally worth having." The headmaster resolves the police paradox intuitively; he knows at a glance what the moral worth of this "wild, haggard brown fellow" is. Hannay tells Sir Walter that he is wanted by the police, and the latter says, "That's all right. Don't let that interfere with your appetite. We can talk about these things after dinner" (TS 97, 98, 100). A more familiar type of headmaster in the thriller is Control, "the cold voice that Bond loved and obeyed" (Amis 72). Bond, by the way, is closer to Hughes's bully Flashman than to Brown; he is the public schoolboy as snob, and he relishes the privileged status his agentry confers; even the sneers thrill him—the gunsmith who criticizes his weapon has "the sort of voice Bond's first expensive tailor had used" (DN 21).

Thriller protagonists in both the Buchan and Le Carré lines often belong to a university elite; they are boys recruited in college by a don still connected with the secret service. Before their extraordinary assignment, they are called in for a solitary conference with another headmaster, the "old man." The two are alone, the apparatus of cabinet ministers and secretaries suspended for this moment of communion (Merry 60). The equivalent structure in hard-boiled detective fiction has the force of an adoption ceremony. In *The Big Sleep*, Marlowe is deeply moved by his initial interview with General Sternwood and will even grudgingly admit it. His perseverance and the pain he endures as a consequence are motivated by a desire, he says, not to let the old gentleman down.[6]

Public school sports provides the missing context for the ethic and aesthetic of analytic detective fiction, for the rule of the rules of the game is to play fair. This is much in evidence in the lists of rules for the genre: "The mysterious stranger who turns up from nowhere . . . spoils the play altogether"; "to solve a detective problem by such means would be like winning a race on the river by the use of a concealed motor-engine"; Chesterton "is too good a sportsman to fall back on such a solution" (Knox 194–95); and undiscovered poison "is not cricket" (Wright 68). Within the fiction as well, the hero must play the game fairly, even though criminals, particularly foreign criminals, are usually unsporting. The sportsman who is most bound to play fair is the amateur, and this, I believe, is the primary locus of that polysemous word and generates its ennobling connotations: the author "does not introduce a professional criminal to take the blame of a private crime; a thoroughly unsportsmanlike course of action, and another proof of how professionalism is ruining our national sense of sport" (Chesterton 1929, 176).

The public school presence is strongest in the amateur thriller established by Buchan where the action is regularly seen as sport: "I am an ordinary sort of fellow, not braver than other people, but I hate to see a good man downed, and that long knife would not be the end of Scudder if I could play the game in his place." Even the American, Scudder, is made to see history as a bizarre game of cricket: "For three hundred years . . . [the Jews] have been persecuted, and this is the return match for the *pogroms*" (TS 23, 10).

The game is best played as an underdog game, and it is not only played manfully but with cheek. When members of the Pimpernel's gang are asked why they risk their lives for French men and women who mean nothing to them, one replies: "Sport, Madame la Comtesse, sport . . . we are a nation of sportsmen, you know, and just now it is the fashion to pull the hare from between the teeth of the hound" (Orczy 32). Popular fiction is itself sport; writing on Buchan, T. E. Lawrence anticipated those defenders of detective fiction who see in it the sacred fire of the lost art of narrative: his books are "like athletes racing: so clean-lined, speedy, breathless. For our age they mean nothing; they are sport only; but will a century hence disinter them and proclaim him the great romancer of our blind and undeserving generation?" (quoted in Watson 43).

The hunt is the most common sporting metaphor because detective stories are, essentially, extravagant hunting tales. In *The Sign of Four*, Watson confesses, "I have coursed many creatures in many countries during my checkered career, but never did sport give me such a wild thrill as this mad, flying man-hunt down the Thames" (SF 138), and Hannay acknowledges that it "was going to be a giddy hunt, and it was queer how the prospect comforted me" (TS 23). The thriller inherited the mantle of this imperial sport from Kipling and Haggard, but many of the metaphoric extensions like cover or going to ground come from the wrong end, from the hunted creature rather than the hunter.

Richard Hannay finds himself alone, burdened by a secret, and suspected of the murder of Scudder; he sighs, "I had no real pal who could come forward and swear to my character" (TS 22). The headmaster and the pal are the valorized males in the Buchan thriller, uncontaminated and attractive people. The spark of identity and love between pals may be set off by a common frame of reference (school or service), shared tastes, or it may be more mystical, for example, anyone who hunts and fishes may be a pal. As Kipling wrote in *The Light That Failed*, "Torpenhow entered the studio at dusk, and looked at Dick with his eyes full of the austere love that springs up between men who have tugged at the same oar together and are yoked by custom and use and the intimacies of toil. This is a good love" (74–75). Needless to say, loyalty to a pal transcends all other imperatives: "So you're going to give me up to the men you're afraid of to do as they like with me. I never expected it of you, Bill. I thought you were the kind of lad who would send any gang to the devil before you'd go back on a pal" (PH 117).

Palling generally involves a recognition of social class; the following quotation both asserts and mystifies this: "I say Class X because there is no definition of it. To talk of an upper or a ruling class is nonsense. . . . It is not, I think, a question of accent, but rather of the gentle voice. It is certainly not a question of clothes. It may be a question of bearing" (RM 36–37). This eroticized redefinition of class corresponds to the fiction of male bonding at the center of Conrad's "Secret Sharer." At a highly framed moment in the tale, the young captain gazes down at a naked man in the lagoon—and sees him wearing an old school tie:

> "A pretty thing to have to own up to for a Conway boy. . . ."
> "You're a Conway boy?"
> "I am," he said, as if startled. Then, slowly. "Perhaps you too—."
> (1976, 658)

The captain unhesitatingly accepts his duty, which is to help his friend escape the law. It is understood that a self-imposed sentence, and a severe one at that, will follow: never to see a white face again. In his unswerving loyalty to his pal, the captain must swerve perilously; he brings his ship dangerously close to the rocks, offering himself and his colored crew up as a sacrifice.

As Conrad's title implies, the pal is that other person that you share your shameful secret with. So it was defined by Thomas Hughes, in sentiments that glorify the English power of repression: "However, you'll all find . . . that a time comes in every human friendship, when you must go down into the depths of yourself, and lay bare what is there to your friend, and wait in fear for his answer. A few moments may do it; and, it may be (most likely will be, as you are English boys) that you never do it but once. But done it must be, if the friendship is to be worth the name. You must find what is there at the very root and bottom of one another's hearts; and if you are at one there, nothing on earth can, or at least ought to sunder you" (245). And so it is in the thriller: when Hannay finds his pal, he tells him his secret—"I thought the time had come for me to put my cards on the table. I saw by this man's eye that he was the kind you can trust. . . . It was the first time I had ever told any one the exact truth" (TS 55–56). What is told, however, is not Hannay's personal secret but the "historical" secret of this thriller.

The notion of sharing secrets with a pal should be an outrageous violation of narrative epistemology (as it is a violation of decency in the Conrad) since the stated condition of survival in all the forms is an unrelenting distrust. The enemy is everywhere, and he is uncannily adept at disguise. The disguises he should favor are the ordinary, cherished images of the hero's homeland. Villains should be expected to disguise themselves as the stuff of which pals are made. And in a sense they do: the headmaster, Sir Walter, and the archcriminal, the Black Stone, are the same image, except that one is certified as true and the other as false. The potential bankruptcy of values equations such as this could support is avoided, although a more cynical second wave of thrillers would flirt with these possibilities. In the thrillers I am discussing, however, pals suspend distrust, as the headmaster suspends the police paradox. In *The Rasp*, Deacon is a mystical pal: "in a party of, say twelve persons . . . I may find a man—perhaps unknown to me before—of whom I can swear before God and man: 'He *could* not have stolen the baby's marmalade—not even if he had tried to! He is incapable of carrying out such a crime.' . . . Deacon was a twelfth man. . . . The gods were good and dropped into my hands a little man who knew as much and a deal more than you. I exulted. I still exult. Like Stalky, I gloat!" But Deacon is also the man whom the police suspect to be the criminal (R 172, 211).

Self-reflexively, the pal is someone who shares the fantasy and who wants the adventure to go on and become more exciting. The hero of *Rogue Male* writes about a pal who claims he wouldn't do this for everyone: "All the same I think he would, given a story that appealed to him" (RM 39). James Bond encounters a similar reaction: " 'Yes, by jove! You were the chap who was mixed up in that treasure business here. . . . Splendid show. What a lark! I say, wish you'd start another bonfire like that here. Stir the place up a bit. All they think of nowadays is Federation and their bloody self importance. . . .' Bond grinned at him. This was more like it. He had found an ally" (DN 46–47).

Pals also come in series, often in the form of an exotic old-boys network that seems to transcend class and race, a community of colorful brigands. They may constitute the links of a chain along which the agent passes, or esoteric resources to whom the analytic or hard-boiled detective can go for information. Insofar as they are identified as comrades in previous adventures, they always hint at a thriller perspective. They can of course be the secret service itself: "They exchanged the sort of professional talk which to those who knew would have stamped them as members of the most exclusive club in the world. It was mostly about their colleagues of the Awkward Shop. One had gone to China;

another had returned from Siam; yet another was finishing a course on explosives. . . . From all corners of the world the frail network of Dombey's contriving—what he himself had once called 'My Giant Cobweb'—shook and vibrated with their messages" (WES 198). This figure is also the "us" of "one of us" that Hemingway adapted from the corps in Kipling—the old fighting and laughing comrades of *The Light That Failed*, for example, disbanded and dispersed in peacetime. It is a flexible structure; it can be used as the multiple protagonist of the spy thriller (*The Kremlin Letter*), the crime thriller (*League of Gentlemen*), or the Western (*The Magnificent Seven*).

Holmes, it has been said, is unthinkable without Watson: the detective cannot be thought without the pal. A central mystery of mystery fiction, however, is the tolerance extended to this figure. Why should a person of extraordinary mental power (and a great aversion to ennui, which includes almost everything except detecting at top speed) burden himself with a companion who understands little and whose talk is all nonsense and bluster:

> "Are you prepared to be the complete Watson?" he asked.
> "Watson?"
> "Do-you-follow-me-Watson; that one. Are you prepared to have quite obvious things explained to you, to ask futile questions, to give me chances of scoring off you, to make brilliant discoveries of your own two or three days after I have made them myself?" (RHM 69)

Holmes apparently chooses to associate on intimate terms not with an intellectual equal but an inferior who can offer him little stimulation; Watson, on the other hand, perversely chooses someone who bullies and humiliates him. Watson may be the representative of the reader, a person of normal, middling intelligence who reenacts within the text the drama of bewilderment and enlightenment that the form is designed to produce; nevertheless, the mystery of Watson is clarified by his difference from other inadequate readers. Both Watson's dimness and his interlocutory function are shared by the obtuse and incompetent policeman like Gregson and Lestrade; yet Gregson and Lestrade are contemptuously dismissed, while Watson is humored. They may be equally dense, but the police are dense and disbelieving, while Watson adores Holmes.

The Watson is the hero-worshipper of boys' fiction and in *this* respect acts as a surrogate for the reader. When the hero-worshipper has no hero to celebrate, when Watson (in *The Hound of the Baskervilles*) is forced into the adventure on his own, what we get is the amateur thriller of Ambler, the story of the sorcerer's apprentice clumsily attempting to restore the glory of a lost script. Watson is also the familiar British figure of Colonel Blimp (certainly as he is portrayed on the screen by Nigel Bruce), although this mask is sometimes worn by the detective himself. Furthermore, Todorov emphasizes Watson's role as a writer of detective fiction (1977, 45). The Blimp is given the task of transforming the adventure into a story, a task for which he should be unfit: the plodding soul writing the biography of the genius, the dull clod celebrating the exploits of the man of ingenuity and imagination. Detective fiction does not exploit the ironies of this tension, as Stevenson did with McKellar's narrative in *The Master of Ballantrae* or Conrad with Captain Mitchell's in *Nostromo*, where the narrative reproduces the moral ambiguity of the totalitarian regime it celebrates as an end to history.

In 1944 Stout wrote an article entitled "Watson Was a Woman" in a vein of insider humor. As Watson describes the relationship with Holmes, it sounds conventionally domestic: "He was a man of habits, narrow and concentrated habits, and I had become one of them. As an institution I was like the violin, the shag tobacco, the old black pipe" (Doyle quoted in Starrett 152). Watson appears on the first page of *The Sign of Four* as a picture of long-suffering irritation in a context of long-standing submission:

> Three times a day, for as many months, I had witnessed [Holmes' taking cocaine] . . . but custom had not reconciled my mind to it. On the contrary, from day to day I had become more irritable at the sight, and my conscience swelled mightily within me at the thought that I had lacked the courage to protest. Again and again I had registered a vow that I should deliver my soul upon the subject, but there was that in the cool nonchalant air of my companion which made him the last man with whom one would care to take anything approaching a liberty. His great powers, his masterly manner, and the experience which I had made of

his many extraordinary qualities all made me diffident and backward in
crossing him. (SF 89)

The bruiser and former criminal Lugg fusses over Campion like a wife.
"Ask me another. . . . Sneaked off on me, that's what 'e's done. 'E
knew I'd 'ave stopped 'im if 'e didn't" (GCM 137). Detective fiction is
aware of this area of slippage:

> "I know," he said. "There are people to whom one need not show off.
> It's a great comfort sometimes. I've got one of that kind."
> "Your wife! But I didn't know—"
> Alleyn sat back on his heels and laughed. "No, no. I'm talking about
> a certain Detective-Inspector Fox. He's large and slow and innocently
> straightforward." (VM 138)

At the end of *Dr. No*, after Quarrel is safely dead, Bond tenderly eu-
logizes that large black man: "Bond thought of the burned twist down
in the swamp that had been Quarrel. He remembered the soft ways
of the big body, the innocence in the grey, horizon-seeking eyes, the
simple lusts and desires . . . the loyalty and even love that Quarrel
had given him—the warmth, there was only one word for it, of the
man" (186).

Erotic loss of this kind often drives the adventure. While hard-boiled
detectives are generally not allowed to have pals, often the absence of
a pal or the memory of an absent pal will be the motive for the investigation. The Spillane books and John D. Macdonald's Travis McGee
series often open with a message from an old buddy saying that he is
in a jam. By the time the detective arrives, the pal is in jail or dead.
These friendships are said to have been neglected for years, and yet
they are extremely powerful. The bond, as it is articulated in *The Phantom Lady*, is worth quoting at length because it is so extravagant and
so exclusively male:

> "Get someone that's close to you, that's all for you. . . . It needs someone
> that'll put passion into it. . . . Someone who's doing it for you, because
> you're Scott Henderson, and no other reason. Because he likes you, yes
> even loves you, because he'd almost rather die himself than have you
> die. . . . That and only that'll swing it. . . . You must have someone like
> that. Everyone has someone like that in his life."

"Yes, when they first start out. I used to, I guess, like everyone else. They seem to drop off along the way. . . . Especially after you get married."

"They don't drop off, if they're what I'm talking about," Burgess insisted. "Whether you keep in touch with them or not has nothing to do with it. If it's once there, it's there."

"There was a guy once, he and I were as close as brothers," Henderson admitted. "But that was in the past—"

"There's no time-limit on friendship." (PL 74–75)

(I hope that you will understand that anyone this good has to be the murderer.)

In analytic detective fiction, the alibi for involvement is the desire to solve a particularly intriguing puzzle, whereas the displaced motive is the need to triumph over the indifference or condescension of the adult community. In hard-boiled detective fiction, the alibi is professionalism; the motive is erotic. Art literature usually balances the ambiguity and pain of intense male friendships with a reluctance to explain why they might matter. In *Much Ado about Nothing*, Beatrice's condition for accepting Benedick as a lover is that he kill his best friend Claudio. The best the plot can do to justify such an improbable condition is to involve an innocent Claudio in a network of flimsy slanders, to divert it indeed to an ado about nothing. William Dean Howells's *Shadow of a Dream* may serve as a gloss: after hearing the story of a helpless love affair between a clergyman and his best friend's wife, the puritanical wife of the narrator states that she has always believed that when a man proposes to marry, he should break with all his male friends. What Beatrice is doing is defining heterosexual passion and the bourgeois institution of marriage.

Popular fiction works over the same ground, uneasy in its unqualified acceptance of adolescent erotics, but willing to deal with the complications in only a fabular way. In Spillane's *I, the Jury*, for example, the old buddy whose death starts the investigation was murdered precisely because he got married and abandoned his old friendships. The most resonant scene in *The Maltese Falcon* occurs at the end, when Spade tells Brigid he must send her to prison. It is the occasion of a rare burst of heated rhetoric from this laconic detective. Most of the reasons he gives support the contention that he is not as corrupt as he seems, and they are not convincing: it doesn't follow that his letting Brigid go will give all detectives a black eye, and so on. I suggest that the driving power of this scene comes from the remaining reason: "When a man's partner is killed, he's supposed to do something about it." Spade does not want to pursue this line of investigation, for he quickly adds, "It doesn't make any difference what you thought of him" (MF 193). Nevertheless, the text bears signs of Archer's powerful valence, considering his brief appearance and regular elisions throughout the text. Spade's dislike of his partner is excessive—he quickly arranges for Archer's name to be taken off the door to the office—and it is confused by his affair with Miles's wife Iva. The reason for this is, again, that he didn't like Miles, but after Miles is shot, he avoids the wife and breaks off the affair. Finally, Spade refuses to touch the pistol that killed Archer.

In both *Farewell, My Lovely* and *The Long Goodbye*, the opening frames Marlowe looking at attractive men. They drop out of sight, and the detective is left with the enigmas that Moose Molloy and Terry Lennox instigated. This leaves a gap in the texts over which the alibis of "none of my business" or "just a job" are allowed to float. The erotic relationship between Marlowe and Terry Lennox has been well discussed, but I would also note that *The Long Goodbye* is the last complete Philip Marlowe novel, suggesting that homoerotic clarity cuts off the generic impulse. Michael Mason writes that *The Long Goodbye* "actually contains a conversation about homosexuality . . . [and] *Playback*, his next [unfinished] novel . . . shows an abrupt change of direction; perhaps Chandler was recoiling from the point his preoccupations had led him to, for in this book Marlowe is transformed almost beyond recognition by a new propensity for aggression and casual lust" (1147). *Playback*, whose title evokes a yearning for prior play, also signifies the death of detection by the fact that in it Marlowe is married.

In the opening pages of *Farewell, My Lovely*, Marlowe is attracted by the image of a monumental man. He continues to stare at him in fascination and follows him without, as he says, intending to. A grotesque moment of bonding occurs between them (grotesque both in its physical contours and in its mediation by a casual racism that has no foundation or consequences): "A hand I could have sat in came out of the dimness and took hold of my shoulder and squashed it to a pulp. Then the hand moved me through the doors and casually lifted me up a step. The large face looked at me. A deep soft voice said to me, quietly: 'Smokes in here, huh? Tie that for me, pal.' It was dark in there. It was quiet. From up above came vague sounds of humanity, but we were alone on the stairs" (FML 2). This connection erupts into violence, and after that Marlowe does not see Moose Molloy for 145 pages.

Molloy is partly replaced by a large former policeman named Red. Red is a reincarnation of the male darling in *The Big Sleep*, Rusty Regan, the wild son-in-law of General Sternwood whom everyone believes Marlowe has been hired to find, although Marlowe keeps denying it. Red is identified with Molloy in a passage that reads like an erotic trance: "He smiled a slow tired smile. His voice was soft, dreamy, so delicate for a big man that it was startling. It made me think of another soft-voiced big man that I had strangely liked. . . . I looked at him again. He had the eyes you never see, that you only read about. Violet eyes. Almost purple. Eyes like a girl, a lovely girl. His skin was as soft as silk. Lightly reddened, but it would never tan. It was too delicate. . . . His hair was that shade of red that glints with gold" (BS 208–9).

Mystery and detective fiction is haunted by the fear that its love is "homosexual." "Juno, the statuesque beauty who has aroused Hammer's lust throughout [*Vengeance Is Mine*] . . . turns out to be a male homosexual" (Grella 425). In such fits of ambivalence, it beckons grotesque homosexual parodies into the tales and mostly sniggers at them or explodes with rage. In other moods, it flirts with sexual connotations through the posturings of the dandyish and effete detectives, for example, Alleyn's inane banter spoken in "a corker sort of voice. Not queeny, but just corker" (VM 57). Or it names one of these detectives Ellery Queen and tells us that he lives in "a veritable fairyland of easy bachelordom" (FPM 173). Sometimes everything in a story goes queer; so, in *The Maltese Falcon*, Gutman takes advantage of the tough talk of hard-boiled detective fiction to travel with his own "punk" and "gunsel," and Cairo and Brigid, like Oberon and Titania, fight nastily over a boy they had once fought over.

Marlowe and Spade (hard-boiled detectives generally) dislike exhibitionistic gay men, the only sort that Marlowe meets or imagines: "It made a sort of high keening noise, like a couple of pansies fighting for a piece of silk" (LS 93). Marlowe is very sensitive to swish connotations, but once in a while his attitude resembles fascination: "He wore a flat black gaucho hat . . . [and] a white silk shirt, spotlessly clean, open at the throat, with tight wristlets and loose puffed sleeves above. Around his neck a black fringed scarf was knotted unevenly. . . . He wore a wide black sash and black pants, skin-tight at the hips, coal black, and stitched with gold thread down the side to where they were slashed and belled out loosely with gold buttons along both sides of the slash. On his feet he wore patent-leather dancing pumps" (LG 97). Sam Spade does not like to be touched by straight men: Dundy "tapped Spade's chest with the ends of two bent fingers. . . . Spade spoke, taking equal pains with his words: 'Keep your damned paws off me.'" Or by gay men: "Get away [he tells Wilbur]. You're not going to frisk me. . . . Get away. Put your paw on me and I'm going to make you use the gun." However, Spade acts as if he likes to touch Cairo: "'This is the second time you've put your hands on me. . . .' 'Yes,' Spade growled. 'And when you're slapped you'll take it and like it.' He released Cairo's wrist and with a thick open hand struck the side of his face three times, savagely" (MF 18, 154, 62). In the film version, John Huston elaborated the erotics of the relationship between Spade and Cairo by having Bogart filmed while rolling and then licking his cigarette as Peter Lorre responds by putting his umbrella handle into his mouth as if it were a lollipop.

Wilbur, "the fairy," makes Spade lose control. He blows up at Wilbur: "'Another thing,' Spade repeated, glaring at the boy. 'Keep that gunsel away from me. . . . I'll kill him. I don't like him. He makes me nervous. I'll kill him the first time he gets in my way. I won't give him an even break. I won't give him a chance. I'll kill him.'" Wilbur had just entered the room and run his gaze over Spade from his shoulders to his knees. Later, a "wooden-faced" and "dreamy-eyed" Spade begins to drive his fists into the boy and threatens to kick him in the face. Wilbur is both a verbal and a visual pun on punk: "What do you let these cheap gunmen hang out in your lobby for, with their tools bulging their clothes?" Spade is so rageful, I believe, because Wilbur is Spade's double. He is the undersized adolescent boy as hired gunman; he is wearing clothes and handling tools that seem much too big for him ("Black pistols were gigantic in his small hands") (MF 175, 99, 85, 154).

6

The Texture of Femininity

WOMEN WHO SIGNIFY SEXUALITY HAVE NO PLACE IN MYSTERY AND detective fiction. On the other hand, the function of women in this fiction is to signify sexuality, to flesh out male desire and shadow male sexual fear. Like most critical conclusions, these are already known, but the pressure of these meanings as structure, image, and language is both fascinating and appalling. A good deal of Western fiction consists of games that women cannot play, although these works are deceptive and a shift in focus often reveals that the woman was the game all along. Nevertheless, women enter the adventure to distract the privileged players, or they play so badly that a lot of time is taken up helping them to their feet. In general, they are said to interfere with the process of male satisfaction: in *Casino Royale*, Bond thinks "And then there was this pest of a girl. He sighed. Women were for recreation. On a job, they got in the way and fogged things up with sex and hurt feelings and all the emotional baggage they carried around. One had to look out for them and take care of them" (CR 25).

Analytic detective fiction has *officially* forbidden women to enter its pages as sexual presence; in striking contrast to the traditions of the novel and romance, it refuses to tell love stories. In the rules drawn up for the conduct of the narrative, this one is number three in Van Dine's list of twenty: "There must be no love interest. The business in hand is to bring a criminal to the bar of justice, not to bring a lovelorn couple to the hymeneal altar" (189–90). It stands alone; there is nothing like it in the other nineteen, except possibly rule number twenty, forbidding literary style.

The detective story and the love story, however, are not incompatible forms. The former tells the story of a heroic male in conflict with a genderless, because unknown, opponent. The conflict is not grounded in any sense of the opponent, and this is an imbalance, a hole in the form. A second hole in the form is the absence of any prize or reward for victory. Detective fiction ignores the question of what fund of desire moves the detective to do his work, make his sacrifices, or risk his life. A number of early alibis—the need to maintain an orderly society, the satisfaction of being a professional—are, as I showed in chapter 4, too much at variance with the overt semantics of the texts to be credible.

The female question was closed in the beginning by Holmes in a well-known passage from "A Scandal in Bohemia":

> To Sherlock Holmes she is always *the* woman. I have seldom heard him mention her under any other name. In his eyes she eclipses and predominates the whole of her sex. It was not that he felt any emotion akin to love for Irene Adler. All emotions, and that one particularly, were abhorrent to his cold, precise but admirably balanced mind. He was, I take it, the most perfect reasoning and observing machine that the world has seen; but as a lover he would have placed himself in a false position. He never spoke of the softer passions, save with a gibe and a sneer. They were admirable things . . . for drawing the veil from men's motives and actions. But for the trained reasoner to admit such intrusions . . . was to introduce a distracting factor which might throw a doubt upon all his mental results . . . [like grit] in a sensitive instrument, or a crack in one of his own high-power lenses. (ASH 161)

The rhythms of this passage imply that erotic indifference is easy, but Holmes also mystifies Irene Adler, refuses to refer to her by name, and uses her against other women. There are also traces of an anger at love that is too strong for the context—the "gibe" and "sneer" that resemble the typical facial gestures of Sam Spade and the "whore" of "abhorrent." And the passage moves helplessly into the current of adolescent voyeurism: the pun on the "false position" and the "crack."

The detective is always more or less afraid of women, but criticism (in this case parody), in obedience to a common law of reversal, gets this backward in the case of the hard-boiled detective and recasts him as a Casanova, a cocksman, a hard-boiled dick: "She . . . had eyes like dusty lapis lazuli, taffy hair, and a figure that did things to me. I kicked open the bottom drawer of her desk, let two inches of rye trickle down my craw, kissed Birdie square on her lush, red mouth, and set fire to a cigarette" (Perelman 191). Marlowe is sexually predatory in his initial interview with Orfamay Quest, but what is turning his quotations of lust is the "little sister's" asexual demeanor: "She was a small, neat, rather prissy-looking girl with primly smooth brown hair and rimless glasses . . . [which] gave her that librarian's look." Marlowe is aroused to anger by what is missing. In this fiction, however, what Orfamay is repressing is both her sexuality and her criminality. He makes a pass, takes off her glasses, and puts an arm around her. When she responds, he jokingly claims that he is forced to kiss her: "It was either that or slug her" (LS 4, 30). But the detective is sexually shy, as bashful in the presence of women as his cousin, the Western hero: " 'No vamping me,' said Mr. Campion nervously. 'My sister—her what married the Squire—would be ashamed of you' " (GCM 133). Both Marlowe and Spade are prudes; Marlowe gets furious when a houseboy suggests that he is sleeping with Eileen Wade, and Spade gets furious when Brigid tries to bribe him with her body (LG 158–59; MF 51–52).

Like Holmes, the protagonist can appear as an adult who is indifferent to female sexuality, or he can, like the hard-boiled detective, move with difficulty through a world bristling with sexual lure and threat. He prefers to drift through a world of pals and chums. The hero of analytic detective fiction is already armed against women, and the hero of hard-boiled is vulnerable and therefore destined to repeat his little dramas of submission and self-disgust. Bond would seem to be exempt from these generalizations. Like the former hero, the professional spy has an allure-proof system that allows him to go through the motions of seduction while remaining inwardly wary.

A pair of texts, Buchan's book and Alfred Hitchcock's film of *The Thirty-Nine Steps*, offers a boundary example of the place of women in detective fiction. In the film, a young woman appears beside the hero in a space for which there is no corresponding language in the book. The woman, Pamela, and Hannay are handcuffed together by spies posing as policemen and remain tied to one another for much of the film. The woman is locked into a structure in which she doesn't belong: between the Buchan of 1915 and the Hitchcock of 1935, this necessary fiction had been anticipated by a chance remark of Dorothy Sayers— "One fettering convention, from which detective fiction is only very slowly freeing itself, is that of the 'love interest'" (1929a, 38). It is a mutually irritating union, established through this grotesque physical connection and the comedy of bickering that classic cinema invariably recuperates as true love. The film registers her presence as an impediment. Pamela and Hannay become unwilling companions, bedfellows even, and Hannay is forced to drag her along in the direction of his narrative destiny—the adventure, the outlands—while she plots and pulls in the opposite direction, the direction of home and society, where adventures are exposed and called off. The woman is at the center of the story, but repeatedly expresses a desire to get out, and the form tells us she can only do this by bringing the story to an end.

What should be clear from the Hitchcock version is that the rule against love stories as often as not will lead to an active presence of romance or sexuality. Detective fiction claims that women are generically useless, and a given work can only fulfill that claim by proving it on the body of an actual woman; the absent woman becomes present, the outside gets inside to show why it should stay out. As discussed in chapter 2, popular fiction devotes much of its space to mapping its own boundaries, and a given text may enact at some length why it may not be a love story. The investigation in *Overture to Death* is dirty work that maps its own structural history: Alleyn "moved like a snail, across and across, between the rows of benches. He felt cold and dirty and he smelled nothing but dust. He could not allow his thoughts to dwell pleasantly on his own affairs, his coming marriage, and the happiness that kept him company nowadays; because it is when his thoughts are abstracted from the business in hand that the detective misses the one small sign events have set in his path." As if the text heard and heeded, Alleyn immediately finds his small sign: "The shining object Alleyn held in his hands was a boy's water-pistol" (OD 113).

The rule against love stories was documented by the Brothers Goncourt in 1856. After reading Poe, they recorded in their journal that here were the "signs of the literature of the twentieth century—love giving place to deductions . . . the interest of the story moved from the heart to the head . . . from the drama to the solution" (quoted in Ford 782). What they observed was not simply the exclusion of a particular subject matter, but a radical recentering of fiction, the replacement of one fictional perspective by another. Evidence of this substitution still remains in the form, and Dorothy Sayers's *Strong Poison* shows how openly plotted this can be: since the woman has been accused of murder, if I want to court and marry her, I must investigate the crime. Various conventions subtly point to absent erotics. The detective must be an amateur, a lover. Another rule stipulates that the crime must be a single murder by someone who is not a criminal, which is a code phrase for overmastering passion. Finally, the detective often investigates or pursues in a state of aroused excitement, and metaphors of bloodlust are frequent in early works to describe the relationship between the detective and the criminal.

The forms I am writing about privilege voyeurism and fetishism. The protagonists are snoopers, peepers, and spies. In *The Big Sleep*, on the night of the first murder, Marlowe has a dream "about a man in a bloody Chinese coat who chased a naked girl with long jade earrings while I ran after them and tried to take a photograph with an empty camera," and this puts him in the place of the dead pornographer in the story (BS 24). Even if the dynamics of the murder, which are reconstructed at the end, and its residue, the scene of the crime, do not patently dissolve into sexually infantile images (the murder of a parent or the primal scene), they still belong to nakedly private moments in the history of a household, and they take place in the domestically sanctified space of the bedroom or the study. Nothing distinguishes the detective more, Dennis Porter writes, "than the fact that he carries a license to snoop and to pry, to peep, eavesdrop, and interrogate" (1988, 11). The logic of the form allows the corpse and all the spilled contents of its life to be prodded and sifted: " 'You see . . .' said Ellery from clenched teeth, as he swiftly passed his hands through coats and gowns, '. . . She probably didn't look in the right garments. . . . Ah, there. . . . Splendid!' " (FPM 149).

If there should be no sexual women in detective fiction, the form tells us this was not always the case; once upon a time (the time of the fiction, although it parallels the literary history of the Brothers Goncourt), the opposite was true. For the presence of the corpse stimulates a cry, Cherchez la femme, find the woman who was here but is now absent: "As our amiable friends in Paris would say, it jumped to the eyes that there was a woman in the case—a woman who had worn a gargantuan hat for the obvious purpose of remaining unidentifiable" ("WBH" 258). She must have been here, or there couldn't be a crime, a corpse, an alluring matrix that calls for solution. The corpse is evidence—a dead record—of prior sexual desire. Futrelle's "Thinking Machine" tells his Watson to find out if the murder victim had a jealous mistress, because the subtler murders are nearly always the work of a cunning woman. " 'I know nothing about women myself,' he hastened to explain, 'but Lombroso has taken that attitude' " (BTM 58). Hammett agrees: "There are many, many murders with never a woman in them anywhere; but seldom a very conspicuous killing" (CO 26). But the extraordinary crime, whether "subtler murder" or "conspicuous killing," is the only crime that the analytic detective is stimulated by.

This woman who is to be found is often recorded as an absence, a diaphanous or aromatic trail, or a peripheral memory (even though she may, as in Collins's *Woman in White*, Chandler's *Farewell, My Lovely*, Woolrich's *Phantom Lady*, or Vera Caspary's *Laura*, dominate the book):

> The Colonel thought again, but shook his head.
> "I couldn't say. I don't remember anyone passing except the conductor. Wait a minute—and there was a woman, I think."
> "You saw her? Was she old—young?"
> "Didn't see her. Wasn't looking that way. Just a rustle and a sort of smell of scent." (MCC 75–76)

Archie Goodwin uses another phrase for the woman that has the glint of parody in it: "It wasn't much of a date, but I put it on the memo pad and hoped she would turn up, for she had the kind of voice that makes you want to observe it in the flesh" (RB 7–8). His is not much of a wisecrack, considering what others, particularly writers for radio, would come up with, but the phrase in all of its versions testifies to the presence of absence. Often the phrase is, "her voice promised—" as if contact on the telephone carried an overcharge of allure. Another phrase, "a woman's work," echoes through these forms: " 'Beastly, underhand, ingenious sort of thing,' he said. 'Sounds more like a woman's work to me. I don't mean to say I think women are particularly underhand, you know; but when they do turn nasty, in my opinion they are inclined to turn crooked-nasty' " (MMF 37). "The fact that M. Renauld was stabbed in the back seemed to point distinctly to its being a woman's crime" (ML 33). " 'No,' I said. 'That's true. It might have been somebody who used a small gun and emptied it carelessly to look like a woman's work' " (LL 97).

Complementing the rule against love stories and the observation by the Brothers Goncourt, Nicolson identifies two other holes in the fabric of detective fiction as female: "Apart from minor characters, the two important roles in the detective story for women are, alliteratively enough, victim and villainess" (123). As one reads, these terms exchange themselves: the victim is the villainess at a prior moment in the criminal history of that world—usually the spiteful, oppressive, withholding mother. The villainess is a victim, the image that the form was designed to entrap; she is exposed as a mad, evil creature, executed, or turned over to the police, because, as Sam Spade implies, she is too attractive to be allowed to roam free in the male imagination.

Laura combines many of the threads I have noted. Outside the text, the woman of the title has become a powerful image of absent allure. She is

> the face in the misty light,
> Footsteps that you hear down the hall
> The voice that floats on a summer's night
> That you can never quite
> Recall.

Within the text, she is a brilliant career woman who is murdered. The detective is drawn to her apartment; he noses into her effects, soaks up her atmosphere, falls in love with her lost possibilities. The book begins as a necrophiliac structure common to haunted house stories: as Carolyn See says of the hard-boiled detective—altering Nicolson's equation—"he is interested in dead bodies, shocked by amorous ones" (210). Sitting one night in Laura's apartment, the detective answers a knock on the door. It is Laura. The identification of the corpse was mistaken: she was a "poor thing" who was using the apartment for the night. In the new case that defines itself, the obvious suspect for the murder is, of course, Laura. It is as if the form determined that if she is not to be the victim, then she must be the villainess.

Encounters with women in detective fiction are never casual. They are moments of fascination or crisis, in either case moments of imbalance. In the course of his investigation, the detective, particularly the hard-boiled detective, will encounter a series of women who are screen images of the criminal. Each one becomes the antagonist of a particular phase of his quest. The criminal will often turn out to be one of these women, ideally the first one he meets. The detective novels of Ross Macdonald, for example, are garbled sexual texts that keep throwing up images of women who are variations of one another.

Hard-boiled detective fiction verifies the fantasy that the other side of sexual attraction is disappointment, and it can only script this as betrayal. In *The Little Sister*, Marlowe rejects all the women; he "refuses the blonde because she has the movie star's professional unreality. 'In a little while she will drift off into a haze of glamor and expensive clothes and muted sex.' He resists the brunette because she is 'utterly beyond the moral laws of this or any world I could imagine. . . .' He rejects the little sister of the title because, though she appears to be an innocent virgin from Kansas, she is a blackmailer and an accessory to murder" (Grella 417). This is such an attractive fantasy that it traps critics as well as detectives, who tend to confirm it as a reality: "The endless come-on to the certain cheat, that is the sort of woman Marlowe dreamily desires. They arouse in him lust's nervous equivalent of infatuation. They are sex appellant, and they do not promise love; yet it is never the pleasure of sensuality they want. They want to use him for some other end of their own. Each time, he escapes; each time he forgets they are all traps . . . he succumbs each time to the glitter girls" (Elliott 358). What is so neat about this passage is that just the opposite is true; the male imaginary of woman is entrapped and held in bondage by images not of her own making, and it is the detective/author/reader who wants to, and does, use them "for some other end of their own."

We are told that the time of the adventure is a time when sexuality must be deferred, but the dismissal of women in detective fiction is the primary symptom of a misogynistic project that has a dual location in the hero and the text. There is no mystery about this in regard to the protagonist, and, apparently, there is no price to pay. The anonymous hero of *Rogue Male* announces, "For me, sex has never been a problem. Like most normal people, I have been able to suppress my desires without difficulty. When there was no need to suppress them, my appreciation has been keen" (RM 80). And Wolfe declares, "It has been many years since any women has slept under this roof. Not that I disapprove of them, except when they attempt to function as domestic animals. When they stick to the vocations for which they are best adapted, such as chicanery, sophistry, self-adornment, cajolery, mystification and incubation, they are sometimes splendid creatures" (RB 84).

At least hard-boiled detective fiction is written against women. At the center of the form, the detective discovers, as if in a dream, that the woman he loves kills men: not only is the attractive woman a criminal, but the extent of her depravity equals his investment in her. The story of much hard-boiled detective fiction allows the hero to come to know his sexual arousal as external danger. Detective fiction protects its protagonist, fictionalizes its own basic rule that the hero is invulnerable and invincible and tells a story that keeps him pure. The form protects him epistemologically by asserting that the story can be successfully told without his ever becoming aware of his own desires and evasions: "I cannot even now explain why I so suddenly commenced to take an interest in her. . . . I knew dozens of women quite as graceful, if not more beautiful. Besides, there was the dark stigma upon her which Sammy had alleged" (MMM 37).

Encounters with women in detective fiction are often fetish moments, except that the woman is seen within an aura of disgust, not attraction. The moment of encounter is frozen through a slick, hard description that, like the advertising image, is a composite of surface gleams, particularly cosmetic saturation. We know that all characters in a detective novel are under indictment and can fall under the glare of the detective's disparaging eye, but women fall particularly hard: "Tall, over-dressed, musquash and those abbreviated sort of shoes with jewelled heels and hardly any uppers—you know the sort of thing. Heavily peroxided; a strong aroma of orifan wafted out upon the passer-by; powder too white for the fashion and mouth heavily obscured with sealing-wax red; eyebrows painted black to startle, not deceive; fingernails a monument to Kraska—the pink variety" (UD 70). "From thirty feet away she looked like a lot of class. From ten feet away she looked like something made up to be seen from thirty feet away. Her mouth was too wide, her eyes were too blue, her make-up was too vivid, the thin arch of her eyebrows was almost fantastic in its curve and spread, and the mascara was so thick on her eyelashes that they looked like miniature iron railings. . . . Her hair was as artificial as a night-club lobby" (HW 39).

Mystery fiction knows the serpentine ways to tarnish women. An early thriller by E. Phillips Oppenheim, *The Great Impersonation*, uses a situation common to adventure romances such as *The Prisoner of Zenda*, where the heroic impersonator finds himself exposed to the hot approach of a wife or mistress who reasonably expects him to be the man she takes him for. He is justifiably amnesiac, since he knows nothing of his history with these women. In the Oppenheim, it is turned around: his "wife," a sylph or "fairy maiden," shrinks from him because her husband's behavior had caused her to dread intimacy with men, and her circumstanced "frigidity" causes disgust in him for all other women: "He saw once more the slight, girlish form . . . the whole sweet appeal for safety from a frightened child to him, the strong man. . . . The woman's passion by his side seemed suddenly tawdry and unreal, the seeking of her lips for his something horrible" (GI 182).

There are various names for these women, but, whether maneater, minx, cat, ice-maiden, mannish woman, lesbian, crone, or witch; or angel, doll, baby-face, or little sister; they all conflate back into the bitch, the name Bond chooses in his curt elegy: " 'She's dead, the bitch,' [he] . . . telephones to his London office, and so ends the romance" (Eco 35). Velma, in *Farewell, My Lovely*, is a striking bitch figure. Marlowe meets her, disguised by culture and peroxide, as Mrs. Grayle, and he identifies her as a reservoir of absent promises: "It was a blonde. A blonde to make a bishop kick a hole in a stained glass window. . . . Whatever you needed, wherever you happened to be—she had it" (FML 78). Although Marlowe is excited by Mrs. Grayle and does eventually kiss her, she initiates all the sexual moves; and Marlowe cannot tell us often enough how much and how quickly he has been drinking. There is another man present during the seduction scene; the seduction of Marlowe is also the humiliation of the husband: "a tall thin sad-faced man with a stony chin and deep eyes and no color in his face but an unhealthy yellow" (FML 104).

The villainous woman is usually countercoded to arouse disgust instead of lust. At the two fantasy extremes, this may be negotiated through the persons of the bitch and the lesbian. At the opening of *The Gyrth Chalice Mystery*, a young man tells his intimate history to Albert Campion. He concludes that "women always seem to muck things up," and at that moment a woman enters who proceeds to muck things up for the rest of the book. She is noticed only when her "high strident voice" drowns the other conversation in the room. She is masculine in appearance, with hair cut short under a felt hat. She sees the young man, bellows his name, catches his coat sleeve and jerks "him backward with a wrist like flexed steel" (GCM 35–36). At bottom, the bitch is also a man-hater, so that when Marlowe finally comes to see Mrs. Grayle as "Grade B Hollywood," she has just admitted that "most men are just lousy animals" (FML 238, 237).

In Sayers's *Unnatural Death*, an able and self-confident woman is known to be the murderer. She is even made to boast that she committed the murder and dare anyone to prove it. She is clearly someone to get, and so she is charged with a repulsive sexuality: she is identified as a lesbian and the revulsion that the fiction generates through and around her is brought to a kind of cutting edge in a scene where Wimsey (who is arguably gay) poses as an ardent lover and makes love to her, and she, as a dissembling criminal, pretends to accept and return his advances: "He knew then. No one who has ever encountered it can ever again mistake that awful shrinking, that uncontrollable revulsion of the flesh against a caress that is nauseous. He thought for a moment that she was going to be actually sick" (UD 153).

As she had been from the Romantic period onward, the bitch is a creature of subtle malice. According to Conan Doyle: "Women are naturally secretive, and they like to do their own secreting" (ASH 171).

> "Ah, *mon ami*, do not set your heart on Marthe Daubreuil. She is not for you, that one! Take it from Papa Poirot!"
>
> "Why," I cried, "the commissary assured me that she was as good as she is beautiful! A perfect angel!"
>
> "Some of the greatest criminals I have known had the faces of angels," remarked Poirot cheerfully. "A malformation of the gray cells may coincide quite easily with the face of a madonna."
>
> "Poirot," I cried, horrified, "you cannot mean that you suspect an innocent child like this!" (ML 66)

In Erle Stanley Gardner's *Case of the Velvet Claws*, Della Street knows immediately that Eva Griffin is crooked: "one of those well-kept little minxes that would double-cross anybody in order to take care of herself," and Perry Mason says to the second woman in the book: "You're one of those baby-faced little liars that always gets by by deceit. Just because you're beautiful, you've managed to get by with it. You've deceived every man that ever loved you. . . . Now you're in trouble, and you're deceiving me" (CVC 11, 40). Not even a woman's intuition, however, is enough to protect the detective against the treachery of women. Della may be able to size up Eva as a bitch instantly, but Effie Perrine feels a deep certainty about Brigid's worth.

As a creature of malice, the bitch intends the downfall of men, and is gratified by it. The deception she practices is not so much the falsification of her part in the story as the tantalizing image she projects of a superlative love object. She is always more than "we" ever expected or deserved, and of course, what the turning of the fiction does is to confirm "our" deserts. Unlike the fatal women of Romanticism, Nathaniel Hawthorne's Beatrice Rappaccini, for example, the bitch is never identified as a dual creature, both innocent and guilty, angelic and foul. Avoiding ambivalence, detective fiction denies the reality of the angel image and declares that it is only a mask, itself a proof of the bitch's demonic cunning. The resistance and unmasking of the bitch is a prominent motif in Hammett, where it culminates in the relationship of Spade and Brigid, but it was used by later writers as well, for instance, Chandler in *The Lady of the Lake:* " 'You do this character very well,' I said. 'This confused innocence with an undertone of hardness and bitterness. People have made a bad mistake about you. They have been thinking of you as a reckless little idiot with no brains and no control. They have been very wrong' " (LL 168).

In an early Hammett tale, the Continental Op tells a woman that her fiancé has been killed: "She broke off with a catch in her voice— the only sign of sorrow she displayed. . . . The impression of her we had received . . . had prepared us for a more or less elaborate display of grief on her part. But she had disappointed us. There was nothing crude about her work—she didn't even turn on the tears for us." The thought is nicely twisted: they expected her to be phony through a display of false grief, but they verified her phoniness through the opposite behavior. Obviously, this woman can't win. In "The House on Turk Street," the Op enacts the Odyssean original of this fiction: "In his place, I might have believed her myself—all of us have fallen for that sort of thing at one time or another—but sitting tied up on the sidelines, I knew that he'd have been better off playing with a gallon of nitro than with this baby. She was dangerous!" (CO 36, 97).

The criminal killer, Brigid O'Shaughnessey, is the most energized female character in detective fiction, but her presence in *The Maltese Falcon* is carried through traces of her absence: she appears first as a voice speaking "so softly that only the purest articulation made the words intelligible"; she advances "slowly, with tentative steps, looking at Spade with cobalt-blue eyes that were both shy and probing." She speaks in broken fragments; she is a catalog of gestures and actions that are almost not there: blushes, chokes, gasps, hushes, puckers, quivers, squirms, stammers, throbs, tremors, and whispers. Brigid is never exposed as a bitch, although her initial description, the "darkly red" hair, "brightly red" full lips, and glistening teeth, alludes to that image. Her performance type is that of the little sister—Spade calls it a "schoolgirl-act"—"stammering and blushing and all that" (MF 4, 189, 49).

Mimi, in *The Thin Man*, is a simplified version of Brigid. Charles warns the police that "the chief thing . . . is not to let her tire you out. When you catch her in a lie, she admits it and gives you another lie to take its place and, when you catch her in that one, admits it and gives you still another, and so on. Most people—even women—get discouraged after you've caught them in the third or fourth straight lie and fall back on either the truth or silence, but not Mimi. She keeps trying and you've got to be careful or you'll find yourself believing her, not because she seems to be telling the truth, but simply because you're tired of disbelieving her" (TM 684).

Brigid cannot be found out in a lie. Entirely superficial, her surface is continually dissolving and reforming. Cairo says to Brigid, "Oh, you dirty, filthy liar," and Brigid willingly admits the truth of this. But her new truths are new lies, as innocent and engaging as the originals: "After a moment in which she seemed confused almost to the point of tears, she laughed and said: 'Very well. . . . I'm not at all the sort of person I pretend to be. . . . But if it's a pose it's one I've grown into, so you won't expect me to drop it entirely, will you?'" Even that is a lie; Brigid is exactly the person she pretends to be, but the pretense is dynamic, a flickering chain of admissions, confessions, and revisions. There is no way of stripping Brigid, the text tells us, in discomfort and triumph, or, rather, she can be too easily stripped, but she has a false name behind every false name. When Spade insists that he must know whether she took the money or not, he literally strips her and finds nothing concealed under her clothes. The relationship between Spade and Brigid is easiest when he accepts her performance and admires her for it: "You're good. You're very good. It's chiefly your eyes, I think, and that throb you get in your voice when you say things like 'Be generous, Mr. Spade'" (MF 66, 31).

Brigid lures men through the language of sexual dependence and trust: "Oh, I'm so alone and afraid, and I've got nobody to help me, if you won't help me. I know I've no right to ask you to trust me. . . . But be generous, Mr. Spade" (MF 32). What frightens Spade is the strength of his own investment in the myth of male strength and female weakness; he knows that somehow Brigid is outside it, running it out as a quotation. When he rejects her, he gives as one of his reasons that he will not protect her because he wants so much to do so, and this is merged with its convolution, that he won't protect her because she counted on his wanting to do so. The final disposition of the criminal—often a complex and brutal act—can usually be read as an act of revenge from some perspective, and when the criminal is a woman that perspective is always a gendered sexuality. Spade tells Brigid that the chances are she will be out of jail in twenty years and he will wait for her: she must be put away until her power to upset Spade is gone.

Women are also avoided in the thriller. As in analytic detective fiction, it is a rule—women have no place in your life while you are on a mission, and the rule is again confirmed through exception. There is also a core of misogynist cruelty here, but it is given to the other, the enemy and his henchmen. Bond's fear that women only get in the way is brutally confirmed in many instances, like that of Else in *The Confidential Agent*. These women are battered or killed because the hero didn't remember the rule or was too soft to abide by it. Their bruised flesh only proves that anyone he dares to love will be hurt. It ends up being treated as his punishment, not hers.

Notwithstanding the anxious pressure of female images in detective texts, every reader knows that smiling young women also appear, supporting and serving the hero cheerfully and sometimes acting as detective heroes themselves. There are various positive ways of easing women into mystery and detective fiction, but the easiest is to dress them in the costume of the pal: "About 1912 it became a deliberate policy [in the boys' magazines] to play up a 'girl chum'—possibly as a concession to the large female readership" (Turner 123).

> When James Bond was not yet popular, *Vogue* and *Esquire* (1956) already had such a model. She was called the "pal-girl." She had to have a past, otherwise her face would not be so intense, expressive, her smile so rich in signifying that I had made her smile. And she had to be innocent, notwithstanding a little of the mysterious, to guarantee my full and complete enjoyment of her performance. . . . The "pal-girl" was sporty and Chanel, was healthy, with little make-up, and her hair was loose, easy to

brush, quite without fixative. The girls of Hitchcock have almost always been "pal-girls." (Columbo 99)

Anne Riordan in *Farewell, My Lovely* is twenty-eight years old and unmarried; she wears no lipstick and has no sexual history. Marlowe never tires of telling us how "nice" and "neat" she is: "It was a nice face, a face you get to like. . . . Glamoured up blondes were a dime a dozen, but that was a face that would wear." But when Randall tells Marlowe how much Anne likes him, he says, "She's a nice girl. Not my type." When Marlowe is hurt, he crawls to Anne's apartment (in which there is "nothing womanish"), but when she tries to take care of him he insists on leaving. In her first scene in the novel, Anne is presented as a hard-boiled detective, as Marlowe's double. Marlowe is just coming to in the vicinity of a corpse and finds someone holding a flashlight and a gun on him. When he suggests that they look at the corpse, she tells him, "Listen, stranger. I'm holding a ten shot automatic. I can shoot straight. Both your feet are vulnerable. What do you bid?" He reaches for his wallet, and she says, "I don't think so. Just leave your hands where they happen to be. We'll skip the proof for the time being. What's your story?" In addition to all her other solidities, Anne is the daughter of an Irish cop (FML 73, 81, 166, 156, 57, 58).

One of the more successful sex changes in American popular culture was the transformation of the tough, wisecracking investigative reporter, Hildy Johnson, into a woman, in Howard Hawks's *His Girl Friday*. Often, to make sure we understand that the pal-girl is really a pal, the text will have a metaphorical mistake, and the pal-girl will be jokingly identified as a man. Nick Charles knocks Nora out to protect her from a gangster's gunplay, and when she comes to she growls at him, "You damned fool . . . you didn't have to knock me cold. I knew you'd take him, but I wanted to see it." And a "copper" in the room laughs and says admiringly, "Jesus . . . there's a woman with hair on her chest" (TM 609). Sam Spade affectionately rubs Effie Perrine's cheek and tells her: "You're a damned good man, sister" (MF 144). Conversely, because Effie is safe, Spade can also utter doting words: angel, darling, honey, sweetheart, dear.

Alison Mackintosh, the daughter of the spymaster in *The Freedom*

Trap, has been raised by her father as if she were a boy, and the hero finds it incongruous that she had been married: "I couldn't see Alison cuddling up on his knee, and saying, 'Darling, you're married to a girl who can shoot a man in the kneecap in impossible light, who can . . . kill a man with one karate chop. . . . Look how handy it will be when we're bringing up the children' " (FT 169).

Because detective fiction can accommodate the woman as pal, it can also recuperate the bitch, since that is a role that the pal-girl sometimes favors, a character she likes to quote.[1] The protagonist can even "put an arm around her slim waist" and rest "his cheek wearily against her hip," after she has shown what she is capable of: "she leaned over and took the tobacco-sack and the paper from his inert fingers. . . . Her thin fingers finished shaping the cigarette. She licked it, smoothed it, twisted its end and placed it between Spade's lips" (MF 24). It is exciting to have the woman invested with a fund of energy that, in another mode, the form exposes; it allows the accepting reader to experience the transformation of the nice woman into the bitch twice, both destructively and playfully. Part of Alison's appeal is her willingness to expose herself as a bitch, and it is offered as proof of her unfitness as a woman:

> "Do you know what I am, Owen?"
> "You're a lovely woman, Alison."
> "No, I'm a Venus Fly Trap. Vegetables—like women—are supposed to be placid; they're not supposed to be equipped with snapped jaws and sharp teeth." (FT 171)

The pal-girl in *Phantom Lady* must transform herself into a bitch in order to trap the real criminal. In disguise she looks to herself like a fire-breathing dragon, and she is ashamed of the necessary veneer of sexuality:

> The clean, tomboyish look was gone from her. The breezy sweep of the hair . . . was missing. In its place was a tortured surface of brassy rolls and undulations, drenched with some sort of fixative and then hardened into a metallic casque. Gone too was the youthful, free-swinging, graceful hang . . . to her clothes. Instead she had managed to achieve a skin-tight effect that appalled her. . . . And now one final ghastly item,

to complete the catalogue of sleazy accessibility . . . a garter of violently-pink satin. . . . Scott Henderson had been watching her . . . and she was ashamed. "You wouldn't know me, darling, would you?" she murmured contritely. "Don't look at me, darling, don't look at me." (PL 133–34)

There is a redemptive fiction in detective fiction, in works such as Sayers's *Strong Poison*, E. C. Bentley's *Trent's Last Case*, and Clemence Dane's *Enter Sir John:* the story of Perseus and Andromeda, or St. George and the Dragon. In painted versions, Perseus or St. George stands aggressively with a downturned sword across from a naked woman tied to a rock. Between the two is a fire-breathing dragon. If the hero kills the dragon, he wins the woman, although this conquest is cast in tones of reluctance by Marlowe in the opening of *The Big Sleep:* "There was a broad stained-glass panel showing a knight in dark armor rescuing a lady who was tied to a tree and didn't have any clothes on but some very long and convenient hair. The knight had pushed the visor of his helmet back to be sociable, and he was fiddling with the knots on the ropes that tied the lady to the tree and not getting anywhere. I stood there and thought that if I lived in the house, I would sooner or later have to climb up there and help him. He didn't seem to be really trying" (BS 3). In *Dr. No,* this story is creakily literalized. Honeychile Ryder tells Bond the story of her pastoral childhood and subsequent rape, and this excites him. Immediately after, Quarrel whispers that the dragon is coming across the water: "a shapeless thing with two glaring orange eyes with black pupils. From between these, where the mouth might be, fluttered a yard of blue flame. . . . The thing was making a low moaning roar that overlaid another noise, a deep rhythmic thud" (DN 104).

If the Perseus-Andromeda scene were not vertical, its title would be "The Rape of Andromeda" and Perseus would be the aggressor. As I read the myth, woman and dragon are one. Attached to the woman, but detachable from her, is a fiery, scaly source of annihilation. As this story is violently retold by Hawthorne in "Rappaccini's Daughter," the peril has become an interior poison. "That dame is pure poison," says a hard-boiled dick, "I'd hate to have her get behind me if she had a knife around anywhere" ("DGRN" 8). And poison (as Christie repeatedly says) is a woman's weapon:

"Did you ever discover what the stuff was that Russian woman put into him? . . ."

"Taken us three months. . . . The drug was *fugu* poison. The Japanese use it for committing suicide. It comes from the sex organs of Japanese globe-fish." (DN 18)

In *Strong Poison,* Harriet Vane is accused of willfully poisoning her lover. She is also tainted by having lived in a state of free love with the deceased. Wimsey falls in love with her as a prisoner in the dock, but in order to marry her he must prove her innocence; he must, that is, detach her from the stigma of poison. " 'And I say,' said Wimsey, 'that it would be better for her to be hanged outright than to live and have everybody think her a murderess who got off by a fluke' " (SP 87). In works like Sayers's or *Trent's Last Case,* the detective investigates a murder case in which the accused or the primary suspect is a lovely woman who will eventually become his wife. The police want to put her to death as a disgusting menace, but the detective transforms her through narrative. That is the way to tell a detective story and a love story—to accuse the fantasy-beloved of the worst crime you can imagine and then clear the record. But, as Bentley's title states, when you tell this story, you are also telling of the detective's last case. The hero of *The Rasp* "was suffering from three disorders: lack of a definite task to perform, severe war-strain, and not having met the right woman. The first and second, though he never spoke of them, he knew about; the third he did not even suspect" (R 10). The first two disorders open and fuel the space of the narrative; the third provides closure.

It is perfectly all right for a critic to announce that "naturally 007, like any hero, cannot have a wife" (Antonini 109), and for Chandler to say that a "really good detective never gets married" and then marry Marlowe off in *The Poodle Springs Mystery* (1984, 70). These are not literal taboos but statements of limits: they tell us what is outside the fiction or what will end the fiction. Despite the rule, one can certainly have a detective operating out of a marriage like Nick Charles, or a married detective pair, like Mr. and Mrs. North.

Nevertheless, love and marriage are formally incompatible with detective fiction. Love paralyzes the investigation in *The Vintage Murder*—"For perhaps the first time in his life, Alleyn found himself unwilling to carry his case a step further" (VM 139)—or spoils it in *The Rasp:* "If it had not been for Her all this would have been great fun" (R 63). Marriage usually ends the detective's career: "Ellery [has] . . . renounced his old profession utterly, now that he is married and do-mesticated [and] . . . has hidden his old cases in the depths of a filing-cabinet" (FPM viii); although it can be easily resumed: "Be-sides, one of the reasons why I went out of business, as you call it, was that my wife has a morbid distaste for crime; but just now she is in the Cotswolds. I am alone and free, like the man in Chesterton; shameless, anarchic, infinite" (TOC 66). Within the context of detec-tive fiction, marriage is, Sayers admits it, murder: "Let me confess that when I undertook *Strong Poison* it was with the infanticidal intention of doing away with Peter; that is, of marrying him off and getting rid of him" (1974 [1937], 210). Marriage ends the detective writers' career for Hammett, Chandler, and Dr. Watson: "I fear that it may be the last investigation in which I shall have the chance of studying your meth-ods. Miss Morstan has done me the honor to accept me as a husband" (SF 157).

7

The Crime,
the Criminal, the Community

CLIVE JAMES SENSIBLY OBJECTS TO THE STATUS OF CRIME IN DE-
tective fiction, and his account of it invokes the boundary between social
and psychological reality: "At least 30 percent of London's population
lived below the poverty line in Sherlock's heyday, but not very many of
them found their way into the stories. Doyle's criminals come almost
exclusively from the income-earning classes. They are clinically, not
socially, motivated. There is seldom any suggestion that crime could be
a symptom of anything more than a personal disorder" (121). Holmes
complains that there "are no crimes [these days]. . . . What is the use
of having brains in our profession. . . . There is no crime to detect, or,
at most, some bungling villainy with a motive so transparent that even
a Scotland Yard official can see through it" (SSt 25); possibly he is ex-
aggerating or is defining his subject matter as an order of event that
should not be confused with what society calls crime.

The simple answer to the riddle of when is a crime not a crime is
"when it is a criminal fantasy." This would help to explain the police
paradox. The official police cannot investigate the crime because they
cannot see it in one way or another: they laugh at the detective, stooped
over and peering at minutiae that are invisible to them. The micro-
scopically fine clue is one figure for the invisibility of the crime. Poe

offered another: speaking of Vidocq, who exemplifies the inadequacies of the police, Dupin claimed that he "impaired his vision by holding the object too close. He might see, perhaps, one or two points with unusual clearness, but in so doing he necessarily lost sight of the matter as a whole." Dupin makes a cosmological analogy: proper detectives are like stargazers who look at heavenly bodies "in a side-long way"; the police look at them directly, "and it is possible to make even Venus herself vanish from the firmament by a scrutiny too sustained, too concentrated, or too direct" (Poe 1902, 4:166).

A variety of figures remove the subject matter of detective fiction from the proximity of "actual" crime. Analytic detective fiction insists on the social marginality of its crimes by specifying that they be murders of passion, the crimes that occur least often and are least likely to be repeated. By choosing such murders, authors buy themselves the freedom to claim that their criminals are not criminals—and are misunderstood: Murderers were not like criminals "and none of them were desperate killers. Murderers were apt to be quite respectable; at least to know nothing of the ways of criminals or of the police either" (TOC 23).

The inaccessible room in which the murder takes place is another image for fantasy: it is a room that can be proved to have no contact with the outside. Often, the crime is first identified as literal fantasy; in *Unnatural Death* the suspicions that will become the fiction are regarded by the community as the paranoid fantasies of a sick old lady: "Then, for some reason, the patient began to take one of those unaccountable dislikes that feeble-minded patients do take sometimes. She got it into her head that the nurse wanted to kill her . . . and earnestly assured her niece that she was being poisoned" (UD 20).

The community responds extravagantly to the crime: it is shocked and convulsed by what has happened. This is, perhaps, the most honest beginning in fiction, for it is a *scandal*, a rupture that opens up an unexpected space for narrative. The corpse, Auden writes, "must shock not only because it is a corpse but also because, even for a corpse, it is shockingly out of place, as when a dog makes a mess on a drawing room carpet" (404). The scandal of the corpse is another version of the crime as a miracle, and as Auden's simile suggests, the corpse is also an obscenity.

Scandal is also what the community most fears; it is afraid that word of this event might leak out into the world of history, and it treats that eventuality as if it carried an explosive charge: "Why, if the thing was exposed there'd be a scandal which would upset at least a couple of thrones and jeopardize the governments of four or five powers" (GCM 26). The crime must be kept inside and under wraps. The fiction of the scandal in Michael Innes's *Hamlet, Revenge!* takes the extreme form of an outside world that is willing to drop everything and come running to the spot, hovering around for a glimpse of the privileged scene of murder and detection (HR 164). The opening of Poe's "Facts in the Case of M. Valdemar" is paradigmatic in this regard: "Of course I shall not pretend to consider it any matter for wonder, that the extraordinary case of M. Valdemar has excited discussion. It would have been a miracle had it not. . . . Through the desire of all parties concerned, to keep the affair from the public . . . a garbled or exaggerated account made its way into society, and became the source of many unpleasant misrepresentations" (6:154). Suppressed through fear of scandal, the crime becomes a scandal. The garbled account is the fictional text, whether a tale by Poe or a detective story. The need to keep the crime an inside story reinforces two conventional constraints: that the detective be an amateur and the criminal an insider. Fear of scandal dictates that a private detective be sent for to solve the crime quietly. Second, as Hartman puts it, the "thrill of a 'thriller' is surely akin to the fear that the murderer will prove to be not an outsider but someone there all the time, someone we know only too well—perhaps a blood relation" (221).

In hard-boiled detective fiction, crime is treated more as an ordinary event. In the thriller, however, the media and the government are kept in the dark or deliberately misled in the name of security. Fantasy is signified through the fiction of a vast threat—often, as shared with science fiction, the end of civilization—which must be dissolved without anyone knowing the threat ever existed.

Speaking of his requirements for crime, Poirot says he wants "the cream of crime":

"It must be no common affair. It must be something recherché—delicate—fine . . ." He gave the last untranslatable word its full flavor.

"Upon my word, Poirot," I said, "Anyone would think you were ordering a dinner at the Ritz." (ABC 13, 14)

The crime of analytic detective fiction is a special event, not only because it is scandalous, but because, as an event, it is ornate, decoratively superfluous, as in the publisher's blurb for *Jumping Jenny* (JJ): "at a party given in honour of a famous writer-detective, the guests impersonate famous murderers and their victim—the hated wife of David Statton—is found hanging from a fake gallows erected as a joke." In *The Seven Suspects,* the crime

> was at once intriguing and bizarre, efficient and theatrical. . . . It was theatrical because of a macabre and unnecessary act of fantasy with which the criminal, it was quickly rumored, had accompanied his deed. . . . Round the head there was swathed . . . the dull black stuff of an academic gown. . . . From the dull dark-oak panels over the fireplace, roughly scrawled in chalk, a couple of grinning death's heads stared out upon the room. Just beside the President's grotesquely muffled head lay a human skull. And over the surrounding area of the floor were scattered little piles of human bones." (SS 7, 17)

One reason the crime may be read as a fantasy is because it is so often a fantastic event.

Even apologists tell us analytic detective fiction is artificial and contrived, and, as its opening statement, it displays a corpse as something artificial and contrived: In *Hamlet, Revenge!* the crime takes place at a particularly dramatic moment in an amateur production of *Hamlet.* It is often discovered that the crime is not a "naturally" theatrical but a theatrically theatrical event. At a certain point in *The ABC Murders,* Poirot discovers that the sign system he has been attempting to read—the murder and its subsequent clues—has been invented by the criminal to mislead him.

The crime is a story written by the criminal. As Flambeau says to Brown, "My friend . . . you must be careful with me and remember I was once a criminal. The great advantage of that estate was that I always made up the story myself, and acted it as quick as I chose. This detective business of waiting about is too much for my French impatience" (AA 38). The criminal is also an artist, and the crime is an expression of his or her creativity: "Now this man had in him a very noble power to be perverted; the power of telling stories. He was a great novelist; only he had twisted his fictive power to practical and to evil ends; to deceiving men with false fact instead of with true fiction" (AA 148). Franco Moretti writes that Holmes "is not moved by pity for the victim, by moral or material horror at the crime, but by its *cultural quality:* by its *uniqueness* and its *mystery*" (135).

As a creative act that intitiates the narrative, the crime is also the structural equivalent of the solution. Analytic detective fiction is framed by two works of art, and the detective's might even be considered the lesser of the two, for what he does at the end is to retell the story of the crime. The detective and the criminal may also be opposed, for if one is writing a detective story, the other has written a work of Gothic fiction: "For the murderer's eye for effect was, in its own peculiar way, excellent; it was a master of the startling and the macabre that was at work" (HR 195).

Like the romantic work of art, the crime is also represented as an idiosyncratic event: "Ask any criminal expert, and he'll tell you that a man's way of killing is as characteristic as his manner of signing a cheque" (MKF 32). When Reik suggested to Freud that the protagonist of his psychoanalytic writings resembled the English detective Sherlock Holmes, Freud evaded that identification and said he preferred to think of him as analogous to Giovanni Morelli, the detector of art forgeries (Hyman 313). Like Morelli, the detective examines a work of art looking for its signature.

Poirot asks Hastings to imagine ordering a crime as one would a dinner at the Ritz, and he decides on "red-blooded murder—with trimmings, of course": "Who shall the victim be—man or woman? Man, I think. Some big-wig. American millionaire. Prime Minister. Newspaper proprietor" (ABC 21). One of Chesterton's victims is Sir Claude Champion: "one of the brightest and wealthiest of England's Upper Ten . . . the great sportsman . . . the great dabbler in art, music, literature, and above all, acting. . . . There was something of the Renascence Prince about his omnivorous culture" (AA 114–15). Sir Claude is killed while dressed for the part of Romeo.

According to Cyril Hare, the choice of a victim is simple, some hateful celebrity or authority figure: "The obvious recourse is to make the victim an unbearably unpleasant person. The millionaire with a shady past, the intolerable old woman with a large fortune who torments her circle of expectant relations, the professional blackmailer with a dozen fatal secrets in his hands" (76). The character of the victim is always extreme; he or she was hateful—"I should say that any one who had anything to do with George was potentially his murderer" (BMD 38)—or lovable, and lovable victims are more tantalizing: "Melhuish—of all people in the world . . . beloved by his patients, esteemed by everyone . . . a man devoted to the highest of human endeavours—a man whose life had been as an open book" (MB 41).

The formula for the victim, then, is the same as one of the figures for the crime that detectives investigate: it must be a crime that appears to be obvious or impossible of solution. Auden offers a rationale for this formulaic split: the victim "has to satisfy two contradictory requirements. He has to involve everyone in suspicion, which requires that he be a bad character; and he has to make everyone feel guilty, which requires that he be a good character. . . . On the whole, the best victim is the negative Father or Mother image" (404). Auden requires that the victim be hateful and lovable at the same time, but mystery fiction refuses to engage complexity, and this requirement is resolved, like the mysteries of the criminal and crime, into an opposition between appearance and reality: "this benevolent white-haired old man, walking sedately about the Cathedral Close . . . is the cruellest and most heartless scoundrel that I have ever met" (CQ 161, 160).

Psychoanalytic critics who look at detective fiction see something uncannily familiar beyond the curtain that is lifted and dropped on the corpse; they see a sexual fantasy: an Oedipal crime and, behind that, the primal scene. This is what the master of psychoanalysis himself saw in the tales of Poe, according to Marie Bonaparte: "in all the detective tales, as Freud first pointed out to me, the unconscious roots of their interest, for us, lies in the fact that the trail the detective follows repeats, though transferred to other activities, the infant's original sexual investigations" (456). In Anna Katherine Green's short story "Missing: Page Thirteen," the crime takes the form of a fencing match, "a duel to the death between this husband and wife—this father and mother— in this hole of dead tragedies and within the sight and hearing of their child! Has Satan ever devised a scheme more hideous for ruining the life of an eleven-year-old boy" ("MPT" 34). These critics see a motive for the narrative dynamics, an equation between the compulsion to read these stories and a "voyeur's inability ever to be satisfied with his peeping" (Rycroft 115).

Ellery Queen is noted for the ornateness of his corpse tableaux, and in *The French Powder Mystery* the corpse appears in a setting that is both public and intensely private. In French's Department Store, "the most popular department store in the city," which "occupied a square block in the heart of the midtown section of New York, on Fifth Avenue," there was a large picture window that demonstrated the latest household fashions: "This window became the focal point for the eyes of all New York. Curious throngs constantly besieged its sheathing of plate glass." On the day of the scandal, what was shown in the picture window was a bedroom. No bed, however, was visible; that article of furniture was concealed in the west wall: "It is of Special Design, Created by M. Paul Lavery, and Is the Only One of Its Kind in This Country." At the stroke of noon, a model dressed as a housemaid pressed the button to lower the bed. What the straining crowd saw "was a marvel indeed—so unexpected, so horrible, so grotesque. . . . It was like a moment snatched out of an unbelievable nightmare. . . . For, as the model pushed the ivory button . . . the body of a woman, pale-faced, crumpled, distorted . . . fell from the silken sheet to the floor" (FPM 25–27). The woman in Mr. French's bed is Mrs. French.

No sexual connotations are attached to these images. The form is schizophrenic and immediately forgets what had convulsed it after the original shock has registered. Detective fiction begins with the brief revelation of a corpse that is almost immediately forgotten in the excitement of the ensuing investigation: "The corpse loses its conclusiveness. . . . It becomes something unreal. It disappears" (Heissenbüttel 91). The corpse is definitely not accounted for. The revelation of the body is often the only imaginative moment in a work of detective fiction. Although Walter Benjamin links the decline of storytelling and the rise of the novel to our loss of access to the dead body and the face of the dying, detective fiction, which exploits its connection with these images, dismisses complexity by dismissing its corpse, its body, and we are correct in saying of the genre as a whole that there is no substance to it (83–109).

Analytic detective fiction is set in a family. If this is not literally the case, there will generally be some easy metaphor for the family, for example, a stable community that shares a continuous and intimate history—"A little town like this is all currents and crosscurrents. Everybody is related to everybody else, or entangled with everybody else through birth, church, or business affiliations, hatred, love affairs, or debts" (TF 58). Or a professional group—"We're a happy little family," says Meyer of the theatrical troupe in *Vintage Murder* whose leading lady is murdered onstage, and another character remembers "the homely, knit-together feeling of back-stage, the feeling that the troupe was a little world of its own" (VM 20, 58). A favorite enclosure in golden-age detective fiction was the circle of family, servants, and guests included in a weekend house party.

Hard-boiled detective fiction is just as firmly set in a family structure, although these relationships are slowly revealed over the course of the fiction; they are themselves items in the ongoing solution. In *The Long Goodbye*, the two spheres of activity centering around Terry Lennox and the Wades are shown to have a family connection; in *Farewell, My Lovely*, characters who seem to appear randomly, for example, Mrs. Florian and Lindsay Marriott, have intimate connections to Velma. This is a trademark of Ross Macdonald's work; one reviewer wrote that in *The Blue Hammer* a complex "series of revelations establishes that everyone is everyone else's parent, child, or sibling" (Edwards 1976, 13). The family is also signified by two familiar conventions: first, the absence of signs of struggle, or the casual dress or undress of the victim, which leads the detective to conclude that the murderer was someone whom the victim knew intimately; second, the common identification of the object of the crime as a family heirloom or inheritance.

Many of the crimes in analytic detective fiction can be identified as crimes against the female, often the mother. Christie's *Mysterious Affair at Styles* is the story of the murder of a wicked stepmother. Conan Doyle's "Case of Identity" stages a fantasy of incest: in order to keep the daughter at home and deprive her of her treasure, a father woos her disguised as a suitor. Charles Rycroft identifies the crime in *The Moonstone* with "a sexual intercourse": the object is a diamond "of exceptional size and beauty and its perfection is only marred by a central flaw. It is called the Moonstone on account of its having the property of 'growing and lessening in lustre with the waxing and waning of the moon.'" The diamond must be given to Rachel Verrinder on her eighteenth birthday, and that task falls to her cousin Franklin Blake, who also falls in love with her. The diamond is given to her and taken from her the same night, and the "essential clue" to this theft is a nightshirt of Blake's which is stained with red paint (116–17).

The daring jewel theft occurs with some frequency in early detective fiction but soon loses its priority in the form and becomes a feature of another genre, the exploits of the gentleman thief. The thief is a suave and dashing rogue, who must often court his victim, a titled dowager: the Lone Wolf talks about violating "the privacy of Madame Omber's strong-box" (LW 166). The woman may refuse to press charges, considering her loss well compensated. This glamorized rape is both displaced and inverted, not a violation but a pleasure, and much could be made of the erotics of penetration as the thief slips silently into the bedroom, freezes when he hears a rustling from the bed, approaches the sleeping victim, and removes her gems from their hiding-place (see Auerbach 126; Freud 1953 [1905]).

A familiar type of analytic detective novel takes place in an ancient estate associated with threatening female sexuality (also the formula for haunted house fiction). John Dickson Carr is obsessed with this formula, as his titles *The Red Widow Murders, Night at the Mocking Widow,* and *Hag's Nook* testify. In the first, the house contains a legendary room (a woman's bedroom), sealed off because of mysterious deaths that have occurred there. The room is mislabeled "Bluebeard's Chamber." The first death took place in 1803, the night spent in the room by Charles Brixton and his new French bride. "It was her room,"

Lord Mantling explains, "but *he* died there" (RWM 18, 21). The murderous energy in the room is associated not only with the first night of marriage but also with France's Reign of Terror. The latter is read as a great explosion of angry female energy by Henry James in *The Ambassadors* and Charles Dickens in *A Tale of Two Cities*—Madame Defarge, knitting as she is splattered with blood from the rolling heads of French aristocrats, marks that historical occasion as a moment of male castration.

Hag's Nook—"where they used to hang witches"—and Margery Allingham's *Gyrth Chalice Mystery* tell the story of murder committed in special rooms set aside for male initiation ceremonies: "the original ancestor decreed that the eldest son must spend an hour in the Governor's Room and see what had been left for him in the safe" (HN 22, 34). In Allingham's book there is a "secret room in the east wing containin' some filfy family secret. There's a winder but there's no door, and when the son o' the house is twenty-five 'is father takes 'im in and shows 'im the 'orror, and 'e's never the same again." The " 'orror" is the mother, represented by a fabulous vaginal object like the Gyrth Chalice; the present "Maid of the Cuppe" is a "rather foolish-looking woman of fifty odd, clad in a modern adaptation of a medieval gown, and holding in her clasped hand a chalice of arresting design" (GCM 45, 22).

While detective fiction often stages sexual fantasy, it can also dismiss it. Stories often begin by framing subjects for their fantasies—sons for the murder of their fathers and husbands for the murder of their wives. In Conan Doyle's "Boscombe Valley Mystery," a father and son have an angry quarrel; the father rushes out of the house, and the son is seen following him with a gun. There is a confrontation in a thicket; witnesses hear angry words, a shot is fired, and they see the son run out afterward. The son's hat and his gun are found by the corpse. The case couldn't be tighter, but Holmes dismisses it because (although this is not his reason) it too closely resembles an Oedipal fantasy.

Spade will not look at Miles Archer's corpse; the corpse of Rusty Regan, which controls the action of *The Big Sleep*, is never seen. While hard-boiled detective fictions and spy thrillers may lack a corpse, they often contain a traumatic and elusive object that serves a roughly equivalent function, as if the insubstantiality of the corpse were re-installed as a lure rather than a prod. The Maltese falcon, Velma, and Ambler's Dimitrios are instances of such elusive objects. Hard-boiled detective fiction, as defined by Chandler and Macdonald, begins as a search for a missing person.

Despite its exotic context, the Maltese falcon refuses to reflect any-thing except the avidity of its pursuers. Nevertheless, Gutman tells Spade that the legend of the falcon will be "the most astounding thing you've ever heard of": it emerges from a Mediterranean romance, a "glorious golden falcon encrusted from head to foot with the finest jew-els," made by Turkish slaves in the castle of St. Angelo and sent by the Knights of Rhodes to Charles V of Spain as tribute, but snatched away by Barbarossa. Thereafter, the bird has an underground existence, sur-facing from time to time at "historical" moments in vaguely "royal" connections until it appears in Paris, "painted or enameled over to look like nothing more than a faintly interesting black statuette." The pat-tern of emergence and evasion continues with increasing violence: the murder of the Greek dealer Charilaos Konstantinides and the burglary of the surburban home of the Russian general Kemidov. Spade himself collaborates in the suppression of the bird; he lets it fall through a seam in the narrative: "Forget this thing. Tell it as it happened, but forget he had a bundle. . . . Everything happened the way it did happen, but without this dingus" (MF 109–10, 112–13, 143).

Hammett's falcon overlaps with the treasure objects of analytic de-tective fiction, like the moonstone, and these overlap with the cursed objects of horror fiction. The moonstone and the Agra treasure of *The Sign of Four* are violently ripped out of context, taken from ancient realms and brought into the detective's civilization, dripping profana-tion and breeding infection. Helen of Troy and the Holy Grail are archetypes of the elusive object, and Velma is a combination of both. Unlike the falcon, which is blackened, she is gilded over and displayed in a glamorous setting as Mrs. Grayle. Velma first appears in the story as a memory cherished by Molloy during his eight years in jail. She is next glimpsed as a photograph hidden in an old trunk full of theatrical memorabilia. Marlowe watches Mrs. Florian hide the photograph and put another in its place. The murders in the book repeat Mrs. Florian's action: they are attempts to suppress traces of Velma.

The elusive object in the spy thriller is usually the criminal, an audacious master-criminal like Dimitrios or Greene's Harry Lime. Like the falcon, Dimitrios recapitulates the secret history of Europe between the wars, as in the conventional history of the criminal parodied by Leacock: "The fact that you have never heard of Blue Edward merely shows the world that you have lived in. . . . Blue Edward is the terror of four continents. We have traced him to Shanghai, only to find him in Madagascar. It was he who organized the terrible robbery at Irkutsk in which ten mujiks were blown up with a bottle of Epsom Salts. It was Blue Edward who for years held the whole of Philadelphia in abject terror, and kept Oshkosh, Wisconsin, on the jump for even longer" (1938, 336). Latimer becomes aware of the existence of Dimitrios, and then dedicates himself to excavating his history. Informed by this desire, he finds Dimitrios in the margins of many public records, revealing behind the patchwork of history what Buchan calls "the leaks in the dyke" (TS 107).

Among the several false moves made by Conan Doyle in *A Study in Scarlet* was his inscription of the corpse within an alien perspective. Dr. Watson describes the appearance of Enoch Drebber, a conspiratorial Mormon, as he lies dead:

> On his rigid face there stood an expression of horror, and, as it seemed to me, of hatred, such as I have never seen upon human features. This malignant and terrible contortion, combined with the low forehead, blunt nose, and prognathous jaw, gave the dead man a singularly simious and ape-like appearance, which was increased by his writhing, unnatural posture. I have seen death in many forms, but never has it appeared to me in a more fearsome aspect than in that dark, grimy apartment, which looked out upon one of the main arteries of suburban London." (SSt 29)

He later writes, "Every time that I closed my eyes I saw before me the distorted baboon-like countenance" (SSt 36).

The corpse is sometimes an anthropological or paleological fantasy: "His face was a face I had never seen before. His hair was dark with blood, the beautiful blond ledges were tangled with blood and some thick grayish ooze, like primeval slime" (FML 60). In *The Mysterious Affair at Styles*, Poirot explains that he cannot solve the crime "unless I can find that missing link" (143). Like most puns in popular fiction, this one is awkwardly accidental—like Conan Doyle's "main artery in London"—but it echoes the monstrously improbable appearance, in the first detective story, of an orangutan trying to shave himself.

The anthropological identity of the corpse in detective fiction belongs with turn-of-the-century portrayals of degeneration theory like the human brutes of naturalism—the hairy apes and *bêtes humaines* of Émile Zola, Theodore Dreiser, Frank Norris, and Eugene O'Neill—as do heroic throwbacks like Tarzan, and Sir Henry Curtis in Rider Haggard's *King Solomon's Mines*. In retrospect, the corpse of Enoch Drebber belongs to Conan Doyle's Professor Challenger series rather than his Sherlock Holmes series and should move us away from detective fiction to a jungle adventure such as *The Lost World*.

Drebber's corpse is both horrifying and scandalous, and it provokes a reaction that is almost too strong for detective fiction. Even in death it excites Watson's rage: he desires to go on beating at it. The first narrator of "Dr. Jekyll and Mr. Hyde" feels a similar rage at the sight of Mr. Hyde. He is overcome by revulsion as Hyde calmly tramples a child's body; he is moved to take his walking stick and beat this creature to death. He finds this reaction strange because there is nothing wrong with Hyde as far as he can see: "There is something wrong with his appearance . . . something downright detestable. I never saw a man I so disliked, and yet I scarce know why. He must be deformed somewhere; he gives a strong feeling of deformity, although I couldn't specify the point" (Stevenson 1967, 65). These moments in Conan Doyle and Stevenson are compatible, however, because the narrator is looking at the phylogenetic equivalent of John Watson's ape. Hyde is almost literally the child in adult clothing. He is physically slighter than Jekyll, and, when transformed, must roll up his sleeves and trouser legs. Wells's Time Traveller moves forward into a world that has regressed; humanity has divided itself into two species, the Eloi who live above ground and Morlocks who live below: they are readily identifiable as child and beast, the phylogenetic and ontogenetic originary forms for the human. Wells also divides the anger provoked by these images of unsuccessful repression: he wants to beat the Morlocks, and to shake the Eloi and toss them about.

The victim may assume a regressive demeanor in death, but the criminal, who is also a brute, cannot be identified in this way. Much time is spent in analytic detective fiction looking at people who might be criminal, but all that can be seen is an appropriate social image. Another mystery of mystery fiction has to do with a primitivism that is so adaptive, and an impersonation so perfect, that it cannot be distinguished from the real thing, that is, social inhibition itself. What is so thrilling about analytic detective fiction is the running conclusion (always called off by the ending), that socialization is unverifiable: the criminal is a character who has "gone civilized."

Another false move made by Conan Doyle in *A Study in Scarlet* was to acknowledge the attraction of the criminal. Like Henry James's Christopher Newman, Jefferson Hope has the name of a democratic hero, and he is tender, faithful, and courageous. The criminal of the first proper detective novel is himself a hero, and the murder of Enoch Drebber is an expression of his virtue. Hope's crime is anachronistic, not culpable; he stands for a repudiated ethos, retributive justice. The criminal in detective fiction is always free to act out anger in defiance of the highly organized and unsatisfying codes of behavior that constitute justice.

Detective fiction obviously shares a border with another literature that expresses the attraction of criminality through such personalities as Robin Hood, Hereward the Wake, the Count of Monte Cristo, and Captain Nemo, and one can understand Conan Doyle to be acknowledging that connection. Jefferson Hope is the hero of some form other than detective fiction. The third false move was to give the criminal a book of his own, the middle book of *A Study in Scarlet*, which is set in the American West at an earlier time than the detective story that occupies the first and last book and that has an urban setting.

Conan Doyle wrote his first detective novel around a Western, and Hope is sympathetic because he is suited to that genre. Hope is guilty of an act of revenge, but that is an acceptable motive for male prowess in almost all other forms of male popular fiction, particularly the Western where "getting even" or "settling a grudge" is applauded. One of the several types of conventional criminal listed by Wodehouse is "men with a grudge which has lasted as fresh as ever for thirty years" (243), like the criminal in *The Rasp:* "I soon found enough reason for the hatred. Look as I looked. You will see that always, always, always was Digby-Coates beaten by the man he killed. Were the race one of scholarship, sport, politics, social advancement, honors, the result was the same" (R 185).

In *The Sign of Four*, the criminal has shrunk to the moral size of Jonathan Small, who is not a good man, merely better than his victim; and that relative ethical discrepancy would be allowed to stay in the form. Small believes his crime to be a justifiable act of vengeance, undertaken out of loyalty to a criminal community against an enemy who broke his word: "I tell you that no living man has any right to [the treasure] . . . unless it is three men who are in the Andaman convict-barracks and myself. . . . I have acted all through for them as much as for myself. It's been the sign of four with us always" (SF 143). Such ethical framing is not uncommon: "There was more in those eyes than any common triumph. . . . They flamed with a hawk's pride. . . . I realised for the first time the terrible thing I had been up against. This man was more than a spy; in his foul way he had been a patriot" (TS 141).

Small, however, does not commit the murder; that was done by the Andaman Islander, Tonga, Small's double and shadow, a racist projection of retributive justice in a repugnant form: "They are a fierce, morose, and intractable people, though capable of forming most devoted friendships. . . . They are naturally hideous, having large, misshapen heads, small fierce eyes, and distorted features. . . . They have always been a terror to shipwrecked crews, braining the survivors. . . . These massacres are invariably concluded by a cannibal feast." Tonga is linked to Small through the repetition of his name: "Their feet and hands . . . are remarkably small," "the smallest race upon this earth," "small, fierce eyes," and "a little black man—the smallest I have ever seen." When Small is himself described, he turns out to be a "brown, monkey-faced chap" (SF 128, 127, 138, 124). One of the names given to the savagery of crime is madness, and, at the end of a work, there is often a brief confirmation of this diagnosis in the form of an explosion of laughter, rage, or obscenity.

If the content of the criminal is savagery or madness, the structural characteristic, in analytic and hard-boiled detective fiction at least, is invisibility: detective fiction often snaps the criminal as an unseen image, a figure moving at night. The criminal is both present and absent; he or she is a split figure with two faces, and the only one showing is a face of social respectability. The criminal is a split figure and the seam of that split is undetectable: "The jealous inspector had taken pains to inform all his colleagues . . . that poor Lecoq, crazed by ambition, persisted in declaring that a low, vulgar murderer . . . was some great personage in disguise" (MLq 134). Various figures for schizophrenia negotiate this split, for example, that of the pathological liar or the consummate actor (who verge on artistic genius): "He is called Colonel Clay, because he appears to possess an india-rubber face, and he can mould it like clay in the hands of the potter" ("EMS" 31). "The big secret of all the famous criminals [is] . . . if you are playing a part, you will never keep it up unless you convince yourself that you are *it*. Those chaps didn't need to act, they just turned a handle and passed into another life, which came as naturally to them as the first" (TS 132).

G. K. Chesterton was fascinated by tropes of undetectability, and he usually worked them out through Flambeau, a master of disguises. His disguises, however, have less to do with the assumption of personality than with the repression of personality itself in the service of social function: the invisible man, for example, in the tale of that name, is a postman. In "The Queer Feet," Flambeau is able to steal an extravagant set of cutlery at the annual dinner of the Twelve True Fishermen where "there was generally at least one waiter to every gentleman who dined" and "the well-trained waiters were told to be almost invisible until they were wanted." Flambeau accomplishes his crime by putting himself into the place of a perceptual fold: "he contrived to lean against the wall . . . in such a way that for that important instant the waiters thought him a gentleman, while the gentlemen thought him a waiter." In this tale, as well as "The Blue Cross," where, disguised as a priest, he steals a valuable relic, Flambeau's crime is also proper behavior for the class or profession he impersonates (IFB 55, 58, 74).

As a creature of multiple identities, the criminal resembles mythical and rhetorical shapeshifters—the old man of the sea, the ogre in "Puss in Boots," the various Harlequin figures of Italian and French comedy, or Falstaff: "The three faces seemed to change before my eyes and reveal their secrets. The young one was the murderer. Now I saw cruelty and ruthlessness where before I had only seen good-humor. . . . The plump man's features seemed to dislimn and form again, as I looked at them. He hadn't a face, only a hundred masks" (TS 139).

This was also one of Holmes's characteristics, but it was largely written out of later detective fiction. As a trope and a fable of identity, shapeshifting belongs most deeply to the spy thriller. The spy, mainly the professional, but even the amateur Richard Hannay, is never himself. The identity of the spy is his *cover story:* "He had a cover story and a part of him believed it already. If he was caught, the whole of him would believe it; and if the Sarratt inquisitors sweated him, he had a fallback—he never travelled without one" (TTSS 88). The cover story, however, may be covering too many people. At the end of *Tinker, Tailor, Soldier, Spy,* Smiley wrote a scenario for Bill Haydon's treason and then "shrugged it all aside, distrustful as ever of the standard shapes of human motive. He settled instead for a picture of one of those wooden Russian dolls that open up, revealing one person inside the other, and another inside him" (TTSS 353). Johnny Vulkan in *A Funeral in Berlin* "changes his motive every time he comes through that East Berlin checkpoint. When men become double agents it's just a matter of time before they lose their grip on reality. They begin to drown in a sea of confusion" (FB 19–20).

Every criminal, however, is at least a double agent, and their deepest cover story is one that incriminates civilization as a whole. The criminal is a *sleeper,* passing as a member of respectable society, usually an Anglo-Saxon gentleman. The master criminal in *The Thirty-Nine Steps* is a "benevolent old gentleman [whose] . . . face was round and shiny, like Mr. Pickwick's" (TS 76). In *Background to Danger,* Colonel Robinson, who is actually a Bulgarian named Stefan Saridza, is "an impressive-looking man in his late fifties, with a smart grey cavalry moustache and a monocle. At first sight, he looked like a cross between a *Punch* drawing of a retired general and a French conception

of what the continent of Europe so oddly terms 'the English sporting' "
(BD 49–50). The thriller criminal is often given a title like "the man
at the top," "the big man," or "the kingpin," titles that also refer to a
refined or powerful cultural elite. What the form proposes is a fantasy
of undetectable criminality packed into images regarded as central to
the enterprise of civilization.

An extravagant version of this type of criminal, the magus, first
appeared in *The Woman in White* as Count Fosco. The magus is a
composite of the two faces of the criminal, the primitive and the gentleman—a mixture of utter ruthlessness and charm. An "immensely fat"
man, Count Fosco is also a great dandy, and Walter Hartright finds
him overwhelming: "Marian had prepared me for his high stature, his
monstrous corpulence . . . but not for the horrible freshness and cheerfulness and vitality of the man." Marian Halcombe's equally fascinated
perception of him also expresses a sense of doubleness: "Fat as he
is and old as he is, his movements are astonishingly light and easy."
Fosco's seamless duplicity produces an uncanny effect; the characters
find him unfathomable (a word repeatedly applied to him and identified with his "grey eyes" of "extraordinary power"). Nevertheless,
Fosco looks "the image of benevolent respectability"; his surface is one
of anachronistic, quaintly foreign charm (Collins 1974, 240, 568, 587,
242, 241, 308).

Fosco's "pitiless resolution," "prompt decision," and "far-sighted
cunning" are devoted to managing people and events: "He can manage
me as he manages his wife and Laura, as he managed the bloodhound
in the stable-yard, as he manages Sir Percival himself, every hour in
the day." Fosco is a criminal agent within the domestic melodrama of
the novel, but he is also quite gratuitously identified as a professional
spy. The word spy—a word which he says he loathes—is first applied to
him in a general sense by the demented heroine, Laura Fairlie. It turns
out to be specifically applicable, and, later in the novel, he is embedded
in a past of professional espionage (Collins 1974, 308, 611, 245).

Caspar Gutman is also a jovial fat man (the magus is the father who
takes everything good for himself), but what is so chilling about Gutman is not his single-minded pursuit of the treasure, but his effortless
maintenance of the mask of geniality and benevolence. When, for ex-

ample, he sacrifices his lover and "son," the punk Wilmer, to secure his own freedom, Gutman smiles "benignly" at Wilmer: " 'Well Wilmer, I'm sorry to lose you, and I want you to know that I couldn't be any fonder of you if you were my son; but—well, by Gad!—if you lose a son it's possible to get another—and there's only one Maltese falcon.' Gutman's sigh did not affect the benignity of his smile" (MF 175).

From the more sophisticated perspective of the spy thriller, the magus (as a person of elegance and charm) can often be seen as a figure of high European culture. The magus codes detective fiction's fear of culture and art: he inhabits a world of chateaux, exquisite furnishings, rare books, and vintage wines. Buchan's Colonel Stumm, a variation of the type, is a Prussian officer who wears scented silk underwear. The magus possesses the charming callousness of jaded decadents like J.-K. Huysman's Des Esseintes or Oscar Wilde's Sir Henry Wotton, and very often the motive for his imperial ambitions is ennui: "The enemy, quite simply, is bored: like Dr. No, or Goldfinger, or Hugo Drax, he sets up an incredibly ambitious operation to gain power or rule the world" (Merry 13).

As a figure of manipulation and power, the magus is a brain or computer (like the analytic detective), chessmaster, or spider. Moriarty is a former professor of mathematics, turned chief of a great criminal syndicate: "He is a genius, a philosopher, an abstract thinker. . . . He sits motionless, like a spider in the centre of its web, but that web has a thousand radiations, and he knows well every quiver of each of them" (MSH 471). The head of SMERSH "is a chess Grand Master and . . . a Pavlovian psychologist who believes that men are basically puppets, whose behavior is easily controllable provided you pull the right strings" (Palmer 7). Earlier avatars of the magus are Merlin, the Gothic wizards of Hawthorne and William Harrison Ainsworth, and George du Maurier's Svengali. Every criminal, though, is a master of control; if nothing else, he or she has committed, unseen, an untraceable murder in the midst of a community while participating in its social life. In the thriller, his ability to control circumstances becomes global; like Dimitrios, he becomes a demiurge whose presence is read in every political scandal. In contrast to the magus, who is a master of the program, the detective or spy hero is presented as spontaneous.

In common with other heroes, particularly the great hunter of outdoor adventure romance, he improvises weapons and strategies; what his starved environment offers he adapts into the tools of victory.

In *A Study in Scarlet*, Conan Doyle incriminates and executes an exemplary man, as if there were a conspiracy afoot to suppress virtues that would be celebrated in other forms of popular fiction. But detective fiction has put a price on his head; he is dangerous, he must be suppressed, because, if not, the reader may begin to see a resemblance between the criminal and the detective, between Hope and Holmes. Jefferson Hope is an earlier version of the hero, and their antagonism signifies his replacement by Holmes. Michel Butor has one of the characters in *Passing Time* make an equation between the detective and the criminal: "Any detective story is constructed on two murders, of which the first, committed by the criminal, is only the occasion of the second, in which he is the victim of the pure unpunishable murderer, the detective" (Butor 152–53). The spider metaphor applied to Moriarty originally belonged to Holmes himself: he "loved to lie in the very centre of five millions of people, with his filaments stretching out and running through them, responsive to every little rumour or suspicion of unsolved crime" (Priestman 94).

The equation of detective and criminal is by now a commonplace: "In fact, the literary figure of the detective typically was and continues to be an extraordinary, marginal figure who frequently bears a closer resemblance to the criminal he pursues than to the police officers with whom he supposedly collaborates" (Black 43). "In the figures of detective and criminal, a single renunciation, a sole sacrifice, is enacted, in different ways. This is seen in 'The Final Problem' when Holmes and Moriarty, 'locked in each other's arms,' plunge into Reichenbach Falls" (Moretti 142). Like the criminal, the detective is driven by revenge: "When a man's partner is killed he's supposed to do something about it" (MF 193); "I am an ordinary sort of fellow . . . but I hate to see a good man downed" (TS 23). But these vengeful impulses are laundered through myth and archetype and linguistic transformation. Many of the names—Gideon Fell, Mike Hammer, Lew Archer, even Sherlock Holmes with its barely disguised Shylock—announce such a connection. In early detective fiction, this connection was announced through allusions to the bloodhound, hounds of hell, or furies: "So swift, silent, and furtive were his movements, like those of a trained bloodhound picking out a scent, that I could not but think what a terrible criminal he would have made had he turned his energy and sagacity against the law instead of exerting them in its defense" (SF 112). The criminal is the *revenger*, the detective the *avenger;* that word carries no illicit connotations. Trent playfully acknowledges, "I should prefer to put it that I have come down in the character of avenger of blood, to hunt down the guilty, and vindicate the honor of society. That is my line of business" (TLC 26).

Literary history has often been read to see the detective as a barely transformed criminal by taking one step back from the first detective, Dupin, to one of his alleged models, François-Eugene Vidoq: "the absolute embodiment of a master criminal and galley slave turned policeman. . . . If Jonathan Wild achieved a legendary efficiency in the apprehension of rogues and the restoration of stolen goods, it was because he himself was a virtuoso thief. . . . Set a thief to catch a thief" (Steiner 141). The detective certainly looks and acts like a criminal; that is one of his most frequent disguises. He is a familiar of criminals, well known to the criminal underworld, and an adept of criminal thinking and criminal techniques. This is implicit in all mystery and detective fiction, although it is more or less dissembled in analytic detective fiction: Auden found hard-boiled detective fiction unsatisfactory because the detectives there "might just as well be murderers" (406).

To a psychoanalyst like Charles Rycroft, the identity of the detective and the criminal is keyed into the nature of literary fantasy: "In the ideal detective story the detective or hero would discover that he himself is the criminal for whom he has been seeking" (115), but only in detective stories that are not detective stories, like Alain Robbe-Grillet's *Erasers*, is such an implication gratified. This lurking equation may be why the rule of detective fiction most stridently advanced is that the detective must never be the criminal, as if this were a crime that would destroy the form. Nevertheless, traces of the ultimate equation persist.[1] Detective fiction always tells the story of a compulsive fascination between the detective and some extralegal other. More than solving the crime or avenging the victim, the criminal is the detective's desire. At one fabulous extreme, the detective and the criminal are connected as worthy adversaries with names that reverberate equally and histories of legendary exploits. This relationship, which begs not to be resolved, is like a competition for supremacy that the detective barely and incompletely wins.

The narrator of *Rogue Male* claims that his story is an act of devotion and, even more, an act of identification with his criminal counterpart: "That is the object of this confession . . . to recover that man with his insolence, his irony, his ingenuity. By writing of him I become him for the time" (RM 108–9). The narrator and the man sent out to hunt him down recognize one another as master sportsmen: "His technique showed that he had experience of big game. He had got into my mind. He knew that sooner or later I should have a look at that sidecar. And his gentle calling of my name to make me turn my head was perfect" (RM 105). In F. L. Packard's "The Gray Seal," Carruthers reminisces about this criminal: "The Gray Seal wasn't an ordinary crook—he was a classic. He was an artist. . . . I actually got to love the fellow—it was the *game*, really, that I wanted to beat" ("GS" 254). In this game, the others—the victims and their families, the police, society—do not count. The relationship between detective and criminal is the true fair play of a form said to be so characterized: "Well, sir, you have been very fair-spoken to me, though I can see that I have you to thank that I have these bracelets upon my wrists. Still, I bear no grudge for that. It is all fair and above-board" (SF 144). Hard-boiled detective fiction pursues Rycroft's ideal in another way: by identifying the criminal with the detective's desire, by criminalizing the detective's beloved. Early in the history of detective fiction, Holmes encountered Irene Adler who was not only "the woman," but also the only criminal that ever outwitted him.

Even if detective fiction only half remembers the ideal detective story, the genre began with such a tale. According to Richard Wilbur, there is a virtual identity asserted in "The Purloined Letter" between detective and criminal, between Dupin and an other represented only as D____ (380). The point, if taken, is more easily written off as an instance of that psychological doubling that convulses Romantic texts than as a structural principle of detective fiction, but Wilbur goes on to argue that it belongs to the genre. In Conan Doyle's notebooks, one of the suppressed names for Holmes was Sherington Hope (Gerber 280–81), and in *The Hound of the Baskervilles,* the criminal identifies himself to a cabman as Sherlock Holmes (HB 697). Wilbur argues that detective method commonly involves a complete identification between the detective and the criminal: "I knew by now every detail of that crime as if I had committed it myself" ("MDUR" 221). Poe's tale also includes this trope in the anecdote of the boy who was invariably successful at playing the game of convolutions, "Even and Odd."

In one of the amateur thriller's most common stories, no one believes that the hero is investigating a crime (except, perhaps, for the woman who irrationally believes in him), but they believe instead that he is the very criminal he claims to be seeking. In *The Thirty-Nine Steps,* Hannay vigorously hunts the murderers of Scudder while the police are hunting him as the murderer of Scudder.

The well-known twistiness of detective fiction allows the form to establish this identification without being responsible for it. In *Trent's Own Case,* a razor without a blade is found lying by the victim's body. Much later, Trent comes across the photograph of the fingerprints on the razor that he had slipped into his pocket and forgotten. Although Trent had at one time made a careful study of the identification of fingerprints, "he had grown decidedly rusty" in his specialty, and he pulls out some old photographs to refresh his memory, "and then Trent exploded in an oath, and the blood rushed to his head. . . . Here were two forefinger-prints exactly alike in every detail. . . . Trent collapsed into a chair and wiped the beads of sweat from his forehead. He felt as if he were in the crisis of a nightmare. The thing was madness; it didn't make sense" (TOC 122–23, 278). The criminal's fingerprints are his own.

The Phantom Lady contains an ingenious duplication: Lombard, the criminal who is also the detective, stands in for Henderson, the hero who is suspected of the murder of his wife. As a last attempt to talk his wife into giving him a divorce, Henderson appealed to their old relationship; he reserved a table "at our old place" and bought two tickets to a musical. When his wife only laughed at him, Henderson got furious, "slammed on my hat and slammed out the door." The prosecuting attorney wrote a different scenario for this moment: "He was at the final stage of his own preparations. He had his necktie open in his hands, measured off, ready to insert it under his collar. Instead, in a blind ungovernable rage . . . he dropped it over her head as she sat there at her mirror. He tightened it around her neck, he twined the ends together with unimaginable cruelty and will to kill." The solution tells this story again, but this time with Lombard in Henderson's place—"He says he got there even before you left, side-stepped you by waiting on the upper flight of stairs." The wife also laughed at Lombard's plans and desires—"that seems to have been her day for laughing at people"— and Lombard strangles her with Henderson's necktie, which he had absently picked up and was holding in his hands without noticing it (PL 39, 65, 231).

The equation of detective and criminal is written into the form in other ways. In "A Case of Identity," Holmes is able to solve the mystery by perceiving that two men are never present at the same time and, therefore, not casually but essentially related, like Jekyll and Hyde. Detective fiction consists of two stories, the story of a crime and the story of an investigation. In one, only the criminal is present, in the other only the detective. On the other hand, the detective and criminal are bound together in any number of nondiegetic ways, for example, they share extravagant characteristics that no one else in the form may possess. The criminal is also a thinking machine and a mind reader: "There's a mind behind this business, make no mistake about that. A very fine brain, cool, calculating and deadly careful. Every step, every single step has been thought out beforehand" (CQ 99); an egoist: "It is a rare pleasure to have an intelligent listener and I shall enjoy telling you the story of one of the most remarkable men in the world" (DN 133); and an exhibitionist: "And then remember, as I said, that nearly every murder is a manifesto . . . of self, a piece of exhibitionism" (HR 188).

Conversely, the detective is also a magus: "When I was watching Stapleton, Cartwright was frequently watching you, so that I was able to keep my hand upon all the strings" (HB 765); and a schizophrenic master of disguise: "a drunken-looking groom, ill-kempt and side-whiskered, with an inflamed face and disreputable clothes, walked into the room. Accustomed as I was to my friend's amazing powers in the use of disguises, I had to look three times before I was certain that it was indeed he. . . . It was not merely that Holmes changed his costume. His expression, his manner, his very soul seemed to vary with every fresh part that he assumed" (ASH 167, 170); and so on. Ideally, the text of a detective fiction should work like that of *The ABC Murders* where, well into the investigation, Poirot knows enough about the elusive criminal to assert, "In my opinion the strength of his obsession is such that he *must* attempt to carry out his promise! Not to do so would be to admit failure, and that his insane egotism would never allow." Both Hastings and the reader should remember that, one hundred pages before, Hastings had observed of Poirot: "Poirot had sustained a defeat. ABC had challenged him—and ABC had won. My friend, accustomed to an unbroken line of successes, was sensitive to his failure—so much so that he could not even endure discussion of the subject" (ABC 153, 54).

Auden's formula for readable detective fiction required a setting in rural England, "the Great Good Place": "an innocent society in a state of grace, i.e., a society where there is no need of the law, no contradiction between the aesthetic individual and the ethical universal, and where murder therefore is the unheard-of act which precipitates a crisis (for it reveals that some member has fallen and is no longer in a state of grace). The law becomes a reality and for a time all must live in its shadow, till the fallen one is identified. With his arrest, innocence is restored, and the law retires forever" (Auden 403). The bucolic English village, however, is also a very bad place, a setting shared with Gothic and horror fiction. Antiquity, as John Aubrey, Walter Scott, and James Fraser discovered, has its bright and its dark sides; behind the charming Elizabethan facades there are often relics of bestial practices. In detective fiction this is expressed through practical jokes, graffiti, or poison pen letters that often precede the murder—texts that appear miraculously in the community and smear eminent citizens with dirt.

Auden's community is also closed or cloistered—"there is a third point which is, I think, decisive. After seven o'clock it is impossible to get in or out of the Close unobserved" (CQ 25)—an English college, an office building with security guards at the door, an isolated railway car, or a deserted stage. The community should not only be closed but also closely related so that "all its members are potentially suspect" as opposed to the thriller, "which requires an open society in which any stranger may be a friend or enemy in disguise" (Auden 402). But even in the open society of hard-boiled and thriller, the fiction operates under the assumption that strangers *are* intimately related to the issue at hand. In the latter two forms there are only secret relationships; in analytic detective fiction there is also the fiction of a community. The crime is a symptom of those hidden relationships and the effort to keep them secret.

As Auden and every list of rules insist, the criminal of analytic detective fiction must be an insider, most clearly so because the community denies this possibility and immediately reacts to the crime by insisting that it must be the work of an outsider: "Who had done the deed? Tramps! answered Stillwater, with one voice" (Aldrich 17). The detective is also an insider, or, more precisely, an outsider who is an insider: The Dean's "hand was actually stretched out for the telephone when he had an inspiration. Bobby Pollock! Bobby was the Dean's nephew. . . . Bobby had joined the Metropolitan Police. . . . Could one call in Scotland Yard over the heads of the local police? . . . But stay—why make it an official matter at all? Why should not Bobby take two or three days' holiday and stop with his uncle" (CQ 19). "Good. You see, no doubt, how well suited you are for the task. As a distinguished Old Boy of the School, you have the best of reasons for being here as my guest. You can talk to both boys and masters without anyone questioning your *bona-fides*. No one, of course, knows or need know why you are really here" (WM 24). In hard-boiled detective fiction, the detective is treated like an insider; he is admitted to the privacy of a family through the insistence of an authoritative older man or a seductive younger woman.

Two incompatible conditions produce the tension in the community that the detective must ease: someone in the community must have committed the murder and yet no one in the community, as the community believes itself to be, could have done it. The innocent community has been suddenly transformed into a community in which someone is guilty, anyone is guilty, everyone is guilty, and this is expressed through the convention whereby the police regard everyone connected with a crime as potentially guilty: "It is always wise to suspect every-body until you can prove logically, and to your own satisfaction, that they are innocent" (MAS 102).

What Poirot concludes in "Murder in the Calais Coach" is that the community is literally guilty; that twelve people acting in concert murdered Ratchett. In a letter to the editor of the paper that serialized his *Big Bow Mystery*, Israel Zangwill thanks the readers who offered solutions while the "tale was running": "When I started it, I had, of course, no idea who had done the murder, but I was determined no one should guess it. Accordingly, as each correspondent sent in the name of a suspect, I determined he or she should not be the guilty party. By degrees every one of the characters got ticked off as innocent—all except one, and I had no option but to make that character the murderer" (202).

The act of murder generates a form of the uncanny called *suspicion*, an anxious atmosphere that renders the casual critical and the familiar strange: "The community was in that state of suppressed agitation and suspicion which no word adequately describes. The slightest circumstance would have swayed it to the belief in any man's guilt" (Aldrich 18). Suspicion can merge with its counterpart in Gothic, the premonition of evil: "Perhaps the nastiness was not in Cope; perhaps it was a poison in the air, a distorting medium that would soon people these stately rooms with knaves, a destructive element that would overwhelm all normal human confidence and make honest people eye each other with suspicion and fear" (HR 142).

Suspicion is intimately associated with looking: "Nothing fosters suspicion like the act of watching; a man spied upon can hardly blow his nose but we accuse him of designs" (Stevenson [and Osbourne] 1909, 345). "It is as if crime alone could make us see again" (Hartman 214–15). Infected by suspicion, individuals look at one another as if for the first time. A random memory of something unremarked at the time will compel speculation. In the acute glare or blur of suspicion, any object can take on resonance and become the signifier of the secret: "Looking round the room amid the ripple of delighted exclamations, Gott saw Lord Auldearn's eyes narrowed upon Clay as upon something suddenly revealed as formidable" (HR 35). The look of suspicion is most like Hitchcock's camera eye, suddenly tracking away from the dramatic center of a scene to discover in some niche or corner an arresting but enigmatic image.

In J. B. Priestley's *An Inspector Calls*, a policeman visits the home of a well-to-do family, investigating the death by suicide of a pregnant girl. The father, mother, son, and daughter all indignantly deny any knowledge of the woman, yet each in turn is taken through a scenario of intimacy that leaves them primarily responsible for her death. Works like J. M. Barrie's *Shall We Invite the Ladies?* and Christie's *And Then There Were None* offer a variation on this structure. In these works, the members of a dinner party or a party weekend are told that they are all guilty of some crime against their absent host. The host (victim/criminal/magus) stimulates and controls their mutual suspicion and panic; he manifests himself miraculously through signs; and, in the Christie, which is set in a series of hermetically sealed rooms as well as the basic setting of an inaccessible island, he kills off the guests one after another.

In hard-boiled detective fiction and the spy thriller, the community is not even apparently "innocent." It is always a more or less overtly collusive or conspiratorial community. But this is very often the case in analytic detective fiction as well, where the two conditions of the community—that it be both innocent and closed—inevitably generate the suspicion of collusion: "I have seven gentlemen in front of me, one of whom shot the—the gentleman behind me, in the presence of the others. Collusion to conceal the fact is a crime. So´whatever you arranged among yourselves before I came, cut it out! It won't do. The Squire of Newplace, a clergyman, a doctor, a naval officer—all trifling with the law and flying in the face of common sense! It's unheard of" (MK 72). Anthony Berkeley's *Jumping Jenny* dramatizes this collusive activity. Ironically, the detective who had been a guest at a masquerade party during which the murder was committed directs a conspiracy meant to mislead the police. The physical scene has to be patched up and the experience of the previous night rewritten to eliminate suspicious details. This activity generates the same anxiety and scrutiny that overwhelms the innocent community: there are too many of these signs once you begin to look for them; patching here creates a hole there which then has to be patched in turn. And as Sheringham, who has worked with the police before, learns or guesses something that the police find suspiciously absent, that absence must be made good through the fabrication of new data (32–38, 85–86).

The community of analytic detective fiction can also be regarded as an inhibited or repressed community. Much of the surface appeal of this fiction is its presentation of models of decorum in the aftermath of trauma. Just as the murderer has gone to great pains to suppress all traces that could connect her or him to the corpse, the impulse to suppress is acted out at almost every moment of the fiction. The criminal, for one, is rarely guilty of guilty behavior.

The community is guilty, however, mostly because it acts guilty out of a desire to protect another who is believed to be guilty of the crime. The suspect, then, is the person who suspects and acts evasively on the basis of that suspicion: in Hecht's *Florentine Dagger*, for example, a girl acts to shield her mother who has murdered her stepfather. The various forms of the community reiterate a Freudian fiction of the family: the members are all guilty of the death of a male or female parent, not in fact but in fantasy. Analytic detective fiction will of course arrive at conclusions that are precisely opposite to psychoanalytic fictions; it will find its destiny in validating repression.

8 Detective Solutions and Their Fictions

ONE OF THE DETERMINING CONVENTIONS OF DETECTIVE FICTION is the absence of the criminal as criminal until the end of the work. Although the pressure of the criminal's behavior behind the scenes has generated the text, deposited a corpse, and led to the presence of a detective, the criminal is no more than a shadow that falls over parts of the work. The criminal is inferred from enigmatic traces; "Only in the false voice of an innocent party does he ever speak" (Woods 17). The criminal may kill only once, or he or she may be at work during the narrative manufacturing new misleading signs. A distinction is generally made between the first murder, which has been prompted by desire, and subsequent crimes that are prompted by the need to elude detection.

Detective fiction ends with the embodiment of the criminal as a graspable object: "If the burglar was now somewhere in the main buildings and had his escape to make through the gates he was virtually in Appleby's hands. . . . If this was the murderer who was operating now the St. Anthony's mystery might be past history within half an hour. It was somehow a disconcerting thought" (SS 60). But that moment is also one of signification: "Sir Charles . . . had been priding himself on the skillful way in which he had been withholding his suspect's name, to bring it out with a lovely plump right at the end after proving his case" (PCC 44). Sergeant Cuff gives Franklin Blake a sealed envelope and tells him to wait "to open the envelope . . . till you have got at the truth. And then compare the name of the guilty person, with the name that I have written in that sealed letter." A few pages later, Cuff tells him to open the letter and then look at a dead sailor with a black beard: the paper and the body bear the same name (Collins 1966, 492, 502).

Very little can happen at this point in the story; the criminal is in the detective's hands. In earlier versions of such pointing/naming forms (riddle forms), the antagonists are allowed one last outburst like Rumpelstiltskin, or a sudden deflation like Shylock. Criminals may bolt for the door to evade or be seized by the waiting police; they may spit curses; they may collapse and confess. We expect nothing more from them as criminals, and were they to escape, the text would simply shift into another popular formula, probably the chase thriller: "The whole affair, the interview, the chase, the capture, appeared to him in a different light—as an impulsive display whose object was not very clear. The chase, in particular, seemed futile. The confession was the thing, and that had been attained in the first twenty minutes. Fane's escape was an extra, something not contemplated, which a wise man would have allowed to pass with a shrug" (ESJ 282–83).

Intimately attached to the pointing/naming of the criminal is another structure, the solution to the crime or mystery. Predecessor genres like the Gothic tale and the sensation novel also end with a solution or explanation. In early detective fiction and the line of adventure romance that preceded and enclosed it (for example, Stevenson and Osbourne's *Wrecker*), this was usually the criminal's story. After the detective found the object of his quest, a new subject took over; the narrator became an auditor and sat down to listen to another story.

In other forms of masculine popular fiction, the neutralization or conversion of the enemy is enough, but detective fiction acts as if narration and interpretation are so important that the form must end with a story. The solution is what detective fiction is "all about." It is a highly protected structure, a revelation surrounded by gestures of veiling and framing, suppression and restoration. It is commonly felt that if the solution is prematurely exposed the book will be damaged, "given away," as one reviewer put it; "in thrillers all material is classified and any comment can be a leak" (Wyndham 626).

The solution is both a narrative and a grammar of narrative. It is the narrative equivalent of the criminal and gives itself to a play of aliases. These interpretive accounts are not logical per se; they merely satisfy the conditions for truth, and therefore closure, established by the genre. They sketch the restoration of a synchronic continuity in the space and time of the fiction, which was broken by the crime, and the restoration of a diachronic continuity in the history of the community or family, the breaking of which led to the crime.

After Conan Doyle, a map of the bounded territory of the crime is often the first text encountered in a detective novel; in Michael Gilbert's *Close Quarters,* it is even a real map, copied from *Residential Closes of England* by Canon J. D. Judd, D.D. (CQ 8). As an inspector briefs Trent, he takes out a thin notebook and "as they talked he began to make, with light, secure touches, a rough sketch-plan of the room. It was a thing he did habitually on such occasions" (TLC 46). After the suspects have been interviewed, a timetable, another synchronic grid, may be folded into the book. In *Close Quarters* this appears on page 33 and is a reproduction of the original map reworked for 8:00 P.M., Tuesday 28 September, followed by a list of people outside the close, where they were, and who says so. Twain's Sherlock Holmes (in "A Double-Barreled Detective Story") demands "the longitude and the latitude, corrected for magnetic variation," and "the altitude, the temperature, and the degree of humidity prevailing" (1958, 49). Finally, detective fiction generally opens with a request for a third map, the map of continuous narrative—a request that the client begin at the beginning and tell everything just as it happened.

According to all the maps, the crime is impossible: it could not have occurred in that time and space. Mysteries involving railroads were prominent in England because the trains were presumed to run on fixed schedules. Mysteries set in a university college or a cathedral close were also attractive because the gates were locked at a certain time of night, and the legitimate inhabitants had keys, all of which could generally be accounted for:

"Yet, as you see, at first sight it would appear impossible for any one of our suspects to have murdered him at that particular moment."

"Then what you say is this." The Chief Constable was displaying a heftyish wit. "Someone in the Close did the job, and yet none of them could have done it, hey?" (CQ 101)

The articulation of a Cartesian frame was also the prefect's method in "The Purloined Letter": "Why the fact is, we took our time, and we searched *every where*. I have had long experience in these affairs. I took the entire building, room by room; devoting the nights of a whole week to each." What he discovered is that the crime has no coordinates, it cannot be located in his graph (Poe 1902, 6:34). It is outside the map or is a hole in the map: it is a miracle. Ernst Bloch uses a different figure for this trope, which he calls the "reconstruction of the unnarrated": "But the main thing always remains: the alpha, where none of the figures appearing in sequence admits to having been present, and the reader least of all: it happens—like the fall of man or even of the angels . . . outside of history" (quoted in Heissenbüttel 83).

The solution is a "true" map on which the murder, the corpse, and the criminal are not merely locatable, but central coordinates. The path of the criminal in *A Study in Scarlet* will eventually be traced on the unknown surface of the American frontier. In addition to solving the crime, a true map must also demystify all Gothic traces and account for all extraordinary phenomena. The secularized fiction of detective novels is that the initial maps are simply false, since they obviously don't do the work that we make maps for: "Very neatly put. . . . And the sum total of it all is this. Every single suspect for our original time of the murder has practically eliminated himself. There's only one answer to that. We must have been wrong about the time. Simple, isn't it?" (CQ 131). "In the stories . . . the dead man's watch is always conveniently smashed, thus enabling the detectives to fix the wrong time of death because the murderer has set the hands at a different hour" (HN 94).

"But the twelve-mile drive?" gasped Hatherley.

"Six out and six back. Nothing simpler." (ASH 295)[1]

Wolfe ruthlessly controls his timetable, and he masters his space by refusing to move at all. Most male popular fiction dramatizes the conquest of time and space. In science fiction it is as easy as a wish: you want to control space, you build a space machine; you want to control time, you build a time machine. Hank Morgan becomes boss of England by knowing "that the only total eclipse of the sun in the first half of the sixth century occurred on the 21st of June, A.D. 528, O.S., and began at 3 minutes after 12 noon" (Twain 1948, 15).

In Poe's "Gold-Bug," Stevenson's *Treasure Island*, and Rider Haggard's *King Solomon's Mines*, the possession or deciphering of a secret map is equatable with vast treasure. So too is the withholding of the map: *Treasure Island* begins with the promise of continuous narrative, with one exception—"Squire Trelawney, Dr. Livesey, and the rest of these gentlemen having asked me to write down the whole particulars about Treasure Island, from the beginning to the end, keeping nothing back but the bearings of the island, and that only because there is still treasure not yet lifted" (Stevenson 1946, 1). If *Treasure Island* is a hole in space, *Murder at the Keyhole* is a hole in time, as its coy framing suggests: "My acquaintance with Veronica, and therefore my entanglement with Roger Pell, began about a quarter to four on a June afternoon on the Hollam Bay road. At fifteen minutes to four, to be precise, I had never seen Veronica and was unaware of her existence. Before fourteen minutes to four I found myself embracing her tightly" (MK 7).

Vast treasure is also the payoff for an uncanny coordination with a timetable that is called "perfect timing," in films like *The Asphalt Jungle, Rififi,* or *The Killing.* The control of time and space can also create a crime; these works are devoted to intercalary fictions in which a safe may be cracked and nothing registers in an airtight security system. In other similar films, a clever convict can effect a Houdini-like escape from an escape-proof prison. Conrad likens these miracles to explosions: "In the close-woven stuff of relations between conspirator and police there occur unexpected solutions of continuity, sudden holes in space and time. A given anarchist may be watched inch by inch and minute by minute, but a moment always comes when somehow all sight and touch of him are lost for a few hours during which something (generally an explosion) more or less deplorable does happen" (1953, 80).

In the spy thriller, a map or a map fragment (the iconic equivalent of the solution) is often the object of pursuit. Map fragments, secret plans, blueprints, and photographs are pieces cut out of the larger map of the known world. The title of *The Thirty-Nine Steps* remains an elusive phrase until we discover that it refers to a specific set of coordinates on the map of England where a momentous work of espionage will take place. However, the rolls of film in *Epitaph for a Spy* never get unrolled. Like the solution, they hold only the promise of an adequate demystification; they can never be developed. To unfold a narrative secret is to have it go dead, blank, dark. The fragments in *The Thirty-Nine Steps* are also photographs and memories, and, in a wonderful final sequence in the film, Hannay feeds a music hall performer named Mr. Memory the title of the movie, and he spews out the crucial information as meaningless verbiage. He is shot just as he is about to utter the criminal's name.

The diachronic form of the solution is the history of the crime, a narrative of events that occurred in the past and, optimally, in a different kind of world. It is a narrative of significance to the community: it frees them from anxiety and guilt, and yet they have no access to it until it is worked into the sequence of historical time and memory by the detective. The history of the crime, then, is a suppressed narrative, and the solution is its restoration.

The history of the crime is a suppressed narrative in several senses. In Conan Doyle's first detective novel, it is still available in a highly visible form, and it can be clearly seen to be suppressed and relocated in the sequence of his first two detective novels, *A Study in Scarlet* and *The Sign of Four*. The first book of *A Study in Scarlet* is a conventional detective fiction narrated by Watson, set in London, and dominated by Holmes's presence. The criminal, Jefferson Hope, is captured at the end as a result of Holmes's investigation. The second book, on the other hand, is the history of the crime, and it is narrated by an unidentified storyteller and set in the American wilderness. It proclaims, in a way that would not be clear in the achieved detective story formula, that if you want to know why a corpse mysteriously appears in London you must know what happened years before in an unknown spot on the other side of the world, the Mormon community in Utah.

In *The Sign of Four*, the history of the crime appears as a much shorter form, in its more familiar and more controlled place at the end of the work. It is spoken as a confession by the criminal in the presence of the detective and the police. It also restores a narrative sequence that took place years before in India; it is a narrative that sounds like the story of *The Moonstone*. If the solution is the restoration of a suppressed narrative, the sequence of Doyle's two books enacts a contrary dynamic, the suppression of the solution, which is also what the detective story is all about. Ellery Queen plays with suppressing the solution completely. Within the context of an unbelievable game that he insists reader and detective play with each other, the first site of the solution is a blank page or a blank screen on which is imprinted the phrase "A Challenge to the Reader." Todorov wrote of a publisher who suppressed the solution completely and "put out real dossiers, consisting of police reports, interrogations, photographs, fingerprints, even locks of hair; these 'authentic' documents were to lead the reader to the discovery of the criminal" (1977, 46).

The sequence of suppression and restoration is often narrative data, particularly in the familiar story of the murder of a blackmailer, a dark version of the detective who may suppress or restore lost meaning sadistically as he is gratified or balked in his desire. The opposition between suppression and restoration is featured in "The Purloined Letter," where the blackmailer is powerful only as long as the letter remains suppressed, where both the blackmailer and his victim desire the suppression of the letter, where the letter is so successfully hidden that the most intense and methodical search cannot uncover it, where the letter has been in plain sight in the open air of the apartment all along, and where the difference between suppression and restoration is the refolding of a piece of paper along its original crease. The blackmail, the dirty letter of the minister, is the rolled-up solution that is threatened with premature exposure.

The crime in detective fiction may coincide with a misplacement of the solution. In *Murder at the Keyhole*, Pell is shot in impossible circumstances, just as he was narrating the solution to a mystery: "Pell was struck dead at the very crisis of his revelation, whatever it was to be. The visitation of Death in such a high-strung moment stunned my nerves" (MK 64). In *The Man Who Killed Fortescue*, the victim is killed for the solution of a previous murder. The book opens with lines that threaten to shut it down immediately: "I have definitely and positively solved the mystery of Fortescue's murder. . . . I'm writing it up in fiction form—and, by George, what a story it makes!" (MKF 55–56). This prior detective story is used in the book for purposes of blackmail.

The solution restores emotionally saturated or infantile material, and this can mean no more than the volatile and excited narration of a crime story within the context of a controlled detective story (see Priestman 101). Moreover, the genres of the solution in Conan Doyle's two novels are relatively infantile compared to detective fiction. In the first, the story is an American Western and in the second it is an adventure story like *King Solomon's Mines*. *The Ipcress File* is a late thriller whose appeal is its cool buttoned-down style and tone, but its solution is a stretch of text where Deighton sounds like Buchan.

The restoration of the solution is a healing act for the community and the detective; in one of the love scenes in *Hag's Nook*, Tod Rampole gives the woman he fancies pretty standard advice for both marital success and narrative closure: "There isn't any need to forget. There's only one thing we've got to do. We've got to explain all this tommyrot, murders and curses and foolishness and everything, and then you'll be free. We'll both go away then, and—" (HN 125). And Prince Julien de Medici, the detective of *The Florentine Dagger*, suffers because he cannot solve: "Unable to keep his thoughts calm and invent something plausible to explain the insane shifting of the past two weeks, the terror from which he had suffered during the early days of the Ballua mystery reinstated itself" (FD 211).

The "detective stories of Edgar Allan Poe and Arthur Conan Doyle," Albert Hutter wrote, "begin with the recent impact of a crime and work backward to restructure the incomplete fragments of present knowledge into a more intelligible whole and consequently to explain the past" (231–32). Nicholas Blake calls it the "Dark Backward" (HT 43). In *The Doomsters*, Archer looks at a woman who is filling in a gap in the story of the crime and thinks, a "pit or tunnel had opened in my mind, three years deep or long. Under white light at the bottom of it, fresh and vivid as a hallucination, I could see the red spillage where life had died and murder had been born" (D 154). In *The Moonstone*, Franklin Blake is literally seeking a "lost recollection" (Collins 1966, 425). Finally, the premise of certain thriller fictions of the 1940s, like Kenneth Fearing's *Dagger of the Mind* or Fritz Lang's *Woman in White* (no relationship to the Collins), is the recovery of lost time, either as amnesia or alcoholic blackout—a time when the hero is accused of having done something criminal. Detective fiction shares a border with a large body of popular fiction distributed over the jungle adventure, fantasy, and science fiction genres—works like *King Solomon's Mines* or Conan Doyle's *Lost World* that dramatize a journey into a "lost recollection" or "lost past."

As someone who must produce continuous narrative from fragments as a means of promoting health, the detective invites comparison with the psychoanalyst. Detective fiction and Freud agree that "an incomplete story . . . produces no therapeutic effect" (Freud 1966, 339). Writing to Wimsey for help, Harriet Vane says, "Perhaps it should be a psychologist and not a detective," as if unclear whether the crime is an inner or outer event; in this case it is a spate of poison-pen letters written to the faculty of a women's college accusing them of sexual perversion and crime (GN 224–25). This relationship coexists with a fear of psychoanalysis within the fiction, and outside the fiction as the enemy that has led the modernist artist astray.

The connection between detective fiction and psychoanalysis has been well discussed.[2] The manners and methods of the detective are much like those of the psychoanalyst as he appears in Freud's writing: the detective listens to repeated accounts of the same incident, listening for gaps or discrepancies; he reads behavior; he identifies secondary formations—"You aren't really telling me your fresh and direct memory of what happened last Monday, you're merely repeating the talk it has been resolved into" (RBx 24); and he uncovers repression—"Shall I tell you why you have been so vehement against Mr. Inglethorp? It is because you have been trying to believe what you wish to believe. It is because you are trying to drown and stifle your instinct, which tells you another name" (MAS 111). Above all, the detective probes slips of all kinds. All of these are signs of guilt, whether or not they have anything to do with the crime under investigation: "She was very up-set—seemed to think we'd think she was a criminal for having made a slip in her memory" (R 54–55). Like the psychoanalyst, the detective is a fixer. Every detective novel is a call for a doctor: "London is sick, Mr. Holmes, come and fix it quick," and a fiction of miraculous healing follows this plea.

Sir Walter Scott's *Waverley* includes a painstaking restoration toward the end of the novel. This is quite unlike the conventional ending of detective stories, but it connects solutions to broader narrative impulses. Baron Bradwardine returns to his estate, which had been devastated by the British army, and finds it exactly as he remembers it: "Every mark of devastation, unless to an eye intimately acquainted with the spot, was already totally obliterated. . . . All seemed as much as possible restored to the state in which he had left it when he assumed arms some months before. . . . While these minutiae had been so heed-fully attended to, it is scarce necessary to add, that the house itself had been thoroughly repaired, as well as the gardens, with the strictest attention to maintain the original character of both, and to remove as far as possible all appearance of the ravage they had sustained." To be given back almost everything is not enough for this possessor. After dinner, Bradwardine "cast a somewhat sorrowful look upon the side-board," noting that the cup with which he normally made his toasts was missing: "Here the Baron's elbow was gently touched by his Major Domo, and, turning round, he beheld in the hands of Alexander ab Alexandro, the celebrated cup of Saint Duthac, the Blessed Bear of Bradwardine" (Scott 1980, 483–84, 490). The scene is extravagant and self-indulgent. Scott demands a restoration complete to the last, or first, detail, just as defenses of detective fiction insist that the solution must explain every floating fact that has called attention to itself in the preceding narrative.

Scott's solution is a way of denying the significance of the narra-tive itself; not merely ending it, but calling it off, as Twain does in the final chapters of *Huckleberry Finn*. Scott's restoration also spills into the meaning of *Waverley* as a whole. Scott claimed that the Scotland his readers could visit was extremely different from the Scotland of his novel, and this transformation was begun by the insurrection of 1745 itself, which is the story that Scott tells. This, both inside and outside the book, was an unsuccessful attempt at still another restoration, the return of the Stuart line to the throne of England.

The conjectural model behind the solution as restoration is the tradition of medical semiotics or "divinatory science"—"the discipline which permits diagnosis, though the disease cannot be directly observed, on the basis of superficial symptoms or signs"—as exemplified in the work of Galen, Giovanni Morelli, Baron Cuvier, Charles Lyell, Charles Darwin, Alphonse Bertillon, and Freud (Ginzburg 87). Darwin begins *On the Origin of Species* by finding fault with the existing timetable of creation. According to the biblical map of Genesis, development is catastrophic, the result of sudden upheavals in time and space. For Darwin, on the other hand, development must be so continuous it is impossible to verify any change is taking place. The solution to the origin of species, the proof of natural selection, would be a vast underground restoration, the geological museum, which would reveal, as we descend, a "finely-graduated organic chain" of existence, displaying the "innumerable transitional links" between species. The geological record, however, is actually "a history of the world imperfectly kept. . . . Of this history we possess the last volume alone, relating only to two or three countries. Of this volume, only here and there a short chapter has been preserved; and of each page, only here and there a few lines" (Darwin n.d., 234, 255). This being the case, the reconstruction that Darwin makes is necessarily imaginative.

In "The Five Orange Pips," Sherlock Holmes compares his method to that of Cuvier: "The ideal reasoner . . . would, when he had once been shown a single fact in all its bearings, deduce from it not only all the chain of events which led up to it but also all the results which would follow from it. As Cuvier could correctly describe a whole animal by the contemplation of a single bone, so the observer who has thoroughly understood one link in a series of incidents should be able to accurately state all the other ones, both before and after" (ASH 224–25). In *A Coffin for Dimitrios*, Ambler compares Latimer's quest to that of a scientist who had built up "the complete skeleton of a prehistoric animal from a fragment of fossilised bone. It had taken the zoophysicist nearly two years and Latimer . . . had marvelled at the man's inexhaustible enthusiasm for the task. Now, for the first time, he understood that enthusiasm. He had unearthed a single twisted fragment of the mind of Dimitrios and now he wanted to complete the structure" (CD 33).[3]

The two parts of the solution, the restoration of a lost past and the true mapping of time and space, are also the two poles of interpretation—interpretation as mystification and as demystification—laid out by Paul Ricoeur in his *Freud and Philosophy:* "According to one pole, hermeneutics is understood as the manifestation and restoration of a meaning addressed to me in the manner of a message, a proclamation, or as is sometimes said, a kerygma; according to the other pole, it is understood as . . . a reduction of illusion" (27). For Ricoeur, these two poles divide interpretation, but in detective fiction they are not in opposition; they coexist happily as a necessary sequence that has as its goal the closure of narrative, not the discovery of truth: "We ought to be able to fake a story that will rock them to sleep" (MF 30).

Detective fiction ends with a story that is a retelling or replay of the crime. In *Enter Sir John*, the solution is a play that Sir John Suarez, an actor-detective, has written about the murder, and the murderer is invited to audition and try out for his own part. *Re-enter Sir John* ends with a home movie of the opening—an alleged incident of cheating at cards—shown to the assembled suspects. Sir John plays the scene with himself.

In certain tales repeatedly identified as sources or original paradigms for detective fiction, the solution is also a crime. In the sixteenth-century collection *Travels of the Three Young Sons of the King of Serendippo*, in a tale reworked by Voltaire in the third chapter of *Zadig*, three brothers "meet a man who has lost a camel. . . . At once they describe it to him: it's white, and blind in one eye; under the saddle it carried two skins, one full of oil, the other of wine. They must have seen it? No, they haven't seen it. So they're accused of theft and brought to be judged. The triumph of the brothers follows: they immediately show how from the barest traces they were able to reconstruct the appearance of an animal they had never set eyes on" (Ginzburg 88–89).

The solution is a crime because it is an apparent act of transgression; it is also a crime because it sounds the death of narrative. But, according to Carlo Ginzburg, this solution, this crime, is the act of narrative itself, and he speculates that the idea of narrative itself may be a product of the mundane acts of inference common to people who must hunt for their meat.

Dennis Porter puts the relationship between the two narratives of detective fiction, the investigation and the solution, generically: "Out of the *nouveau roman* of the offered evidence he constructs a traditional readable novel that ends up telling the story of the crime" (1981, 30). Detective fiction is about the manufacture of narrative, a story about story that we tell repeatedly and obsessively, like Scheherazade. The first fiction, the investigation, is quite literally the ground of narrative in *Monsieur Lecoq:* "Now I know everything. . . . I mean all that is connected with the episode of the drama which ended in that bloody bout in the hovel. This expanse of earth covered with snow is a white page upon which the people we are in search of have written, not only their movements, their goings, and comings, but also their secret thoughts, their alternative hopes and anxieties" (MLq 27). In "The Adventure of the Beryl Coronet," Holmes declares, "when I got into the stable lane a very long and complex story was written in the snow in front of me" (ASH 315).

The first detective, C. Auguste Dupin, insisted that the mystery of the purloined letter could only be solved by someone who was a poet as well as a mathematician; the Sherlock Holmes of *A Study in Scarlet* who was a laboratory technician had been remodeled by the time of *The Sign of Four* as a fin-de-siècle Bohemian and aesthete. There is remarkable coincidence between his method and that of Henry James, as laid out in "The Art of Fiction," where he describes an exemplary novelist who is blessed "with the faculty which when you give it an inch takes an ell. . . . The power to guess the unseen from the seen, to trace the implication of things, to judge the whole piece by the pattern" (James 1956, 13).[4] Holmes, in his "Book of Life," claims that "by a momentary expression, a twitch of a muscle or a glance of an eye, [it was possible] to fathom a man's inmost thoughts" (SSt 23). Wolfe makes quite grand artistic claims for his craft: "It is true that I hire out my abilities for money, but I assure you that I am not to be regarded as a mere peddler of gewgaws or tricks. I am an artist or nothing. Would you commission Matisse to do a painting, and, when he had scribbled his first rough sketch, snatch it from him and crumple it up and tell him, 'That's enough, how much do I owe you?'" (RBx 32–33).

The detective is also doubled by an artist, a writer of narratives, usually a writer of detective stories. Watson is such a writer. In the thriller it is the hero who is sometimes a writer of popular fiction (but that hero, as I have argued, *is* the Watson). The protagonist of *The Third Man* is a writer of Westerns, and Latimer, in *A Coffin for Dimitrios*, is a university lecturer in political economy who wrote his first detective story in the hope of dispelling a black depression that resulted from his study of Nazi propaganda. The telling of a complete and continuous story has another name in the thriller—the "debriefing." In more recent works it is sometimes told to its author: the criminal is the agent's control and the debriefing consists of the agent telling his control the story of his own treachery.

The setting for the murder in Anthony Berkeley's *Jumping Jenny* is a masquerade party to which guests come as famous murderers and their victims. It is itself a highly elaborate crime fiction; doubly so, for the host is a writer and the party "exactly carried out the lighthanded treatment of death in his books" (JJ 8–9). The detective, Roger Sherringham, is a writer of detective stories as well as a theatrical director; he stages a collusive drama to disarm the police. It is not a detective story that he produces, but the record of an unspectacular, accidental death. In *Hamlet, Revenge!* Giles Gott, a writer of detective stories, is asked if he is going to use the Scamnum theatricals—an amateur production of *Hamlet* in the course of which the lord chancellor of England will be murdered—as the setting for a new detective novel. During the investigation, Gott and John Appleby, the detective, take turns detecting and formulating theories.

After Gott has delivered his solution, Appleby admits that it was convincing but that he doesn't believe it, and tells Gott, "you were having it all your own way." To Gott's defense that it "all fits," he says, "Quite so. I think it is a triumph. But do you think they'll miss the point that it's a triumph of your own craft—a bit of ingenious fiction? . . . The case is yours, Giles—is so brilliantly yours. Don't misunderstand. I'm simply scared by a sense of your extraordinary facility in these matters. You created a magnificent case—or at least a magnificent effect. But some people would say that you could have done the same with half a dozen other suspects." "Giles, it's such a pity," a young woman says, "that it wasn't true, I mean. It was such a good story" (HR 261, 264, 284). And Poirot says of Hastings's solution to the crime in *Murder on the Links:* "You should write for the cinema, *mon ami.* . . . It would make a good film, the story that you have recounted to me there—but it bears no sort of resemblance to everyday life" (ML 158).

At the end of detective fiction, the detective *relates*, and he does so in two senses: he tells a story and he makes, or makes up, relationships. Since a condition of intimate and secret relatedness governs all the signs, animate and inanimate, of mystery and detective fiction, the detective tells the story of those secret relationships; he relates relatedness. The ideal condition of the solution is that it should relate everything in two ways: tell a story about all the signs and relate them to one another: "The solution must account for everything. And it must account for it in the way which, when all is revealed, is seen to be the only logical explanation of the whole mystery, red herrings and all" (Hare 60).

This is, of course, one of the genre's lies about its relationship to logic: "The detective's final summation offers not a maximal integration of parts into whole, but a minimal one: what is totalized is just—and no more than—what is needed to solve the crime" (Miller 1980, 153). Detective fiction may even self-consciously expose this as a lie: "Everything needn't fit—there lay the difference between his activities and Gott's. In a sound story everything worried over in the course of the narrative must finally cohere. But in life there were always loose ends . . . details that never found their places" (HR 162); yet still pass itself off as a story of "maximal integration." The solution also enacts a rage for order that leads to the calling in of a detective to clean things up in the first place, as well as the rage for order that makes Poirot wince at undusted tabletops and straighten pictures on the wall and makes Wolfe growl when his private timetable is disturbed.[5]

The hard-boiled detective lived in a world of "stories": "Sit quiet," Marlowe says in *The Long Goodbye*, "and let me tell it another way"

(LG 306). "When you get tired of it, let me know," he says in *Lady in the Lake*, "I'll have something else" (LL 73). "I think that's an all-right spread," Spade tells his lawyer,

> "It seems to click with most of the known facts. It ought to hold."
> Wise . . . studied Spade's face with curious eyes and asked: "But you don't believe it."
> Spade plucked his cigarette from between his lips. "I don't believe it or disbelieve it, Sid. I don't know a damned thing about it." (MF 103)

A penultimate solution or "false bottom" was a common feature of analytic detective fiction. We are meant to accept it as the solution, to believe that all the clues have "been caught up into a satisfactory pattern" (Kermode 1972, 12). In *The Poisoned Chocolate Case*, this is multiplied many times as the crime is solved successively by the eight members of the "Crimes Circle" and the police: "practically speaking no two members have agreed on any one single matter of importance. The divergence of opinion and method is really remarkable. And in spite of such variations each member has felt confident that his or her solution was the right one" (PCC 166). But even the "truth" may be a false bottom: What the Op "soon discovers is that the 'reality' that anyone involved will swear to is in fact itself a construction. . . . And the Op's work therefore is to . . . defictionalize that 'reality.' . . . [Yet] the reconstruction or true fiction . . . is no more plausible—nor is it meant to be—than the stories that have been told to him by all parties" (Marcus 16).

In Chesterton's "Honour of Israel Gow," the investigators make their way to the "strange castle of Glengyle," at the dead-end of "a grey Scotch valley," on a stormy evening and find "a long oak table . . . occupied by detached objects arranged at intervals; objects about as inexplicable as any objects could be. One looked like a small heap of glittering broken glass. Another looked like a high heap of brown dust. A third appeared to be a plain stick of wood." Brown remarks, "You seem to have a sort of geological museum here," and Flambeau answers, "Not a geological museum . . . say a psychological museum." The official policeman is, as usual, baffled: "But suppose the worst in all this, the most lurid or melodramatic solution you like. . . . Invent what Wilkie Collins's tragedy you like, and you still have not explained a candle without a candlestick, or why an elderly gentleman of good family should habitually spill snuff on the piano. . . . By no stretch of fancy can the human mind connect together snuff and diamonds and wax and loose clockwork" (AA 26, 28).

Brown thinks he sees the connection and accounts for the four items. When asked if his explanation is the truth, he says, "I'm perfectly sure it isn't. . . . The real truth I am sure lies deeper." He then accounts for the items again: "I don't think it the true explanation. . . . The true tale, of course, is something much more humdrum"; and he accounts for the items a third time (AA 30, 31). As a critical fable, this reminds us of the anxiety of interpretation, the feeling that the true story always lies at the other end of a convolution from the story we are telling—more superficial if we are being complicated, far deeper if we are being simple. Yet these false fictions can also constitute the only truth we know, the truth, for example, of scientific reality, which consists of a succession of scientists telling the same story a little differently in an effort to fit in all the facts.

9

Methodological Items:
The Clue, the Trifle, and Dirt

In CHAPTER TWO, I DISCUSSED A BASIC CONVENTION OF DETECTIVE
fiction, that the agencies of law enforcement are peculiarly inadequate
to investigate and resolve crime. This is one of the prominent forms
taken by a larger principle of perversity I call *the paradox of the obvious*,
a law that stipulates that anything that is obviously true or significant
must, for that reason, be insignificant and false. It governs the crime
(obvious crimes, or "open and shut" cases, will be extremely difficult
to solve), criminals (obvious suspects will not be guilty), and signs—
evidence will be either false or misleading: "Charles, acushla," Wimsey explains, "distrust the straight-forward case, the man who looks
you straight in the eyes, and the tip straight from the horse's mouth.
Only the most guileful deceiver can afford to be so aggressively straight.
Even the path of light is curved—or so they tell us" (SP 45). The deceptive banality of the obvious belongs not only to the crime and the
criminal, but to the narrative as well, as Watson's perceptions and as
bad writing.

According to this paradox, ordinary cases can be transformed into
extraordinary crimes by a principle first elaborated in "The Mystery
of Marie Rogêt": "there is nothing so extraordinary as the ordinary."
Conan Doyle got this, like so much else, from Poe, and he often has

Holmes lecture in this Dupinesque vein: "This is an *ordinary*, although an atrocious instance of crime. There is nothing particularly *outré* about it. You will observe that, for this reason, the mystery has been considered easy, when, for this reason, it should have been considered difficult, of solution" (Poe 1902, 5:19).

From the Watson's perspective, the detective's assumptions are perverse if not mad. Watson feels there is "some radical flaw" in Holmes's reasoning, that he is suffering "from some huge self-deception [likely] . . . to fall into error through the over-refinement of his logic—his preference for a subtle and bizarre explanation when a plainer and more commonplace one lay ready to his hand" (SF 131). Hastings thinks Poirot "was rather too much given to these fantastic ideas. In this case, surely, the truth was only too plain and apparent" (MAS 67). And another Hastings, in *The Rasp*, tells Gethryn: "this is a bit too much. When you get such a lot of circumstantial and presumptive evidence as there is against this man Deacon and then add to it the fact that his fingerprints were the only ones on the weapon the other feller was killed with, it does seem insane to blither: '*He* couldn't have done it! Just look at his *sweet* expression!' " (R 95). In hard-boiled detective fiction, in keeping with the morally corrupt ambience, the discrepancy is made to seem like a frame-up: "You mean you're going to poke around and twist the facts and try to prove that Carl didn't do—what he did do?" (D 56).

The most crucial form of the paradox of the obvious is the a priori rejection of obvious signs, or *evidence*. Evidence is rejected as meaningless precisely because it seems to be bursting with meaning, pointing aggressively in the direction of the criminal and the solution:

> "You surely cannot still believe in the possibility of Alfred Inglethorp's innocence?"
>
> "Why not now as much as before? Nothing has changed."
>
> "But the evidence is so conclusive."
>
> "Yes, too conclusive." (MAS 90)

Evidence is fact that announces its importance: the fingerprint on the murder weapon, the monogrammed handkerchief stained with blood; these announce that they are centrally connected to the crime and give explicit directions for resolving it. "And now . . . we are invited," says Trent, "by this polished and insinuating firearm to believe the following line of propositions" (TLC 73). Most actual crimes are solved through the obvious interpretation of evidence, yet, in detective fiction, evidence is misleading.

In *A Study in Scarlet*, Holmes dismisses the evidence collected by the police. In "The Adventure of the Noble Bachelor," Lestrade, stung by Holmes's flippant dismissal of the evidence, tries to confront him: "I suppose you know all about it. . . . Oh, indeed! Then you think that the Serpentine plays no part in the matter? . . . Then perhaps you will kindly explain how it is that we found this in it?" He opens a bag and tumbles onto the floor a "wedding-dress of watered silk, a pair of white satin shoes, and a bride's wreath and veil, all discolored and soaked in water." In this pile is a piece of evidence as neatly framed as one could hope: "In the dress is a pocket. In the pocket is a card-case. In the card-case is a note. And here is the very note." Holmes takes up the paper "in a listless way, but his attention instantly became riveted." He admits that the paper is important and congratulates Lestrade on his discovery. Lestrade rises in triumph, but then shrieks, "you're looking at the wrong side!" (ASH 295–96).

Holmes's dismissal and inversion of signs is perverse, and readers respond to the arbitrary nature of his act. We accept this convention, although it should outrage common sense; unlike the Watson we are not flabbergasted, and unlike the police we do not laugh. When the convention is freed from its generating context, however, it does excite laughter. In Twain's parody of detective fiction, "The Stolen White Elephant," this is one of the first conventions seized upon. The tale is narrated by an Indian civil servant responsible for escorting an elephant to England as a present for Queen Victoria. On a stopover in Jersey City the elephant is stolen, and the celebrated Inspector Blunt and his force of detectives are called in to investigate. The narrator is impressed by their ingenuity, particularly when he reads a newspaper account of the first fruits of their investigation:

There were eleven . . . theories, and they covered all the possibilities; and this single fact shows what independent thinkers detectives are. No two theories were alike, or even much resembled each other, save in one striking particular, and in that one all the other eleven theories were absolutely agreed. That was, that although the rear of my building was torn out and the only door remained locked, the elephant had not been removed through the rent, but by some other (undiscovered) outlet. All agreed that the robber had made that rent only to mislead the detectives. That never would have occurred to me or to any other layman, perhaps, but it had not deceived the detectives for a moment. (1958, 205)

Ignoring the fact that evidence might make the game dissolve, the problem with evidence within the fiction is that there is too much of it and it reads like a bad story—evidence is too bright and too insistent: "my views as to Mr. Inglethorp's guilt were very much shaken. There was, in fact, so much evidence against him that I was inclined to believe he had not done it" (MAS 171). Lew Archer discounts evidence that shows up with "clockwork regularity" (D 84).

Possessing an infallible sense of design, the detective instinctively knows a piece of evidence was put there for him to find. Ultimately, evidence is dismissed because it is a product of art, although it is hard to tell from the following quotation whether the obvious case is being dismissed because it is a work of art, because it is a bad work of art, or because it is not a work of art: "I don't like it. I don't like it a little bit. It's too rule-of-thumb. The Profligate Secretary, the Missing Bank-notes, the Finger-printed Blunt Instrument! It's not even a good shilling shocker. It's too damnation ordinary, that's what it is!" (R 57).

The *front* and the *cover* are the equivalents of evidence in hard-boiled detective fiction and the spy thriller. The front, as opposed to the back, is deceptive—" 'My dear doctor. . . . We know something of Saxe-Coburg Square. Let us now explore the parts which lie behind it.' The road in which we found ourselves as we turned round the corner . . . presented as great a contrast to it as the front of a picture does to the back" (ASH 184–85); "Now it is easy to be mistaken in faces, but almost impossible not to recognize a back" (UD 221). The back generally gives access to a deep truth: Archer says to himself, "The trouble with you . . . you're always turning over the postcards and reading the messages on the underside. Written in invisible ink, in blood, in tears, with a black border around them, with postage due, unsigned, or signed with a thumbprint" (D 29).

This paradox was commented on in 1852 by Hawthorne's analytical voyeur Miles Coverdale: "It is likewise to be remarked, as a general rule, that there is far more of the picturesque, more truth to native and characteristic tendencies, and vastly greater suggestiveness, in the back view of a residence, whether in town or country, than in its front. The latter is always artificial; it is meant for the world's eye, and is therefore a veil and a concealment. Realities keep in the rear, and put forward an advance guard of show and humbug" (1964, 138). In "The Simple Art of Murder," Chandler writes of fronts and tie-ins from a familiar social perspective: the realist in murder writes of a world run by men "who made their money out of brothels, in which a screen star can be the fingerman for a mob, and the nice man down the hall is the boss of the numbers racket" (1944, 398).

The detective assumes the truth is hidden and distrusts anything "up front": "I spent most of my working time waiting, talking and waiting. Talking to ordinary people in ordinary neighborhoods about ordinary things, waiting for truth to come up to the surface" (D 134). Richard Hannay, at the end of the trail leading him to the criminals, stops, profoundly perplexed by the logic of surfaces: "I rubbed my eyes and asked myself if I was not the most immortal fool on earth. Mystery and darkness had hung about the men who hunted me. . . . It was easy enough to connect these folk with the knife that pinned Scudder to the floor, and with fell designs on the world's peace. But here were two guileless citizens . . . soon about to go indoors to a humdrum dinner, where they would talk of market prices and the latest cricket scores (TS 129)."

Buchan's opposite number, Eric Ambler, also stresses how ordinary spies look and how impossible it is to identify them as spies. In *Epitaph for a Spy*, Vadassy is arrested by the police as a spy. To clear himself, he must return to his vacation hotel, maintain his front and keep his eyes open for the real spies. "This man could not be a spy," he later ruminates. "There was something about him that made the idea seem absurd. A certain dignity. Besides, did spies quote Hegel? . . . Well, his own answer would do there: 'Why shouldn't they?' "; "The Vogels?

The temptation was to eliminate them also. No spy could be so grotesquely unlike a spy as Vogel" (ES 64, 140). Looking at the "huge chocolate-colored *coupe de ville*" of a successful retired spy, Latimer finds it unreasonably "odd that there should be no evidence in the car of the sinister origin of its purchase" (CD 96), while the agent in John Marquand's *Stopover Tokyo* stands by his window, "looking at it—an inconspicuous American car, one of thousands of its vintage, and one which must have had several owners. It was exactly the sort of car he would have picked if he had wanted to tail someone" (ST 93).

Reversing the examples given above, which suggest that nothing is more ordinary than the ordinary, one could also say that nothing is more sinister than the ordinary. Criminals in analytic detective fiction are invisible because they are passing as ordinary persons. In Chesterton's "Invisible Man," an eyewitness swears he did not see the murderer, because the latter had passed in and out of the house dressed as a postman. Detective fiction repeatedly collapses the distinction between the ordinary and the outré. Even Watson becomes sensitized, and when, in "The Adventure of the Blue Carbuncle," he sees a worn and cracked hat hanging on a chairback, he remarks, "I suppose . . . that, homely as it looks, this thing has some deadly story linked on to it—that it is the clue which will guide you in the solution of some mystery and the punishment of some crime." Holmes laughingly demurs (ASH 245).

Mystery and detective fiction thematizes the particular pressures I have been discussing as a distrust of and contempt for the ordinary—one is grounded in the paranoia and the other in the escapism of the form. Merry presented it as a "scorn for wife, children, a fixed address" (7). Fleming wrote of "cottagey, raftery nooks where elderly couples with Ford Populars and Morris Minors talked in muted tones about children called Len and Ron and Pearl and Ethel, and ate in small mouthfuls with the points of their teeth and made not a sound with the tea things" (Fleming quoted in Amis 40), and Chandler wrote, "Tired men in dusty coupes and sedans winced and tightened their grip on the wheel and ploughed on north and west towards home and dinner, an evening with the sports page, the blatting of the radio, the whining of their spoiled children and the gabble of their silly wives" (LS 61).

Obedient to the paradox of the obvious, a detective will deny meaning to the customarily meaningful fact, the piece of evidence. But he will also deny meaning to its opposite, the apparently meaningless fact, the accidental fact. It is taken for granted that the contents of detective space cannot be tangentially related: that, for example, the grease stain on the doorknob, the wilted rose under the piano, and the scraps of insulated wire on the floor cannot be the respective droppings of a plumber on Monday, an insurance salesman on Tuesday, and a radio repairman on Wednesday—"He took his cap off and the carnation dropped to the floor. He bent and picked it up and twirled it between his fingers, then dropped it behind the fire screen. 'Better not do that,' I told him. 'They might think it's a clue and waste a lot of time on it' " (LL 115). Ronald Knox's sixth rule proscribes both external and internal accident on the grounds of fair play: "No accident must ever help the detective, nor must he ever have an unaccountable intuition which proves to be right" (195).

A briefcase is lying next to a potted plant in my living room. It is there because that is where I set it down when I came home last night. To the left of the plant is an armchair, and on a small table next to that, there is a book. But it is there because I set it there when I finished reading it three days ago. Yet Holmes and Brown assume that arrangements such as this express a unified meaning and an underlying design; and in the fiction they turn out to be right:

> Poirot closed his eyes. What he perceived mentally was a kaleidoscope, no more, no less. Pieces of cut-up scarves and rucksacks, cookery books, lipsticks, bath salts; names and thumbnail sketches of odd students. Nowhere was there cohesion or form. Unrelated incidents and people whirled around in space. But Poirot knew quite well that somehow and somewhere there must be a pattern. Possibly several patterns. Possibly each time one shook the kaleidoscope one got a different pattern. . . . But one of those patterns would be the right pattern. . . . The question was where to start." (NRM 187)

The assumption, or faith, that all signs in a bounded space must be relatable is generally regarded by the Watson or the police as fanciful, demented or paranoid activity. The solution is a confirmation of that faith. According to psychoanalysis, such an assumption is justified in the psychological realm, and so this premise, like so many others in detective fiction, announces that the fiction is like a fantasy. Within the discipline of literary criticism, such an assumption is justified within the space of a text. Dupin's pronouncement in "The Mystery of Marie Rogêt"—"experience has shown, and a true philosophy will always show, that a vast, perhaps the larger portion of truth, arises from the seemingly irrelevant" (Poe 1902, 5:39)—is an apt description of critical reading.

Mystery and detective fiction strains to connect various moments of the text. It shares this feature with the sensation novel from which it partly derives: "If I had not dived for Professor Pesca when he lay under water on his shingle bed, I should in all human probability never have been connected with the story which these pages will relate—I should never, perhaps, have heard even the name of the woman who has lived in all my thoughts" (Collins 1974, 37). This echoes the persistent connecting that goes on within the text.

> Judging by the ordinary rules of evidence, I had not the shadow of a reason, thus far, for connecting Sir Percival Glyde with the suspicious words of inquiry that had been spoken to me by the woman in white. And yet, I did connect him with them. Was it because he had now become associated in my mind with Miss Fairlie, Miss Fairlie being, in her turn, associated with Anne Catherick, since the night when I had discovered the ominous likeness between them? Had the events of the morning so unnerved me already that I was at the mercy of any delusion which common chances and common coincidences might suggest to my imagination? (Collins 1974, 101)

Hard-boiled style, on the other hand, suppresses relatedness. These works tell a story of total design in a style that refuses to bind or invest its elements, or, conversely, parodies that tendency: "On the back of the photos was written '5' 11"; muscular, inclined to overweight'. . . . I looked at the familiar face again. I knew the eyes were blue, even though the photograph was in black and white. I'd seen the face before; most mornings I shaved it" (IF 30).

In analytic detective fiction, the law of compulsory relationship governs objects; in hard-boiled detective fiction and the spy thriller, it governs people. In a hard-boiled story, a number of people from different walks of life may enter the detective's office claiming to have picked his name out of a telephone book and wanting help on very different kinds of cases. The detective refuses to believe that their appearance is accidental—he believes that it is coincidental—and he waits for the connections he knows are there. The hard-boiled detective assumes that everyone he meets is related, that their relationships were manifest in the past, and that they are crucial to the particular mystery he is investigating: "If any real solid work had been done on the Lennox case at the time, somebody would have dug up his war record and where he got wounded and all the rest of it. Somewhere along the line a connection with the Wades would have turned up" (LG 268). The professional spy assumes that everyone he meets is in some way connected with the conspiratorial apparatus he is attempting to uncover and defeat, even though this passage from *The Ipcress File* dismisses such a notion as absurd: "There was nothing to make me sure it was a matter for us to deal with even, let alone to connect it with Jay. It's only writers who expect every lead the hero meddles in to turn out to be threads of the same case" (IF 71).

If signs that are obviously significant are false, does it then follow that everything that is not obvious points the way to the truth? It does, and this equally perverse law inaugurates the reign of the *clue*. The terms "evidence" and "clue," which are antithetical in this book, are often used indistinguishably: "There was something in that case— some piece of evidence, slight in itself perhaps, but still enough of a clue to connect the murderer with the crime" (MAS 64). I am restricting the word clue, however, to those insignificant (accidental or trivial) signs that stand in a direct, if obscure, relationship to the lost or hidden truth: As Brown says, "All those things that 'aren't evidence' are what convince me" (AA 123).

The terms *evidence* and *clue* belong to the police and the detective, respectively; each is blind to the other and identifies the other as a blind. The concept of the clue can be initially understood as the apparently accidental fact—the object that seems to have no reason for being where and what it is. The absence of relationships in itself indicates how significant those missing connections are, and, when they are found, they will constitute a new story. The task of the detective is so to interpret and integrate the clue that, far from being accidental and peripheral, it will become the central fact of a new history.

The term *clue* has a continuous but limited distribution in the prose fiction of the eighteenth and nineteenth centuries. The primary context for the clue is the story of Theseus, Ariadne, and the Minotaur, and the word refers to the thread that guided Theseus out of the labyrinth. Clues are thus minute, almost unseen connections between a place of baffled obscurity and the ordinary world of light. "Yes, X___ is a nut not to be cracked by the tap of a lady's fan. . . . I think that to try and get into X___, enter his labyrinth and get out again, without a clue derived from some source other than what is known as 'knowledge of the world'—that were hardly possible, at least for me" (Melville 1962, 74). "Invaluable and uninterrupted line of philosophers, to whom wisdom, like another Ariana, seems to have given a clue, which they have gone on unwinding from the beginning of the world through the labyrinth of human affairs" (Hugo 25). "[I] was not without hopes, that through his means I might obtain some clew of guidance through the maze in which my fate had involved me (Scott 1956, 335). "The postilion pointed to the hill—I then tried to return back to the story of the poor German and his ass—but I had broke the clue" (Sterne 65).

A thread given by a woman to guide the hero-son from the darkness into the light has obvious psychosexual implications, and detective fiction has a crazy way of getting things right: "She—she's morbidly sensitive, of course, about having the case reopened, and I know it may be impossible to do so, but if it should be possible—if you should ever happen on some clue that has been overlooked, some chance of tracking the beast who is hiding behind her skirts" (MKF 12). The clue is also the key, and, by extension, the keyhole.

Like most conventions, the significance of the clue in detective fiction seems to be arbitrary, if not absurd. Poirot explains his model of reality in the first novel in which he appears, *The Mysterious Affair at Styles:* "*Voyons!* one fact leads to another—so we continue. Does the next fit in with that? *A merveille!* Good! We can proceed. This next little fact—no! Ah, that is curious! There is something missing—a link in the chain that is not there. We examine. We search. And that little curious fact, that possibly paltry little detail that will not tally, we put it here. . . . It is significant!" (MAS 30).

Poirot is anal-compulsive, but there is no reason why the world should exhibit the excessive neatness he demands of it. Nevertheless he asserts that the fact that does not fit into a chain of related facts must fit the one gap in that chain. "How often have I said to you [Watson] that when you have eliminated the impossible, whatever remains, *however improbable*, must be the truth" (SF 111). The jigsaw puzzle is a common metaphor for figuring the clue; for example, "it was a queer thing that fitted nowhere into the pattern within whose corners he had by this time brought the other queer things in the case" (TLC 92); or, "suddenly the most annoying pieces of my jig-saw puzzle fell into place" (R 201). All of the pieces but one have been fitted into place, and the box contains one last piece which, to the eye, cannot possibly fit the shape defined by the nearly completed puzzle. Acting on faith, however, the detective applies it to the hole, and it fits: "My friend . . . I have a little idea, a very strange, and probably utterly impossible idea. And yet—it fits in" (MAS 67). Ideally, it should also be the piece that allows the pictured scene to be identified.

Poirot calls the clue a "little curious fact," because it suggests no associations into which it can enter; it does not want to fit anything, and yet its great virtue is that it fits whatever gap there is. As we know from the legend of Sherlock Holmes and the dog that didn't bark, the clue may also be the gap itself: "I am always," Ellery Queen tells his father, "worried by omissions" (FPM 61). "Father Brown, I don't know how you do it. You seem to have known he was a murderer before anybody else knew he was a man. He was nobody; he was nothing; he was a slight confusion in the evidence; nobody in the hotel saw him; the boy on the steps could hardly swear to him; he was just a fine shade of doubt founded on an extra dirty glass" (AA 171).

The clue is not any old fact, but a "curious," "queer," or "odd" one. These words are equivalents of Freud's "uncanny," and the concept of the clue is central to both detective fiction and psychoanalytic method, as it is fictionalized by Freud. In a tale by T. S. Stribling, Professor Poggioli lectures one of his disciples: "When anything seems queer . . .

that is merely a psychological signal that it has connections with some-thing we do not understand. In any crime, queerness may well be a clue" ("C" 43). It may take the form of a ridiculous but irresistible thought: "He started for the veranda door. Half-way he stopped, sud-denly. . . . The idea was ridiculous. But, after all—well, he'd spend ten minutes on it, anyhow" (R 40); "you have been trying to believe what you wish to believe. It is because you are trying to drown and stifle your instinct, which tells you another name" (MAS 111); "Oh, don't say it! It isn't true! I don't know what put such a wild—such a dreadful—idea into my head. . . . It can't be so—it's too monstrous, too impossible" (RBx 30).

The clue may take the form of a nagging thought—"That *wrong* something was troubling him again. He clutched his head, trying vainly to fix the cause of this feeling . . . that something about the mark was definitely wrong because the mark itself was so undoubtedly right"; an elusive memory—"But there was still something missing—a link which would complete the chain of reasoning. Nigel knew he had been given this link, perhaps without recognizing it; now he had mislaid it" (HT 146–47); or an unconscious fact—"There's something you can tell us, and I doubt whether you know it yourself" (HN 164). Closer to the text, it may be a slip, the wrong word: "If the woman's fierce temper once got beyond her control, and once flamed out on me, she might yet say the words which would put the clue in my hands" (Collins 1974, 508); and "I assure you, Revell, it was convincing enough to me. That little word 'up' was the one morsel of truth that the woman couldn't help letting escape" (WM 238). Despite detective fiction's official re-pudiation of the morbid subjectivity of modernism, this last detective assumes that criminals or suspects cannot tell false stories without re-forming the true story that lies buried beneath. And Freud approves of this trope: "The distortion of a text is not unlike a murder. The diffi-culty lies not in the execution of the deed but in the doing away with the traces" (Freud quoted in Mehlman 34).

Chesterton's "Blue Cross" provides a wonderful (and absurd) model of a world in which absolute relationship reigns and the clue is king, a model worked out through the equivalence of opposites and the reality of coincidence. A Parisian policeman, Valentin, has come to London to apprehend Flambeau, the most famous criminal in the world. He knows only that his prey is in London, but, since Flambeau is a master of disguise, he can be "anyone, rich or poor, male or female, who was well up to six feet." Is there a method for finding someone in the world's most populous city, when the only identifiable characteristic is size—and even that can be altered? Of course. One must begin by rejecting the obvious: "In such cases, when he could not follow the train of the reasonable, he coldly and carefully followed the train of the unreasonable. Instead of going to the right place . . . he systematically went to the wrong places; knocked at every empty house, turned down every *cul de sac*, went up every lane blocked with rubbish. . . . He defended this course quite logically. . . . There was just the chance that any oddity that caught the eye of the pursuer might be the same that had caught the eye of the pursued" (AA 7, 9).

The "oddities" that Valentin seeks appear as insistent exchanges. He drifts on impulse into a restaurant and orders a cup of coffee. After his first sip, he realizes that he has poured salt instead of sugar. He tastes the condiment in the saltcellar and finds that it is sugar. The proprietor has no idea how this could have happened, but Valentin associates it with another event that occurred that morning, simply because both were outré and meaningless: before leaving the restaurant, a clergyman had picked up his cup of coffee and thrown it against the wall. Valentin is immediately on his feet and out the door: "He had already decided that in the universal darkness of his mind he could only follow the first odd finger that pointed." He walks feverishly down a street, and "something in a shop front went by him like a mere flash; yet he went back to look at it." The price card for oranges is lying in front of a pile of nuts and vice versa. He finds that the clergyman was also there, and that he and a companion boarded a train for Hempstead. Valentin and two policemen ride north looking for queer things. "What sort of queer thing do you mean?" an inspector asks. "Any sort of queer thing." Finally Valentin waves his stick: "Our cue at last . . . the place with the broken window." One more meaningless sign brings the police to Hampton Heath where Flambeau is about to rob Brown of church treasure (AA 12, 14–15).

Such a model of reality compels other, more appropriate, contexts, like the mental economy in the works of Freud or the invention of hypotheses in Albert Einstein. The activity of the analytic detective has often been identified with the "reading" of clues: "It is no exaggeration to say that the truth we pursue across the text is the detective's *reading* of it. For if the exemplary tool of classical detection, the magnifying glass, belongs as much to a technique of reading manuscripts and uncovering palimpsests as to criminology, this is because detective stories conceive reading and detection as fully analogous, often overlapping, at times perfectly identical activities" (Miller 1979, 101). In *Hamlet, Revenge!* the clues are provocative messages with which the criminal bombards the guilty community: a quarto sheet of typescript containing a couplet from *Titus Andronicus;* a telegram with the message "*Hamlet, revenge!*" (not "actually from Shakespeare's play. It was probably a line in an earlier play, now lost, and is first quoted as a joke in Lodge's *Wits Miserie* in 1596"); a tape recorder that, instead of playing the butler's interesting reading of the Lord's Prayer, speaks, in a high falsetto, "I will *not* cry Hamlet, revenge"; a recording from *Macbeth* that wakes the household in grotesquely loud tones; and a telephone call consisting of a line from *Hamlet* (HR 21, 33–34, 45–46, 68–69, 242). Since the occasion of the crime is an amateur theatrical performance of *Hamlet,* the clues also announce the infection of all contemporary modes of communication and expression by the privileged and oblique language of that anachronistic but classic center.

The model of understanding proposed often seems close to textual interpretation: "Briefly, Watson, I am in the midst of a very remarkable inquiry, and I have hoped to find a clue in the incoherent ramblings of these sots, as I have done before now" (ASH 232). In E. C. Bentley's "Ministering Angel," certain plants in the victim's garden are labeled with botanical names in Latin. These mean nothing to Trent, but a sense of duplicity seizes upon him when one of the names, "*Ludovica Caroli,*" clicks in his mind. The labels translate into the works of Lewis Carroll which have been combined into the salutory communication that solves the crime ("MA" 82–85). All linguistic clues are basically ciphers: words and phrases that do not fit a context or messages that read deceptively. As in "The Gold-Bug," the cipher is an unintelligible text, but it is also the map of a new world, otherwise impenetrable; its successful reading rewards the interpreter with unimaginable riches.

The cipher is an extraordinary linguistic performance that has an arcane or nonsensical surface. In the same series, detective fiction can give prominence to song and riddle forms, allusions and quotations; it can treat the traditional verbal reservoir as code. Colonel Methuen, in Lawrence Durrell's *White Eagles over Serbia*, is told by a drunken old man on a Yugoslavian train that he will understand what the Russians have done to his country "when the white eagles come again," which "produced a quite extraordinary effect of alarm in the carriage" (WES 36).

He is told later that the agent whose death he is investigating had in his pocket a small volume of Serbian folk songs; the one marked passage was "about white eagles." As he is waiting to be taken to the opera, he amuses himself by idly running over a list of Belgrade radio broadcasts and notices one devoted to an "apparently endless series of national poems" read every evening by the famous actress Sophia Maric: "Methuen saw, with some emotion, that the little poem . . . was the first to be broadcast and was repeated twice during the first week" (WES 47, 55). The clue, which here takes a repetitive, coincidental, and semantically shifting form (like the elusive object), is literally a code that governs the culture and ideology of a nation.

Ordinary texts may become clues by being torn or partially burnt: a page from a private diary, "the fragment of a hotel bill," or "a small piece of half-charred paper" (ASH 223, 296). "The inanimate things around us," says Dr. Thorndyke, "have each of them a song to sing to us if we are but ready with attentive ears" (BDT 108). As Appleby stares thoughtfully at a little weapon, Dodd says: "You seem to be waiting for it to jump up and out with the whole story" (SS 93).

The largest class of clues is the *trifle* or *minutia*. "It was little—very little—but still it was something. It was a clue; and in this absolute darkness even the faintest gleam of light was eagerly welcomed" (MLq 54). Dickens on Inspector Field: "Every clue seems cut off; but the experience of a Detective guides him into tracks quite invisible to other eyes" (Dickens quoted in Kayman 108). Detective fiction regularly announces the supremacy of the trivial as the cornerstone of its revolutionary method: "You know my method," Holmes tells Watson, "is founded upon the observation of trifles" (ASH 214).[1] And Thorndyke tells Jervis, "there is one rule which I follow religiously in all my investigations . . . and that is to collect facts of all kinds in any way related to the case in hand, no matter how trivial they may be or how apparently irrelevant" (BDT 257). Watson responds to Holmes's summary of his monograph upon ashes by remarking, "You have an extraordinary genius for minutiae," and Holmes replies, "I appreciate their importance" (SF 91). This focus is also a feature of the detective's instructions to witnesses—" 'Can you remember *everything* he said?' Hewitt asked. 'If you can tell me, I should like to know exactly what he did and said to the smallest particular' " (ROSH 51). "And begin right at the beginning," says Wimsey, "if you will, please. I have a very trivial mind. Detail delights me" (UD 17). This focus provides early detective fiction with many images of detective-like method, like the following:

> Without waiting for a reply, he commenced his survey of the coach. . . . The off-side footboard occupied his attention specially, and when he had scrutinized minutely the part opposite the fatal compartment, he walked slowly from end to end with his eyes but a few inches from its surface, as though he was searching for something. Near what had been the rear end he stopped, and drew from his pocket a piece of paper; then, with a moistened finger-tip he picked up from the footboard some evidently minute object, which he carefully transferred to the paper, folding the latter and placing it in his pocket-book. (BDT 141)

The detective is not only an observer of trivia but also a possessor of them: Thorndyke "is a most remarkable man, sir, a positive encyclopedia of out-of-the-way and unexpected knowledge" (BDT 220).

This is one of the few conventions distinctively present in the work of Conan Doyle, Freeman, and Chesterton that is not anticipated by Poe, although it somewhat resembles part of the distinction between "oddities" and essences (or "evenses") in "The Purloined Letter," and between the ordinary and the outré in "The Mystery of Marie Rogêt." But the stress on trivia is fully present in James Fenimore Cooper, who is closer to the ground: "Some of the leaves which were exposed to the sun had drooped a little, and this slight departure from the usual natural laws had caught the quick eyes of the Indian; for so practiced and acute do the senses of the savage become, more especially when he is on the warpath, that trifles apparently of the most insignificant sort often prove to be clues to lead him to his object" (1961, 60).

The concept of the trifle plays through the fiction of Wilkie Collins without being firmly embedded there. In *The Moonstone*, Sergeant Cuff announces that he "made a private inquiry last week. . . . At one end of the inquiry there was a murder, and at the other end there was a spot of ink on a tablecloth that nobody could account for. In all my experience along the dirtiest ways of this dirty little world, I have never met such a thing as a trifle yet" (Collins 1966, 136). In *The Woman in White*, the word "trifle" gratuitously enters the text about the middle of the book and then appears unable to get out. It occurs first in a speech by Marian Halcombe; it is repeated in her journal, echoed by Madame Fosco, and picked up many pages later by Walter Hartright as a pompous generalization: "Through all the ways of our unintelligible world the trivial and terrible walk hand in hand together." It informs a climactic statement by Mrs. Catherick in her continuation of the story: "And what do you think was the something? The merest trifle. Nothing but the key of the vestry, and the key of the press inside it"—and these trifling keys are, of course, the keys to the mystery (Collins 1974, 304, 325, 546, 549).

The police are attuned to an inventory of certain shining facts, while the detective and his predecessors devote exhaustive attention to the overwhelming graininess of the actual. The detective is characterized by an infinite capacity for details, no matter how small (the smaller the better) although the record treats this selectively. The trope is more pointed from the criminal's side, for his or her success also depends on exquisite housekeeping, and the criminal is often said to be defeated as a result of one overlooked piece of trivia.

The detective's investigation of trifles upsets the other players, the police, and the Watson. They respond to it with incredulity or scorn, behind which I hear a degree of anxiety. The detective is continually observing signs that do not matter to them, that they insist may not matter:

> "You have omitted one fact of paramount importance."
> "What is that?" I asked.
> "You have not told me if Mrs. Inglethorp ate well last night."
> I stared at [Poirot]. . . . Surely the war had affected the little man's brains. (MAS 31)

And this is the reader's proper response as well.

Although the detective is always theoretically correct, this is the real challenge to the reader. The form nominally insists that the detective shall account totally, and that this total account shall depend on an order of sign intimately wedded to anxiety and culturally taboo; an order of sign, in fact, associated with mental illness: "Though in the course of his continual voyagings Ahab must often before have noticed a similar sight, yet to any monomaniac man, the veriest trifles capriciously carry meanings" (Melville 1964, 315). The environment drops its traces on us; we live in the midst of continual fallout; and, like unconscious Hansels and Gretels, we leave a continuous trail: "Uncas, you are right; the dark-hair has been here, and she has fled, like a frighted fawn, to the wood. . . . Let us search for the marks she left; for to Indian eyes, I sometimes think even a hummingbird leaves his trail in the air" (Cooper 1962, 218).

The program of the detective—the program it is duplicitously suggested we compete in—involves the constant and concentrated inspection of such signs. From this perspective detective fiction embodies a fantasy of pain as clearly as pleasure. Twain's detective badge is a "wide-staring eye, with the legend, WE NEVER SLEEP" (1958, 213). The genre claims that detectives have an inordinate fund of psychic energy: noticing a smear on Rachel's door, Sergeant Cuff asks Superintendent Seagrave how it happened, and is told "the petticoats did it." Asked if he noticed which one, Seagrave replies, "I can't charge my memory, Sergeant" (Collins 1966, 136). Something very like toughness must lie behind the detective's ability to tolerate the strain of his method (although it is texted not as strain but as easy-flowing behavior).

Like all other elements the trifle spreads through detective fiction, appearing in variant forms. With "people of that sort" (the lower classes), Holmes lectures, one must never "let them think that their information can be of the slightest importance to you. If you do they will instantly shut up like an oyster" (SF 124). Spies are provided with trifles as part of their cover story: "Next came the odds and ends which Hartbeck would plausibly have about him: a bunch of keys on a chain—the key to the suitcase was among them—a comb, a khaki handkerchief stained with oil and a couple of ounces of substitute coffee in a twist of newspaper; a screwdriver, a length of fine wire and fragments of metal ends newly turned—the meaningless rubble of a working man's pocket" (LGW 195). Spies are alerted to danger by the dropping of a thread from the door or a minute shift in the position of their shirts and underwear. Detective fiction capitalizes on a fetishism of detail that was featured in Western art in the nineteenth and early twentieth centuries: following Imagism, Fernand Léger called for a filmic art devoted to the close-up and the blow-up (7); and in fiction, the "exhausting intensity of attention to detail" in Balzac is " 'demonic'; this passion to see, never to stop feeling, what it means for this tawdry woman to walk into the dining room in the morning, to sum up the whole of her life in her first momentary appearance—this demonism . . . is the investment of all the observer's passion in the smallest facts" (Sennett 158). The fit is theoretically close here except that detective fiction equivocates between an endless stream of detail and the one detail in a thousand that constitutes a clue; moreover, detective fiction denies the fatigue and dissembles the passion.

In *Background to Danger*, Ambler declares that "the more fanciful among recent interpretors of history have frequently drawn attention to the grotesque intrusion of the trivial on the larger affairs of mankind" (BD 86–87). Ambler is making a move from a history of pre-World War II crisis to the back-corner espionage of his private fiction, but he might very well be announcing the clue as the concept that underlies various revolutionary systems of scientific thought associated with Darwin, Freud, and Einstein—or the system of modern capitalism fictionalized by Ben Franklin as he relates the transformation of his vegetarian lunches into capital gains or Andrew Carnegie who heeds the disposition of pennies as well as pounds.

Lyell and Darwin try to subvert an older view of the world's master plot as classical narrative or melodrama and to replace it with a model of absolutely trivial change, a model that they read in dirt, on the ground: "By the consideration of [recent and fossil species] . . . the mind was slowly and insensibly withdrawn from imaginary pictures of catastrophe and chaotic confusion, such as haunted the imagination of the early cosmogonists, . . . [and] the geologist proved that it had been the theater of reiterated change, and was still the subject of slow but never-ending fluctuations" (Lyell 498). The primacy of the trivial is sounded on virtually every page of *On the Origin of Species:* "infinitesimal variation," "very slight changes," "very trifling change," "variations, however slight"—"It may metaphorically be said that natural selection is daily and hourly scrutinizing, throughout the world, the slightest variations" (Darwin 13, 16, 51, 66).[2]

In an article that considers the detective as the epistemic hero of a paradigmatic conceptual system, Carlo Ginzburg chooses to begin with Giovanni Morelli, author of a system for detecting art forgeries. According to Morelli, to properly attribute a painting "one should refrain from the usual concentration on the most obvious characteristics. . . . Instead one should concentrate on minor details . . . earlobes, fingernails, shapes of fingers and toes." Ginzburg illustrates Morelli's influence on Freud by quoting from a neglected passage in "The Moses of Michaelangelo": Morelli "achieved this [revolution] by insisting that attention should be diverted from the general impression and main features of a picture, and by laying stress on the significance of minor details . . . unconsidered trifles." What Freud found in Morelli was "an interpretive method based on taking marginal and irrelevant details as revealing clues. Here details generally considered trivial and unimportant, 'beneath notice,' furnish the key to the highest achievements of human genius." Ginzburg then brings Conan Doyle into the constellation. Holmes's method is canonized in an article he wrote bearing the title "The Book of Life." Watson skims it and dismisses it as "ineffable twaddle" because "it attempted to show how much an observant man might learn by an accurate and systematic examination of all that came his way. . . . The writer claimed by a momentary expression, a twitch of a muscle or a glance of an eye, to fathom a man's inmost thoughts" (Ginzburg 81–82, 84, 86).

It should be apparent by now how many of the clues or trifles cited in the foregoing pages belong to a category that could more properly be called *dirt* or *garbage*. When Holmes reads individuals by their traces, such signs become paramount: "By a man's finger-nails, by his coat-sleeve, by his boots, by his trouser-knees, by the callosities of his forefinger and thumb, by his expression, by his shirt-cuffs—by each of these things a man's calling is plainly revealed" (SSt 23). Sample moments of investigation from *The Sign of Four* feature dirt: "Twice as we ascended, Holmes whipped his lens out of his pocket and carefully examined marks which appeared to me to be mere shapeless smudges of dust upon the cocoanut-matting which served as a stair carpet"; and "here is a circular muddy mark, and here again upon the floor, and here again by the table. See here, Watson! This is really a very pretty demonstration." Investigating the scene of the murder, the first sign Holmes encounters is a footstep in the dust, the second a "strong tarry smell," and then, after climbing to the roof of the house, he finds a pouch full of poisoned darts (SF 108–13).

One of Father Brown's many lectures is on the subject of dirt; here, as elsewhere, Chesterton saw the patterns that were to be central to detective fiction. In "The Quick One" an "officious" servant has washed out the glasses left on the bar where the murder had taken place, and Brown declares, "I sometimes think criminals invented hygiene. Or perhaps hygienic reformers invented crime; they look like it, some of them. Everybody talks about foul dens and filthy slums in which crime can run riot; but it's just the other way. They are called foul, not because crimes are committed, but because crimes are discovered. It's in the neat, spotless, clean, and tidy places that crime can run riot; no mud to make footprints; no dregs to contain poison, kind servants washing out all traces of the murder; and the murderer killing and cremating six wives and all for the want of a little Christian dirt" (AA 164).

In the "junior-executive residential" tract houses in Redwood City that Archer visits as part of his trail, everything in the living-room is "so new and clean, the furniture so carefully placed around it, that it seemed forbidding." Earlier, Mrs. Galton can tell him nothing about her son: "I know nothing of his life after he left the university. He cut himself off from all decent society. He was perversely bound to sink in the social scale. . . . I'm afraid my son had a *nostalgie de la boue*—a nostalgia for the gutter." She says of her husband's letter, which she burned the day she got it, that it "felt like it was dirt tracked into the house" (GC 76–77, 16, 40).

This category exposes one of the secret places of detective fiction, another of its mysteries: this literature is obsessed with telling dirty stories or the story of dirt. Crime leaves dirt, crime is dirt, dirt solves crime; criminals are dirt; crime that gets out, scandal, is dirty, both in itself and in its effects—"Even if the poison campaign led to no open disaster . . . a washing of dirty linen in public was not calculated to do Shrewsbury any good. Because, though nine-tenths of the mud might be thrown at random, the remaining tenth might quite easily be . . . dredged from the bottom of the well of truth, and would stick" (GN 65). Victims are often killed by dirty food and drink, by poison.

Freud describes clues as dirt or garbage: "It seems to me that his [Morelli's] method of inquiry is closely related to the technique of psychoanalysis. It, too, is accustomed to divine secret and concealed things from unconsidered or unnoticed details, from the rubbish-heap, as it were, of our observations" (Freud quoted in Hyman 371). We must "turn our attentions precisely to those associations . . . which are normally dismissed . . . as worthless rubbish" (OD 18). Trifles, for Freud, are "the refuse, so to speak, of the phenomenal world" (1920, 31); and Freud defines dirt as if it were a clue: "dirt is matter in the wrong place" (Freud quoted in Kubie 390).

Perhaps the most familiar clues in detective fiction are the marks of an absent shoe on the ground and the traces of absent ground on shoes; the proximate image, Friday's footprint, is one of the most famous clues in literature. In another limit-text for detective fiction, Wells's Invisible Man is perceived as the end of a trail of muddy footprints. A crowd pursues what it inferentially calls "Feet running!" but the Invisible Man is able to evade them after his feet grow hot and dry, and the last he sees of the chase is "a little group . . . studying with infinite perplexity a slowly drying footprint . . . in Tavistock Square—a footprint as isolated and incomprehensible to them as Crusoe's solitary discovery" (Wells n.d. [1897], 270).

Analytic detective fiction repeatedly presents the image of a man stooped over, reading the ground, which, as Ralph Waldo Emerson announced, "is all memoranda and signatures, and every object covered over with hints which speak to the intelligent" (quoted in Irwin 25). Although this image may have been inspired by the success of Cooper's woodsmen, Gaboriau and Conan Doyle take it back to the natural, unerring activity of the bloodhound.

> A bloodhound in pursuit of his prey would have been less alert, less discerning, less agile. He came and went, now turning, now pausing, now retreating, now hurrying on again without any apparent reason; he scrutinized, he questioned every surrounding object . . . nothing escaped his glance. For a moment he would remain standing, then fall upon his knees, and at times lie flat upon his stomach with his face so near the ground that his breath must have melted the snow. He had drawn a tape-line from his pocket, and using it with a carpenter's dexterity, he measured, measured, and measured. (MLq 27)

"Lestrade showed us the exact spot at which the body had been found, and, indeed, so moist was the ground, that I could plainly see the traces which had been left by the fall of the stricken man. To Holmes, as I could see by his eager face and peering eyes, very many other things were to be read upon the trampled grass. He ran round, like a dog who is picking up a scent" (ASH 212). In 1834 Cuvier praised the methods and successes of the new science of paleontology: "Today, someone who sees the print of a cloven hoof can conclude that the animal which left the print was a ruminant, and this conclusion is as certain as any that can be made in physics or moral philosophy. This single track tells the observer about the kind of teeth, the kind of jaws, the haunches, the shoulder, and the pelvis of the animal which has passed" (Cuvier quoted in Ginzburg 102).

The detective sifts through garbage and garbage cans like an augur: Father Brown regarded "for some minute and a half; then he . . . put his head inside. . . . He remained thus for a measurable period, as if engaged in some mysterious prayer" (AA 101). A house that has been used in connection with the crime in "31 New Inn" has been cleaned out by the time Thorndyke arrives to investigate it. Nevertheless, he rakes up a little heap of rubbish from under the grate. Jervis notes that it looks "unpromising enough, being just such a rubbish-heap as may be swept up in any untidy room during a move." In it, Thorndyke finds a battered pair of spectacles, a tiny stick of bamboo, a small wide-mouthed bottle, a screw, and a trouser button. However unpromising this rubbish heap looks, it is enough, and enough precisely because it is unpromising: "A poor collection . . . and yet not so poor as I had feared. Perhaps, if we question them closely enough, these unconsidered trifles may be made to tell us something worth hearing, after all" (BDT 242–44). "My brain has been more than usually free from occupation lately," Ellery Queen tells his father. "It's been clear enough to grasp the amazing fundamentals this case has spewed up today" (FPM 158).

Spade finishes his search of Brigid's apartment by looking at the places where waste collects, as if he could find there the truth behind all her poses and pretenses: "He emptied the garbage-can on spread sheets of newspaper. He opened the top of the flush-box in the bathroom, drained the box, and peered down into it. He examined and tested the metal screens over the drains of bathtub, wash-bowl, sink and laundry tub" (MF 81). A. J. Weberman has attempted to analyze the character of various celebrities through their garbage; the assumption is that the facade presents a false message, and the truth is only to be found through a careful examination of what is unceremoniously shoved out the rear (113–17): "anything to do with that quite amazing house is important. . . . Blamelessness above stairs; and yet, and yet, below stairs that sinister dustbin" (RSJ 180).

The dustbin that the detective is scrutinizing is Darwin's "tangled bank." The clue that provided Darwin with his discovery of natural evolution, the clue that he got from Thomas Malthus and the city streets, is *waste*. This was eventually to become the wasteland of T. S. Eliot, Nathanael West, and Thomas Pynchon; but it is already present in the nineteenth century, in the following infernal vision by John Ruskin, which he links to the new literature of Wells and Doyle:

The lane itself, now entirely grassless, is a deep-rutted, heavy-hillocked cart-road, diverging gatelessly into various brickfields or pieces of waste; and bordered on each side by heaps of—Hades only knows what!—mixed dust of every unclean thing . . . that can rot or rust in damp: ashes and rags, beer-bottles and old shoes, battered pans, smashed crockery, shreds of nameless clothes, door-sweepings, floor-sweepings, kitchen garbage, back-garden sewage, old iron, rotten timber jagged with out-torn nails, cigar-ends, pipe-bowls, cinders, bones, and ordure, indescrib-able; and . . . remnants, broadcast, of every manner of newspaper, ad-vertisement or big-lettered bill, festering and flaunting out their last publicity in the pits of stinking dust and mortal slime. (436)

What the detective is examining, questioning, and interpreting is the garbage of civilized life, everything that culture demands we hide, and he is doing this in a form culture calls *junk*. The civilization that produced detective fiction also devotes itself to denying the existence of dirt by washing, flushing, bagging, and burying. The dirt of detective fiction takes the form of those minute assaults upon our fastidiousness that must be immediately removed from sight and smell. Trifles assault us, dust on surfaces, mud on shoes, cigarette ash on clothing. We are reluctant to read them as signs: if there is mud on my shoes, I must have walked in mud; when and where I did so is of no conceivable interest to me. What does concern me is getting the mud off as quickly as possible. The symmetry is intense; the detective only wants to look at what we don't. The detective goes after what we want to be rid of, as if he knew why we were so driven to keep ourselves clean. But of course he doesn't; in this, as in almost every other instance, detective fiction hasn't a clue about the potential of the tropes and structures that, until the advent of postmodern fiction, it almost exclusively treated.

The detective can be treated either as a cleansing agent or as an ex-tension of the dirt. Crime is a mess, and clues are indexes to that mess: "Of course, it's all very untidy, this evidence. Very untidy! Not at all neat!" (R 94). The detective straightens things out; as he discovers foot-prints, picks up cigarette-ends, he might almost be the groundskeeper. The dirt that the detective is impervious to in the way of business becomes the fastidiousness of Hercule Poirot: he "alone seemed per-fectly at his ease, and dusted a forgotten corner of the bookcase" (MAS

57), and Marlowe's "domestic life is partly chess and booze, but consists equally of fastidious routines of cooking and tidying (he is forever emptying ashtrays)" (Mason 1147). Holmes, however, is not irritated by ash; instead he distinguishes the varieties. In his monograph "Upon the Distinction between the Ashes of the Various Tobaccos," he enumerates "a hundred and forty forms of cigar, cigarette, and pipe tobacco, with colored plates illustrating the difference in the ash" (SF 91).

Within the space of the crime, the primary dirt is the corpse itself and the corpse, therefore, is one standard form of the clue. Hartman states this equation in reverse: "What is a clue, for instance, but a symbolic or condensed corpse, a living trace or materialized shadow"; he is referring to the "deadness" of the detective scene (208).

Trivia and dirt are, finally, mystery and detective fiction itself, conventionally "trash": "A mind too proud to unbend over the small *ridiculosa* of life," says Christopher Morley, "is as painful as a library with no trash in it. There must always be a shelf of detective stories and desert-insular romances for after-supper dissolution" (quoted in Mierow 1).

The most incredible thing about miracles is that they happen. A few clouds in heaven do come together into the staring shape of one human eye. A tree does stand up in the landscape of a doubtful journey in the exact and elaborate shape of a note of interrogation . . . and a man named Williams does quite accidentally murder a man named Williamson; it sounds like a sort of infanticide. In short, there is in life an element of elfin coincidence which people reckoning on the prosaic may perpetually miss.

—G. K. CHESTERTON, *THE AMAZING ADVENTURES OF FATHER BROWN*

10 Methodological Moves: Coincidence and Convolution

MYSTERY AND DETECTIVE FICTION REVELS IN COINCIDENCE AS ITS primary means of mystification, exposes coincidence as "mere" coincidence or as a type of fraud, and then redeems coincidence through further mystification. In the above quotation from Chesterton, coincidence is made to mean a miracle.

Coincidence is also presented as the order of art in fiction that is generally wary of art (the classic novel on the contrary is wary of coincidence). In the opening of *The Gyrth Chalice Mystery*, Percival St. John Wykes Gyrth is down and out in London. A policeman has just asked him to move on, and it is a little after midnight as he walks toward Piccadilly Circus. He keeps "as much in the shadow as possible," and soon comes upon a dirty world, a fallen garden: a "dishevelled little square whose paved center was intersected by two rows of dirty plane trees, beneath which, amid the litter of a summer's day, were several dilapidated wooden benches." Gyrth becomes "obsessed with a curious feeling of apprehension" that he cannot explain; it seems to this "unimaginative boy . . . that something enormous, and of great importance was about to happen." As he is about to lift his feet out "of the miscellaneous collection of paper bags, orange skins, and cigarette cartons," he stiffens and stares at the ground. He is "looking at his own name, written on a battered envelope lying face upwards among the other litter" (GCM 9–11, 13).

This is a pointed act of contrivance on the part of both the detective and the detective-story writer, but it is dressed up in a language of prescience common to much popular literature: "His mind had accepted the astounding coincidence which had brought him to this particular seat in this particular square and led him to pick up this one envelope which bore his name." Like a miniature detective story, it is itself explained—Campion has staged the whole affair because Campion has a desire and a great flair for showmanship of this kind—and repeated: Gyrth is led by this envelope to an eating-house, where he is given another envelope; an engraved card falls out, which he stares at in "stupefaction":

> Mr Albert Campion
> At Home . . . . Any evening after twelve.
> Improving Conversation.
> Beer, Light Wines, and Little Pink Cakes.
> Do Come. (GCM 13)

The figure of the opening is the impossible accident that spells the death of the novel and its values, even though it is later explained as a natural event involving a high degree of intention. The classical model of such transitions is Lewis Carroll's *Through the Looking-Glass*, as Gyrth would be the first to admit: "There was a faintly nonsensical, Alice-through-the-Looking-Glass air about it all" (GCM 15).

The concept of coincidence, as it had been mysticalized in Romantic fiction of the nineteenth century, is crucial to the paradoxical metaphysics of mystery and detective fiction, and the function of coincidence is to signal that we are close to the place of the secret. From the vantage point of the ordinary world, coincidence produces a startling sense of significance; but, lacking a sufficient context, we explain the event and the feeling away as an accident, a function of the law of probability. In a world to which such things could properly belong the significance can be realized as meaning: the accent on the word would shift, coincidence becomes coin*cid*ence, and it now expresses relationship and design.

Coincidence as the structural matrix of mystery fiction is another of Poe's bequests. It is the subject of his tale "The Mystery of Marie Rogêt," which most readers have understood as a self-dramatizing tour de force—Poe's attempt to solve the historical murder of Mary Rogers in New York through the flimsy fiction of Dupin investigating the Parisian murder of Marie Rogêt. Critics have taken their revenge on Poe's arrogance by exposing the illogic of many of Dupin's arguments and conclusions (see Roth).

Poe, however, begins this tale with a dissertation on coincidence: "There are few persons, even among the calmest thinkers, who have not occasionally been startled into a vague yet thrilling half-credence in the supernatural, by *coincidences* of so seemingly marvellous a character that, as *mere* coincidences, the intellect has been unable to receive them. Such sentiments . . . are seldom thoroughly stifled unless by reference to the doctrine of chance, or, as it is technically termed, to the Calculus of Probabilities." The tag to Poe's tale also speaks of coincidence; it is a quotation from Novalis that may be paraphrased as follows: for every worldly series of events, there is an ideal series that parallels it exactly. These two sequences, however, rarely coincide for long. Human agents and circumstances modify the worldly train of events and cause it to move out of parallel with its ideal counterpart (5:2).

What is all this talk of coincidence and the supernatural doing in the tale? Surely we know that Poe took the facts of an American murder, translated them to a fictitious Parisian setting and set C. Auguste Dupin to solve it. Poe, however, tells us otherwise; he tells us that the Parisian murder is "the primary branch of a series of scarcely intelligible *coincidences*, whose secondary or concluding branch will be recognized by all readers in the late murder of MARY CECILIA ROGERS, at New York." And he further tells us that Dupin cannot solve the crime because the point of divergence postulated by Novalis will intervene:

And farther: in what I relate it will be seen that between the fate of the unhappy Mary Cecilia Rogers . . . and the fate of one Marie Rogêt up to a certain epoch in her history, there has existed a parallel in the contemplation of whose wonderful exactitude the reason becomes embarrassed. . . .

But let it not for a moment be supposed that, in proceeding with the sad narrative of Marie . . . it is my covert design to hint at an extension of the parallel, or even to suggest that the measures adopted in Paris for the discovery of the assassin of a grisette, or measures founded in any similar ratiocination, would produce any similar result. (5:65)

Todorov calls this order of explanation *pandeterminism:* "everything, down to the encounter of various causal series (or 'chance') must have its cause, in the full sense of the word, even if this cause can only be of a supernatural order" (1973, 110).

Writers of detective stories are not as high-flying as Poe; they have instituted laws forbidding the genre to meddle in the supernatural. Yet it encodes forms of magical coincidence that are distinguished from chance, or "mere" coincidence. Coincidences in detective fiction are often described as junctures, points of intersection where one can cross over into the place of the secret:

"Ellery, this is really amazing! In every case the *day* coincides with the first two letters of the author's last name!"

". . . Pretty, isn't it? *Wedjowski*—Wednesday. *Throckmorton*—Thursday. . . . Coincidence? Hardly, hardly, dad!"

"There's dirty work at the crossroads, all right, my son," said the Inspector with a sudden grin. (FPM 179)

Exclamation points signal that we are at such a significant juncture.

In "The Blue Cross," Valentin defends his method of turning into every cul de sac; he is looking for points of contact, contiguities that are also coincidences: "there was just the chance that any oddity that caught the eye of the pursuer might be the same that had caught the eye of the pursued. Somewhere a man must begin, and it had better be just where another man might stop" (AA 9). Coincidences are connections, and they show up on maps and timetables as points of intersection between the public map of the ordinary world, on which no murders or miracles can be plotted, and that terra incognita whose only known point is the crime.

In *The Cask*, the detective La Touche has been searching for the typewriter on which a certain letter was written. After reporting his failure, an "idea flashed into his mind and he stopped as if shot." One of the typewriters he examined had been a new machine. He returns and questions the typist, but she cannot tell him how long this machine has been in the office, since she herself has only been there six or seven weeks: "Six or seven weeks! And the murder took place just over six weeks before! Could there be a connection, or was this mere coincidence?" (C 259, 262). On the other hand, when Harriet Vane reflects that Miss de Vine "was the 'learned lady' whose arrival had coincided with the beginning of the disturbances," that intersection (along with the tantalizing echo in their names) will merely be a coincidence, a provocative but accidental point of contact (GN 104).

Despite the guarantee seemingly offered by the fair play thesis, there is no determinable difference between co*in*cidence and coin*cid*ence. The web of circumstantial evidence that binds an obvious but innocent suspect to the crime is usually a network of coincidence: "And now, observe the accumulation of circumstantial evidence against him. He was the last person seen in company with the murdered woman . . . he appeared to be quarrelling with her when she was last seen alive, he had a reason for possibly wishing for her death, he was provided with an implement—a spiked staff—capable of inflicting the injury which caused her death, and, when he was searched, there was found in his possession the locket and broken chain, apparently removed from her person with violence" (BDT 138–39).

Coincidence is often a structural pun: in *Hamlet, Revenge!*, the victim is playing Polonius in a production of *Hamlet,* and he is killed when Polonius dies in the play, so that anything he might cry out would be determinately misconstrued. Moreover, whatever local fiction may be in place to anchor the coincidence, it is a sign of bookishness, and it is commonly read in that way: "It's too coincidental. . . . You keep reading them dime thrillers and you give yourself ideas" (GSM 46).

Like puns, coincidences are folds in time and space. Comparing detective fiction to a tale of the marvelous, Balzac's *La Peau de Chagrin,* Hartman asks, is "it less oriental, magical, or punning when, in a Ross Macdonald story, the same gun is used for killings fifteen years apart or the murders of father and then son take place in the same spot also fifteen years apart?" (208). Merry finds the trope of "global simultaneity" to be typical of the modern thriller: "While Thomas and Lloyd [in Frederick Forsyth's *Day of the Jackal*] were talking above the waters of the Thames, and the Jackal was scooping the last drops of his Zaba-glione from the glass in a rooftop restaurant in Milan, Commissaire Claude Lebel attended the first of the progress report meetings in the conference room of the Interior Ministry" (53).

A distinctive form of spatial coincidence can be found in the novels of Buchan and Fleming, that of going exactly where you don't want to go: Hannay's flight away from his pursuers into the wilds of Scotland— a place of spatial diffusion—leads him to the very heart of the con-spiracy, as if there were no free space in that world, only lines leading back to the center. This is a common figure in romance fiction: encoun-tered in prison, the elder Rudge is asked how he was taken: "Because I went there [to Chigwell] to avoid the man I stumbled on" (Dickens 1966, 458). In Hawthorne's "Roger Malvin's Burial," the trek out West to settle new land is a retracing of steps that leads Reuban Bourne to the very spot where he left his father-in-law unburied eighteen years before.

Coincidence distributes itself across the texture of detective fiction as false and true sign, chance and relationship, evidence and clue. Such semantic crisscrossing is stimulated by the nature of the word coincidence, which is a primal term, asserting itself and its opposite, covering itself, concealing and exposing its mystery—a criminal of a word (Freud 1910).

Coincidence, for example, is sometimes design that has no meaning, and, therefore, in George Smiley's universe, "there is no such thing as coincidence" (TTSS 328). In the following exchange, however, co-incidence cannot guarantee design: after the murder of a man named Ascher at Andover and a note from a criminal who signs himself A.B.C. hinting that the next murder will take place at Bexhill-on-Sea, Poirot suggests that the surname of the next victim will possibly begin with the letter B. The doctor comments: "It's possible. . . . On the other hand, it may be that the name Ascher was a coincidence—that the victim this time, no matter what her name is, will again be an old woman who keeps a shop. We're dealing, remember, with a madman. So far he hasn't given us any clue as to motive" (ABC 57).

Madness is here a codeword for the absence of design, yet madness can just as easily be used to privilege design: " 'I mean,' continued Rénine, in a clear voice, sounding each syllable separately, 'I mean that you see before your eyes three Christian names which all three begin with the same initial and which all three, by a remarkable coincidence, consist of the same number of letters, as you may prove. . . . The obsession of an idea and the continual repetition of an act are characteristics of the maniac. I do not yet know the idea by which the lady with the hatchet is obsessed but I do know the act that results from it and it is always the same' " ("LH" 231, 230).

These are also the common movements of romance texts, for example, *Oliver Twist*, where the leader of the London underworld is named Fagin and the leader of the London criminal courts is named Fang. Discussing "The Gold-Bug," Jean Ricardou suggested that the image of Jupiter catching the bug with a piece of parchment on which is inscribed "the still secret skull traced on the parchment by Kidd" and Legrand drawing an image of the beetle on the reverse of that piece of parchment illustrate a law of texts, that "Birds of a Feather Flock Together" (35).

Christie's doctor uses the fact of coincidence to deny the legibility of crime, and it can also be used to deny the existence of crime. In James Hilton's *Was It Murder?* a boy dies at school in a way that seems accidental. Sometime later the headmaster finds a handwritten will in the boy's algebra book. He tells Revel, "I daresay the whole thing is just pure coincidence. I certainly don't want you to assume that there is more in it than meets the eye." And yet—"And yet—there's that little demon of curiosity in my mind—why *was* the boy thinking of death on that Sunday evening?" After another accidental death occurs, the same word will be used to refer to criminal significance: the "two accidents present a most terrible and remarkable coincidence" (WM 22–23, 50).

Finally, coincidences are signs that block investigation because they are read as pointing inward, to the imaginary—"It's difficult to explain . . . but I was quite sure in my own mind that what I had seen was an hallucination—not of this world. I had some reason for thinking so. A month ago I went over to the organ shed on a similar errand and at about the same time at night. It was raining then, I remember, and as God's my witness I saw then—what I saw last night" (CQ 88–89); the fantastic—"Men believe the oddest things if they are in a series; that is why Macbeth believed the three words of the three witches" (AA 190); or the fictitious—"Then, unless a coincidence occurred greater than any invented by a novelist in difficulties, your visit was in some way connected with the murder" (R 67).

Coincidence is a sign that blocks investigation, and yet it is the very thing that must be investigated. Coincidence is the line of the investigation, and detective fiction, which prides itself on its classic metonymy, actually proceeds through metaphors of identity: "He had it in the back of his head that somewhere in this case was a relationship, a resemblance, between two phenomena. What it was he had not been able for his life to think; but somewhere in the events of the last two days he had come across something that reminded him strongly of something else" (MSY 94). Coincidences are lines of criminal intent, but they are always registered "as if by accident": in Poe's *Narrative of Arthur Gordon Pym*, the hero notices that as "we passed along, the party of Too-wit . . . was momentarily strengthened by smaller detachments, of from two to six to seven, which joined us, as if by accident, at different turns in the road. There appeared so much of system in this that I could not help feeling distrust" (152). Coincidence, therefore, is always suspicious, and yet coincidence also erases suspicion:

> "Is that, or is it not, a darned suspicious circumstance?"
> "So suspicious that it is probably the purest coincidence." (MMA 58)

Freud's 1919 essay "The 'Uncanny'" is not nominally about coincidence, although it eventually becomes the story of Freud meeting himself in a railroad compartment, meeting a double whose appearance, Freud says, he thoroughly disliked. He tells us twice that the word *uncanny* means coincidentally: "equally certainly, too, the word is not always used in a clearly definable sense, so that it tends to coincide with what excites fear in general. . . . Thus *heimlich* is a word the meaning of which develops in the direction of ambivalence, until it finally coincides with its opposite, *unheimlich*" (1953 [1919], 216, 226).

The uncanniness of the images or events cited as examples by Freud generally involve a vague perception of coincidence, doubleness, or polarity. A conventional thriller image involves two torn halves of a bill, which, when fitted together, authenticate two random individuals as part of a conspiracy. The two halves are meaningless in design until they come together and meet, when those ragged edges become precise and perfect.

Edgar Allan Poe and E. T. A. Hoffmann are among the primary authors of the uncanny, and the most powerful images of coincidence in Romantic fiction are the ones that Poe uses to annihilate his tales: Ligeia squeezing herself back into life through the form and contours of the Lady Rowena; William Wilson fighting a duel with that other William Wilson, both wearing the same costume of a Spanish cloak of blue velvet, a crimson belt and a black mask. The narrator finally plunges his sword repeatedly through the bosom of the other. Hearing a sound at the door, he hurries to it and, turning back, sees a large mirror standing where his double had been, and another double, his own mirror reflection, moves toward him in the rhythms of his own tottering gait. A perfect, but impossible, example of coincidence in Poe would be an ideal reading of the final image in "The Fall of the House of Usher" where the house and its mirror reflection fall down and up into one another in immaculate bilateral inversion (in my reading the reflected image is not dispersed by the agitated water).

Most of Poe's tales locate themselves at points of coincidence, identified as such through a state of mind and feeling analogous to the uncanny. The longest of such positioning exercises comes at the beginning of "The Fall of the House of Usher." Traveling through a "singularly dreary tract of country," the narrator is "unnerved" at the sight of the house by a feeling that he cannot analyze. Believing that "a mere different arrangement of the particulars of the scene" might annihilate or modify this painful effect, the narrator looks instead at the "remodelled and inverted images" of the house in the tarn. He remembers a remarkable fact about the family, that time and genealogy have made it coincide with the house. Thereafter, he meets a Roderick who resembles the house in several intricate ways.

The narrator finds Roderick Usher to be both friend and stranger, familiar and unfamiliar. This condition is one of Freud's formulas for the uncanny, and a version of it opens Poe's "Black Cat" (in a form that uncannily evokes Freud): "For the most wild, yet most homely

narrative which I am about to pen, I neither expect nor solicit belief."
Another formulation for the uncanny—an object or event that is both
trivial and significant—occurs at the opening of Hoffmann's "Sand-
man," the example-text of Freud's essay: "But now you will, I suppose,
take me for a superstitious ghost-seer. In a word, the terrible thing
which I have experienced, the fatal effect of which I in vain exert every
effort to shake off, is simply that some days ago, namely, on the thirti-
eth of October, at twelve o'clock at noon, a peddler of weather glasses
and thermometers came into my room and wanted to sell me one of
his wares. . . . I hear you laugh and Clara say, 'What's all this childish nonsense about!' Well, laugh at me, laugh heartily at me, pray do.
But, good God, my hair is standing on end'" (183–84).[1] The unfamiliar familiar, the trivially significant, these are also phrases for the
Romantic image and the poetic symbol—the world that William Blake
sees in a grain of sand, Immanuel Kant's purposiveness without purpose, Samuel Taylor Coleridge's and Hawthorne's familiar object seen
under the alienating influence of moonlight. And they are also phrases
for the clue, that uncanny object that is simultaneously meaningless
and meaningful, isolated and integrated.

The Woman in White opens with Walter Hartright meeting Anne Catherick, a woman dressed in white, who is a double of the woman Laura
Fairlie, whom Walter will soon come to love. The two women are
brought together in various ways; eventually they will be related to one
another as half-sisters. The women are not precise doubles, although
Walter is able to imagine such a duplication: "Although I hated myself
even for thinking such a thing, still, while I looked at the woman before
me, the idea would force itself into my mind that one sad change, in
the future, was all that was wanting to make the likeness complete"
(Collins 1974, 120). This is precisely what the narrative will make happen. The design of the conspiracy in the book is to make the two women
coincide, to bring them together, have them pass through one another
and out the other side like Ligeia and Rowena, so that Anne becomes
Laura and is buried by her mother's grave, and Laura becomes Anne
and is shut up in a lunatic asylum—and no one can tell that this coincidence has occurred. Conversely, the object of Walter's quest, the

information that will defeat the conspiracy, is that Sir Percy Glyde is also an imposter, a bastard son passing as an heir. Glyde's impersonation is figured in the book by an image of coincidence that anticipates Jorge Luis Borges's "Tlon": two identical texts, except that in one "a certificate of his parents' marriage" occupies the bottom of the page, while in the other: "I looked again—I was afraid to believe the evidence of my own eyes. No! not a doubt. The marriage was not there" (Collins 1974, 550, 529).

Exchanges of this kind abound in mystery and detective fiction, and the more undetectable they are, the greater the surprise when the invisible fact is announced. *Epitaph for a Spy* takes place because identical cameras were accidentally exchanged. In *Re-enter Sir John*, Sir John "has no need to make his point. Her voice broke in: 'But Peter's left-handed!' " and this sinister bombshell reverses everything else (RSJ 74). In John Stephen Strange's *Man Who Killed Fortescue*, a solution (in the form of a confession) is destroyed at the beginning of the novel, but it is, coincidentally, there all along, reversed on a sheet of carbon paper; and it is read at the end, reversed yet again in a mirror (285–88).

Coincidences and clues are transfer points in the text, polar moments where meaning is transformed into its opposite. Hartman identifies the model as a schizophrenic one, its "rhythm of surprising reversals— from casual to crucial or from laconic detail to essential clue" (221). At certain points in the narrative, it is announced that a certain signifier is not important but obstructive; another signifier is not trivial but tremendous; and, on another level, that a third signifier is not a fact but a fiction. Other common itineraries are between accident and intention—"I can't figure out, in this business of the disguised corpse . . . if he's made a slip, or if we're trotting along in line just as he expected" (MSY 144)—and from innocence to guilt: "If Felix had acted in this way, it followed that either he was the murderer and wished to get the body to his house . . . or else he was an innocent man upon whom the real criminal wished to plant the corpse" (C 155). The motive power for these shuttles is suspicion, a state of mind that is also induced by coincidence.

In thrillers such movements are entitled, as in Ross Thomas's *Cold*

War Swap or Derek Lambert's *Yermakov Transfer,* and the thriller persistently tracks such twisty movements. The double agent can act out multiple transfers as he may be turned two or more times. At the end of his book, Quiller engages his tag in an operation known as the switch, where "the tag is noticed, flushed *and followed.* The switch has been made, and the tag is now tagged." *The Quiller Memorandum* is devoted throughout to the unraveling of "double-think": Oktober "wanted me to think that he thought I was dead, so that I would at once go to ground, change my open tactics, and lead him to my base" (QM 125, 105). The switch is the model for larger forms, particularly a tale like Richard Connell's "Most Dangerous Game" and other hunt stories that are coiled to allow hunter and hunted to change positions. These stories will reverse themselves at least once, but they have the potentiality of reversing themselves at any time.

"Double-think" appears at an originating moment in detective fiction, in "The Purloined Letter," as the game of even and odd, where it is offered as a paradigm for detection. It is also a paradigm for the reading of detective fiction. One player holds a number of marbles in his hand, and the other guesses whether that number is even or odd. In the tale, the analysis in the second round of play goes as follows: "This fellow finds that in the first instance I guessed odd, and, in the second, he will propose to himself . . . a simple variation from even to odd, as did the first simpleton; but then a second thought will suggest that this is too simple a variation, and finally he will decide upon putting it even as before. I will therefore guess even" (Poe 1902, 6:41). In *Exile's Return,* Malcolm Cowley describes a similar game called *convolutions,* the name I use for this type of movement in detective fiction (Cowley 21–22): "It is a generally practiced rule that the most suspected person is innocent and the least suspected the criminal; naturally, the validity of this rule is not annulled, but only confirmed, when the author for once reverses the procedure in consideration of the clever reader and permits the really guilty party to seem so suspicious that he seems unsuspicious" (Alewyn 70).

The turning point of Jane Austen's *Pride and Prejudice* is a letter that is read and reread. Elizabeth reads Darcy's account of what happened at Netherfield as a register of falsehood, pride, and insolence.

As she rereads later "with the closest attention," deliberating "on the probability of each statement," the text reverses itself, and "every line proved more clearly that the affair, which she had believed it impossible that any contrivance could so represent, as to render Mr. Darcy's conduct in it less than infamous, was capable of a turn which must make him entirely blameless throughout the whole" (182). Arthur Dimmesdale's sermonistic confession in *The Scarlet Letter* is so caught up in the polarities of Puritan rhetoric that every earnest statement he makes about his criminal condition is taken by his audience as a statement of personal worth; and Melville's Benito Cereno has to channel his communication through its opposite: to save Amasa Delano from imminent peril, he must keep telling him that everything on board the slave ship is proper and ordinary.

Poe's argument proving there can be no such thing as a long poem moves to the rhythms of convolution. Because poetry is an exhausting burst of supernal energy, it is humanly impossible to read a work like *Paradise Lost* as a unified whole. We are forced to register it as an alternation of poetic peaks and prosaic troughs, corresponding to the alternations of excitement and consequent depression that such energy produces in us. "But if, upon completing the work, we read it again; omitting the first book—that is to say, commencing with the second—we shall be surprised at now finding that admirable which we before condemned—that damnable which we had previously so much admired" (Poe 1902, 14:267).

In the examples from Austen and Poe, the proper reading is a rereading. *The Narrative of Arthur Gordon Pym* is given over to convolutions of structure and discourse, and it contains a simple model for the process of rereading that these examples engage. In chapter 14, Pym describes the construction of an albatross and penguin rookery on Kerguelon's Island. It is work of mathematical nicety: between the albatross and the penguin "the most singular friendship exists," and their "nests are constructed with great uniformity upon a plan concerted between the two species—that of the albatross being placed in the center of a little square formed by the nests of four penguins." But the next time we survey this ground plan it is subtly but radically different: "At each intersection of these paths the nest of an albatross is constructed, and a penguin's nest in the center of each square" (Poe 124–25).

Adventure fictions such as *Treasure Island* literally consist of an alternation of peaks of excitement and troughs of despair. Movement in such works is a great zigzag: peril inevitably turns into salvation that gives way, often with a great economy of means, into the imminence of new peril. In the Stevenson romance, this is figured by the boys' game of feints and dodges that Jim plays with Israel Hands: "Seeing that I meant to dodge, he also paused; and a moment or two passed in feints on his part, and corresponding movements upon mine. It was such a game as I had often played at home" (Stevenson 1946, 164).

Certain conventional structures in detective fiction, such as the frame-up or the double cross, are already convoluted, and many of these texts function overall like frame-ups and double crosses. All of these forms testify to the pleasure of betrayal. *Jumping Jenny* deals with a case of apparent suicide in a highly theatrical setting. Because the death threatens to incriminate a friend, the community decides to forestall the rewriting of this death as a murder (which the police are certain to do) by restaging it as a simpler, more obvious, case of suicide. The community later learns that it truly was suicide and not the murder they had feared, and their manipulations created suspicion where none need have been. They learn even later that it was a murder: "I was just thinking on what small points these cases depend. One single piece of evidence is enough to turn an apparently obvious case of suicide into a still more obvious case of murder, or an accident into a suicide, or what you will" (JJ 81).

It would be wearying to give many examples of convoluted thinking and dialogue. The following long extract, however, is offered by Sayers as an example of the type of thinking manufactured by an ideal reader at every moment of the investigation, as this reader responds to the challenge of detection:

> At the opening of a story, the servant Jones is heard to say to his master, Lord Smith, "Very good, my Lord. I will attend to the matter at once." The inference is that, if Jones was speaking to Smith, Smith was also speaking to Jones. . . . But that is a false conclusion. . . . Lord Smith

may be absent; he may be already dead. . . . Nor can we draw any safe conclusion about the attitude of Jones. If Jones is indeed present in the flesh, and not represented merely by his voice in the form of a gramophone record . . . (as may well be the case), then he may be addressing some other party in the belief that he is addressing Smith; he may have murdered Smith and be establishing his own alibi; or Smith may be the murderer and Jones his accomplice engaged in establishing an alibi for Smith. Nor, on the other hand, is it safe to conclude . . . that *because* Smith is not heard to reply he is *not* therefore present. For this may very well be the Double Bluff, in which the reader's own cunning is exploited to his downfall. (1947, 232)

The intensifiers "too" and "so" are clues to convolution: "Some accidents," Wimsey says, "are too accidental to be true" (MMA 197). In the teasing display at the opening of "The Purloined Letter," the Prefect sits, stupidly suspended between a misunderstood *so* and two perverse *toos:*

> "But then I thought Dupin would like to hear the details of it, because it is so excessively *odd*. . . . The affair *is* so simple, and yet baffles us altogether. . . ."
>
> "Perhaps the mystery is a little *too* plain," said Dupin. "Oh, good heavens! Who ever heard of such an idea?"
>
> "A little *too* self-evident." (Poe 1902, 6:29–30)

"Don't you see, my dear fellow? *There's too much glass,*" Dr. Thorndyke exclaims (BDT 30), and Poirot worries, "there is altogether too much strychnine about this case. . . . It is confusing" (MAS 140).

"Too" is also the mark of coincidence—"Yet, of course, Ena Stratton must have committed suicide. . . . But he was not satisfied. It was too neat, too tidy altogether, too convenient that Ena Stratton should have committed suicide just at this juncture, when so many people desired it" (JJ 71)—or the coincidence of coincidence: The results "fell into my lap. It's one of the things that made me suspicious. Too many coincidences came together. . . . I can't help feeling that the whole business may have been planned to come out this way" (GC 90).

More than any of the other mystery forms, the spy thriller features convolutions. In the 1960s and 1970s, at the hands of Le Carré,

Deighton, Thomas, and William Haggard (and in the 1980s and 1990s by Richard Littell and Stan Lee), the game was pressed to the limit. In *The Yermakov Transfer*, for example, seven Jewish fanatics plan to kidnap the Soviet premier from a train bound for Siberia. They will demand the release of a number of Jewish nuclear scientists, who will be given safe passage to Israel, where they will work at making that country a major nuclear power. None of the seven has "Jew" written on his passport; in fact, most of them are minor members of the KGB who have been acting as agents provocateurs in Jewish circles, informing on Zionist activities in the Soviet Union—activities that have been invented or aggravated by them in order to please their Soviet masters.

The context of their fanaticism is the rabid anti-Semitism of the Soviet Union since 1932, and this anti-Semitism has been anchored in Zionist conspiracies aimed at disrupting the Soviet regime—but these conspiracies have themselves been invented by the Soviet authorities. To combat the consequences of a grim hoax created by the Soviets, the conspirators are about to become the reality of that fantasy. The thriller shuttles back and forth along the axis of fact and fiction and doubles that play of inversions along the axis of text and reader.

The labyrinths of Borges provide a model for the later convolutions of the thriller. One, "The Theme of the Traitor and the Hero," he claimed to have written under Chesterton's influence. It is the sketch for an unwritten story about an unwritten biography of Kilpatrick, the great Irish hero who died on the eve of the successful revolt that he had planned. Kilpatrick's great-grandson, Ryan, wants to write his ancestor's biography for the centenary of his death. The circumstances of the death betray blatant resemblances to elements in the death of Julius Caesar, but Ryan chooses to read them as signs of a secret coincidence in time that governs the margins of history, an effect of the transmigration of souls. The discovery of a further analogy to *Macbeth* shifts the base of the coincidence from history to literature. Ryan finally discovers that Kilpatrick's oldest companion, Nolan, a translator of Shakespeare and theatrical scholar, had discovered that Kilpatrick was not only the leader of the conspiracy, but also a traitor who was planning to betray it. Nolan proposed a plan that would function both as a punishment of Kilpatrick and a stimulus to revolt: Kilpatrick would die at the hands of an assassin in dramatic circumstances. Kilpatrick's death was scripted and staged by Nolan and became the sacred history of Ireland. The event was made to resemble the Swiss *Festspiele*, a theatrical event that repeats historical events in the places where they had originally occurred; but he wrote into his history obvious and detectable plagiarisms from Shakespeare so that his achievement would eventually be identified as his own work of art.

Reading mystery stories is convoluted, the apologists claim, because the stories must do justice to complex crimes and conspiracies. Early detective fiction often staged the exchange and confusion of identical opposites. When Chandler attempted to expose the artificiality of analytic detective fiction in "The Simple Art of Murder," he went straight to three versions of this elaborate story: A. A. Milne's *Red House Mystery*, *Trent's Last Case*, and an unnamed mystery by Freeman Wills Crofts. In all of these the criminal and victim are twins or doubles, and the mystery hinges on the criminal impersonating the victim, keeping him alive after he is dead. Ironically, this particular story had been ruled out of the genre by Chesterton—"He does not introduce suddenly at the end somebody's brother from New Zealand, who is exactly like him" (1929, 176)—but apparently to no avail.

Plautus and Shakespeare aside, detective fiction again seems to acknowledge the paternity of Twain who was extremely fond of this story and mined it in *The Prince and the Pauper* and *Pudd'nhead Wilson*. Detective fiction shares this story with nineteenth- and early twentieth-century romances like Alexandre Dumas's *Corsican Brothers* and Anthony Hope's *Prisoner of Zenda*. When Laura Fairlie is put into an asylum in *The Woman in White*, a letter is written to her guardian telling him that Anne Catherick (the woman in white, Laura's half-sister) has been returned to the asylum, and the writer warns him "that Anne Catherick's mental malady had been aggravated by her long freedom from control, and that the insane hatred and distrust of Sir Percival Glyde" took "the idea of annoying and distressing him . . . by assuming the character of his deceased wife," that is, Laura herself (Collins 1974, 438).

A literature that regularly inverts its fictions and devotes itself to legitimizing conspiratorial thinking would neatly fit the context that the detractors of mystery and detective fiction contemptuously evoke, the context of addiction. Poe's critical persona, that petulant rationalist of the reviews and the essays, has often been identified as a detective and associated with Dupin, and, like Dupin, his art is primarily an art of convolution. Dupin's companion says to him, "You surprise me . . . by these opinions, which have been contradicted by the voice of the world. You do not mean to set at naught the well-digested idea of centuries" (Poe 1902, 6:43). The critic overturns outrageously and advances incredible positions as matter of fact: he can prove deductively that there is no French poetry; that no one before him has ever been able to define "plot" or even talk about it precisely; that all philosophical methods for determining the truth are philosophically inadequate; that "for centuries, no man, in verse, has ever done, or ever seemed to think of doing, an original thing" (Poe 1902, 14:261, 13:44, 14:203).

Nevertheless, mystery and detective fiction insists on an external justification for its addictive moves. The various paradoxical figures that the crises of detection or espionage bring to the surface are grounded in the existence of a second world, an *other* world. The second world of detective fiction is accessible to reason, but only along the underside of coincidence and convolution. The detective knows that one is at the edge of a convolution through an invisible resistance and symmetry:

> "When did you change your mind?"
> "When I found that the more efforts I made to clear him, the more efforts he made to get himself arrested." (MAS 171)

The divided territories have the same extreme economy of form as do the contradictory readings of the convoluted text: the other world is just the same as ours, "only the things go the other way"; "the books are something like our books, only the words go the wrong way" (Carroll 110). The data of this second world are indistinguishable from the indices of ordinary experience. We no longer have to regard the police as fools, they are simply locked into a world where lines of perception and thought only negotiate an irrelevant surface.

Detective and mystery fiction has made much use of a model of reality that has two opposed domains coinciding with one another. It shares this with a high vein of postmodern fiction: Borges's labyrinths (particularly "Tlon"), *Pale Fire* and *Ada* by Vladimir Nabokov, or the work of Pynchon, Julio Cortázar, and Italo Calvino. This is partly a coincidence, the result of a radical change in traditional influence, for these later fabulators are drawing not on the novel but on the "low" tradition of romance and popular fiction, the work of Kipling, Wells, Stevenson, Jules Verne, and Conan Doyle.

The most exciting and perplexing relationship between the two orders of things is one in which they are both the same and different, in which they coincide or present a convoluted boundary like the Don Quixotes of Miguel de Cervantes and Pierre Menard. Carroll brought this kind of space and its epistemology into focus, and the *Alice* books, which are sources of imaginative energy for postmodern writers, also serve as master-texts for analytic detective fiction and the spy thriller. Titles alone announce this: *The Mad Hatter Mystery, Malice in Wonderland, Twinkle, Twinkle, Little Spy, The Looking Glass War.* In works that contain no other literary allusions, sentences like the following from *Tinker, Tailor, Soldier, Spy* can still appear: "Like the Cheshire cat, the face of Bill Haydon seemed to recede as soon as he advanced upon it, leaving only the smile behind" (TTSS 157).

Alice's looking glass reflects a world that moves along with ours in time, repeating every gesture made from this side. But Alice suspects the resemblance may be deceptive: "Oh, Kitty! now we come to the passage. You can just see a little *peep* of the passage in Looking-glass House . . . and it's very like our passage as far as you can see, only you know it may be quite different on beyond" (Carroll 111). Once on the other side, she notices that what could be seen from the room was quite common and uninteresting, but all the rest was as different as possible.

The world beyond the looking glass is a world of coincidence in a special sense, for it is a chess game, and the imagery and language of chess also sprinkles detective fiction because it is a game that demands convoluted thinking: "I walked that green for a quarter of an hour . . . thinking the thing out like a game of chess. I had to think ahead and think coolly; for my safety depended on upsetting the plans of one of the longest-headed men who ever lived. . . . At every turn the cunning of Manderson had forestalled me" (TLC 195). As a metaphor for reality, chess is influential in modern fiction as well; at the borderline between art and popular fiction is a collection of detective stories by William Faulkner entitled *Knight's Gambit.*

Detectives operate on the assumption that the ordinary world is deceptive and not to be trusted. Analytic and hard-boiled detectives and professional spies presume such a second reality below or beyond the surface of things. The amateur thriller protagonist, on the other hand, discovers the second world abruptly; he falls into Wonderland or underland. *Newsweek* described the Ambler formula: "An innocent bumbler accidentally stumbles into an undercover operation. He doesn't understand what's going on; he can't go to the police; he probably won't survive the ordeal" (10 July 1972, 91).

The heroes of mystery fiction are continually "stumbling on" something or other—a clue, a secret, sometimes a whole world. In *The Red Box*, Wolfe asks Helen Frost to arrange for the cooperation of her relatives to help him "stumble on a path that will lead us away from ignorance" (RBx 114), and in *Background to Danger*, Maillor tells Kenton he regrets the necessity of killing him but it is Kenton's misfortune that he "stumbled on an affair that is not yet ready for the attention of the world at large" (BD 142). In *The Three Hostages*, Hannay is told "there is some superlative cunning on the other side. That is why I want *you.* You have a knack of stumbling on truths which no amount of ordinary reasoning can get at" (TH 33). One stumbles upon something through the agency of the trifle—hints, whiffs, stray and scattered signs. Richard Hannay asks Scudder how he got the story of the unknown but ubiquitous conspiracy, and Scudder says: "I got the first hint in an inn on the Achensee in Tyrol. That set me inquiring and I collected my other clues in a fur-shop in the Galician quarter of Buda, in a Stranger's Club in Vienna, and in a little book-shop off the Racknitzstrasse in Leipsic. I completed my evidence ten days ago in Paris" (TS 12).

After stumbling, what one falls through is a familiar romance trope, "the thin veneer of civilization," a provocative limit previously engaged by Conrad and Henry James in their espionage novels *The Secret Agent* and *The Princess Casamassima.* Nella, the adventurous millionaire's daughter in Bennett's *Grand Babylon Hotel,* falls through this surface: "Twenty-four hours ago she would have declared it impossible that such an experience as she had suffered could happen to anyone; she would have talked airily about civilization and the nineteenth century, and progress and the police. But her experience was teaching her that human nature remains always the same, and that beneath the thin crust of security on which we good citizens exist the dark and secret forces of crime continue to move" (Bennett 80). Richard Alewyn associates the detective with the romantic artist and sees the latter inhabiting a "thin layer of deception over an abyss of dark symbols which . . . [he] seeks to penetrate" (Alewyn quoted in Holquist 156). In Buchan's *Power House*, the magus, Andrew Lumley, lectures Leithen on the "precarious . . . tenure of civilization" to explain his equally invisible conspiracy: "You think that a wall as solid as the earth separates civilization from barbarism. I tell you the division is a thread, a sheet of glass. A touch here, a push there, and you bring back the reign of Saturn." Leithen later echoes the theme: "Now I saw how thin is the protection of civilization. An accident and a bogus ambulance—a false charge and a bogus arrest—there were a dozen ways of spiriting me out of this gay, bustling world" (PH 46–47, 141).

Traditional cosmologies are usually unlike that of detective fiction, as in the contrast between the apparent multiplicity of the ordinary and the transcendental unity of the ideal realm in Platonic versions, but they can also resemble it: for example, the emblematic relationship between the Calvinist world and its heaven, as it is detailed in Ann Bradstreet's poem "Here Follows Some Verses upon the Burning of Our House" where every item she has lost on earth is waiting for her, in its proper place and in an ideal form, in heaven. A nightmare of Western cosmology, Descartes's supererogatory belief in a *mauvais génie*, holds precisely the mixture of coincidence and deception that is implicit here: "A certain evil spirit, not less clever and deceitful than powerful, has bent all his efforts to deceive me. I will suppose that . . . [all] objective things are nothing but illusions and dreams that he has used to trick my credulity" (22).

11

Messages from the Underworld

THE ORDINARY WORLD OF MYSTERY AND DETECTIVE FICTION MAY BE randomly meaningful, but the other world, the underworld, is wholly organized; it is identified by figured versions of the totality of relationship that governs the form. The most common of these is a conspiracy of deception or evil. Conspiratorial reality is the fiction that validates the masochistic and paranoid bent of the composite dreamer, the writer-hero-reader. The second world is in the condition of Milton's hell: a ruthlessly dedicated band of fallen angels, ruled over by a magus, are devoting all their thought and energy to penetrating the ordinary world and causing disruption.

The spy thriller is the most overtly conspiratorial of the three forms, and Edmund Wilson singles that out as an index of its potential superiority: "It is not simply a question here of a puzzle which has been put together but of a malaise conveyed to the reader, the horror of a hidden conspiracy which is continually turning up in the most varied and unlikely forms" (1945, 395); and Michael Gilbert makes "the continuous and threatening presence of the enemy" the thriller's defining characteristic, the trait that separates it from the "adventure story," with which it otherwise shares some of its most distinctive features, like perilous adventure and hairbreadth escapes (1959b, 109).

One of the "realistic" elements of the spy thriller is the use of a historical conspiracy as a cover story in much the same way as the Gothic novel appropriated the Spanish Inquisition and the secret societies of Freemasons, Illuminati, and Rosicrucians. The thriller, therefore, shares a boundary with a class of fiction that appeared in the Edwardian period, conservative novels that reflected the threat of contemporary socialist and anarchist movements in Europe and America —novels like J. M. Barrie's *Better Dead*, Joseph Conrad's *Under Western Eyes* and *The Secret Agent*, William Dean Howells's *Hazard of New Fortunes*, Henry James's *Princess Casamassima*, Jack London's *Assassination Bureau* (and several of his tales, for example, "The Minions of Midas"), and Robert Louis Stevenson's *Dynamiter*, which uses the American "Mormon conspiracy." When Conan Doyle reinvented analytic detective fiction, he located some of his stories and novels among actual conspiracies: the Mormon conspiracy in *A Study in Scarlet* (taken from Stevenson), the Ku Klux Klan in *The Adventures of Sherlock Holmes*, and the Molly Maguires in *The Valley of Fear* (see Priestman 99). Conspiracy is in the fictive air of this period, which also sees a wave of "Yellow Peril" romances—particularly Sax Rohmer's three novels about Fu Manchu, " 'The Devil Doctor,' the head of the great Yellow Movement against the entire white race" (Mierow 16; see also Rosenberg 15; and Wu)—and the rise of science fiction, of which one line of development is devoted to extraterrestrial invasions, as in H. G. Wells's *War of the Worlds*.

Although Conan Doyle used conspiratorial fictions in his detective fiction, he also ruled them out of the genre when he had Holmes declare in *A Study in Scarlet* that the mark of a secret society left at the scene of the crime was a ruse to throw detection off the track. Collins had done this earlier; in *The Moonstone* he would not allow the Indians who came to England for the sole purpose of regaining the jewel to have any part in the theft, partly because they were the obvious criminals and partly because they were Indians. Chesterton and others announced the rule: "He does not introduce into the story a vast but invisible secret society with branches in every part of the world, with ruffians who can be brought in to do anything or underground cellars that can be used to hide anybody" (1929, 175–76). But if public conspiracies are ruled out of analytic detective fiction, this is partly because these works choose instead to delineate the family or the community as conspiracies of suppression. Analytic detective fiction likes to keep crime in the family.

The ultimate gratification of mystery and detective fiction is its invocation of a paranoid universe that can be experienced without shame; it "is a paranoid representation of the world, the world seen through paranoid eyes" (Palmer 86). The situation of the hero also fulfills a condition of paranoia: he "always appears to be at the center of a great deal of attention—some persecutory, some grandiose, but in any case, all focused on him. Something is always happening to him" (Swanson, Bohnert, and Smith, 15); he is "the true paranoid for whom all is organized in spheres joyful or threatening about the central pulse of himself" (Pynchon 95). The romance tradition is generally devoted to the celebration of positive paranoia; in this respect, it is opposed to the later nineteenth-century novel, which energetically denies and dissembles paranoia, but reproduces it nevertheless. *Caleb Williams* and *Frankenstein*, for example, are fictions in which an implacable enemy, with virtually superhuman energy, tracks and threatens to punish the male subject. One line of the British novel consists of paranoid fantasies that roughly anticipate the shape of the thriller.

Robinson Crusoe is convinced he lives in a world of imminent peril where he is at risk of being eaten by cannibals, and this threat is all the more terrifying for being invisible. Despite his constant surveillance, there are no signs of the conspiracy, and when he finally does encounter a sign (actually half a sign), it turns out to mean the opposite—a kindly, loving "savage." The absence of verification, however, only intensifies his anxiety; he remains acutely on guard for many years scrutinizing nature and prodded by his anxiety into radical modes of protection—building series of fences and walls as well as erasing traces of himself. Like the hero of *Rogue Male*, he eventually goes to ground in an attempt to become invisible. This story, moreover, is framed by an anterior paranoid fiction: all this is happening because he once disobeyed his father.

In Scott's *Waverley* and Dickens's *Oliver Twist*, well-intentioned, dutiful young men drift against their will into conspiratorial situations: Waverley into the heart of the 1845 Jacobite rebellion against the English throne and Oliver into the London underworld where there exists a conspiracy of boys ruled by Fagin. In both cases the protagonist finds himself trapped in an incriminating circumstantial web of appearances: Waverley as a traitor and Oliver as a thief, a boy who was born to be hanged. In the Scott novel, the web of entrapment (the frame-up), is hidden from Waverley and the reader by a fiction of Romantic drift. On holiday, following the trail of the picturesque, Waverley finally awakes to find himself clothed in tartan, on the battlefield, witnessing the death of his old commander. He is accused by the eyes of the dying man and subsequently finds himself the object of detestation of his countrymen.

Both Waverley and Oliver have a talismanic relationship to the conspiracies in which they become involved. Both Fergus Mac-Ivor and Fagin, once they have glimpsed the erotic innocence of a Waverley or an Oliver, must have them as figureheads for their projects. In *Oliver Twist* and *Treasure Island*, the child keeps slipping loose, and must be regularly brought back into the bosom of the conspiracy. This is a trait these heroes share with Jim Hawkins, Huck Finn, and Kim, an early form of the unique necessity of the hero in detective fiction. This convention suggests a very special relationship between the detective and the tangle of events he resolves. A crime solved by Holmes or Poirot is a crime only they could solve. This implication is sometimes announced in a title like John Creasey's *Send for Inspector West*, or in narrative units where clients are told to move heaven and earth to get a particular detective to take the case.

Conspiratorial reality is a pervasive presence in the fiction of Dickens, and this is certainly the reason behind his great appeal to Franz Kafka, a later producer of paranoid fictions. In so many of Dickens's works there is either a conspiratorial system or a more ordinary system recast in that mode: the proletarian revolt in *Barnaby Rudge*, the Eden Land Company in *Martin Chuzzlewit*, Chancery and Tom All-alone's in *Bleak House*, the factory system in *Hard Times*, the Reign of Terror in *A Tale of Two Cities*.

In Wilkie Collins's *Woman in White*, the paranoia of British fiction is enhanced and married to the structures and language of later mystery and detective fiction. *The Woman in White* yearns to be a spy story; at the end, Fosco is identified as an actual spy and associated with an anarchist secret society. But quite apart from this gratuitous historical identification, Fosco is the first omnipotent and ubiquitous spy: he sees and hears everything. He walks with noiseless tread into any scene or any dream. The protagonists find it virtually impossible to speak or act outside his knowledge. Walking to town, Marian Halcombe looks back from time to time to make sure she is not followed. Nothing is behind her but an empty country wagon, but as it passes she looks at it "more attentively than before, [and] I thought I detected at intervals the feet of a man walking close behind it." Fosco has a magical ability to merge with objects; he is discernible only as a shadow or a pair of footprints (Collins 1974, 332, 359).

In this novel, a man and two women—Walter Hartright, Marian Halcombe, and Laura Fairlie—are subject to sustained but invisible persecution. Other people act toward them in mean and vicious ways, but they cannot conceive explanations for this behavior, and when they confront the others, they always have a story to tell that acquits them of blame. The three not only cannot explain this persecution to the authorities, they cannot even accept one another's reality. After leaving Limmeridge House, Walter seems to degenerate utterly. He was the first exposed and the first infected, so the paranoid condition is most extreme in him. Marian reads a letter from him and believes that he has sunk into madness: "After mentioning that he has neither seen nor heard anything of Anne Catherick, he suddenly breaks off, and hints in the most abrupt, mysterious manner, that he has been perpetually watched and followed by strange men ever since he returned to London. He acknowledges that he cannot prove this extraordinary suspicion by fixing on any particular persons, but he declares that the suspicion itself is present to him night and day. This has frightened me, because it looks as if his one fixed idea about Laura was becoming too much for his mind" (Collins 1974, 188–89).

Like the crime that initially manifests itself as a miracle, the criminal conspiracy is so successful that it feels omnipotent. It is associated with a demonic underworld even though it will eventually be (dis)solved by a single man who often identifies himself as "ordinary" (just as the miraculous crime becomes "elementary" or "a simple affair"). According to Todorov, the miracle and the conspiracy are closely related: the traditional endings of fantastic tales either confirm the miraculous occurrences or offer a "rational solution for them." The latter, however, inevitably involves an extraordinary degree of conspiracy and is "altogether improbable; supernatural solutions would have been, on the contrary, quite probable" (Todorov 1973, 46). The solution in the fantastic tale is either a miracle or a conspiracy; in analytic detective fiction, the solution, by law, may not be miraculous, but it is an epistemic conspiracy in its claim to relate all the facts.

The consummate nature of the conspiracy is also figured through hyperboles of strength and magnitude, powers of foresight, ubiquity, and an ability to remain undetectable. These powers, however, are waning properties: the conspiracy will break down, gaps will develop, simply as a function of reading. Nevertheless, it is initially presented as an all-powerful fact: "My bald words can give no idea of the magnetic force of his talk. . . . I was proposing to match my wits against a master's—one, too, who must have at his command an organization far beyond my puny efforts. . . . It was a boy's mechanical toy arrayed against a Power-House with its shining wheels and monstrous dynamos" (PH 66). The conspiratorial agency in *The Gyrth Chalice Mystery* is "half a dozen of the wealthiest men in the world" who hire thieves to procure "that portrait of Marie Antoinette which is in the Louvre" and "the Ming vase which is in the British Museum," and "they are untouchable" (GCM 23–24).

The conspiracy enters popular reality as a "machine" (one of the basic metaphors for the analytic detective and the great threat of early science fiction), or an "organization." Jerry Palmer has identified the villain of the thriller as an organization man and the hero as an improviser: "The object of the programming that typifies the villain . . . is to initiate a series of actions that unfold with machine-like precision and predictability" (10). Bruce Merry wrote: "The agent's mission is to neutralize both the operator and the machine. . . . The writer tends to combine the moments when the enemy is neutralized and his machinery destroyed" (100).

The power of the conspiracy appears as organization or technological surplus, for example, systems of miraculous surveillance. In their ability to penetrate sealed spaces, conspiracies perform the criminal equivalent of the locked-room mystery. In Stevenson's *Dynamiter*, the woman who believes she has escaped from the Mormons finds them everywhere on her journey back to London: "In every place, on every side, the most unlikely persons, man or woman, rich or poor, became . . . spies to observe and regulate my conduct" (n.d. [1885], 49). The Mormons of *A Study in Scarlet* are also able to branch out and penetrate all the spaces of the civilized world: "The victims of persecution had now turned persecutors of the most terrible description. Not the Inquisition of Seville, nor the German Vehmgericht, nor the secret societies of Italy, were ever able to put a more formidable machinery in motion. . . . Its invisibility . . . made this organization doubly terrible. It appeared to be omniscient and omnipotent, and yet was neither seen nor heard" (SSt 62). Scudder, the noble spy of *The Thirty-Nine Steps*, takes great pains to disappear and reach London by "a mighty queer circuit": five cities and five different identities; like Huck Finn, he even fakes his own death. He believes he has erased his trail, and then a note is dropped in his box bearing "the name of the man I want least to meet on God's earth" (TS 13). In these episodes, we see from a different angle the theatricality of the crime and the mystification and exhibitionism usually attached to the detective.

The paranoid fantasy validated as a conspiracy was a common feature of suspense novels like *The Phantom Lady* that began by framing the narrator for murder, usually the murder of a wife or girlfriend. He is then forced to become a detective to save himself. In the Woolrich novel, Scott Henderson has had an argument with his wife and storms out of the apartment determined to ask the first woman he meets to share the dinner and evening at the theater he had planned. In a bar he meets a woman in a flaming orange hat, "so vivid it almost hurt the eyes. . . . Not one woman in a thousand would have braved that color." They agree to spend the evening together and then part, "No names, no addresses, no irrelevant personal references and details" (PL 7–9).

When he returns home he finds that his wife has been murdered. A police detective agrees to trace his movements on the previous night. The bartender denies seeing the woman, even claims that "there was no one else at the bar at that time *for* him to speak to"; and the bar tab only registers his drinks. Henderson accuses the bartender of lying: " 'Don't do this to me,' he protested in a choked voice." The cabdriver also insists that he was alone, and so does the headwaiter in the restaurant where they ate: "There must have been a case of mass-astigmatism all over town that night. Sometimes they've got me wondering myself if there really was such a person, or if she wasn't just a hallucination on my part, a vagary of my own feverish imagination" (PL 48, 50, 90). They are, of course, all lying, all part of a conspiracy to erase some primal event. Similar collusory fictions can be found in Christie's *Murder in the Calais Coach* or Alfred Hitchcock's *Lady Vanishes*.

The conspiracy has an uncanny ability to hide itself behind respectable surfaces. The surface of the conspiracy is convoluted, presenting both an over- and underside of ordinary and extraordinary, respectable and criminal behavior. In *The Woman in White*, observers look at a set of facts and conclude, "Why, this is lovely, perfectly fine"; while Marian is protesting "No, can't you see, they're foul, they're destroying us." Criminals are so successful in their arrangement of surfaces that they discredit reading:

> Yet I am convinced that did I attempt to establish his innocence merely by the means I have employed so far, the very people who already accept his guilt as certain would accuse me of having nothing but trivialities upon which to base my version of the affair. Further, it could be said . . . that I have read between the lines writing what was not there; that I have so ingeniously twisted the interpretations of what are, in fact, merely ordinary meaningless signs as to make them appear a grim and coherent indictment against another man; that I have seen an anarchist bomb in a schoolboy's snowball and a Bolshevik outrage in a "varsity rag." (R 183)

Mistrust, suspicion, and the anxiety of scrutiny are the affective tropes of the paranoid or conspiratorial regime instituted by detective fiction. Works set in a police state take such behavior as given, whether they are thrillers involving the penetration of Cold War Russia or China by agents, such as Alastair MacLean's *Secret Ways* or Noel Behn's *Kremlin Letter*, or works of science fiction, such as *1984* or *Brave New World:* "He had no sense of safety. . . . The one person you trusted was yourself. One friend was found with a holy medal under the shirt, another belonged to an organization with the wrong initial letters. . . . And the watcher—was he watched? He was haunted for a moment by the vision of an endless distrust" (CA 4).

In naive thrillers like John P. Marquand's *Stopover Tokyo,* the American agent is continually watched by others, and the fiction tries to reproduce the anxiety of this way of life. The agent, for example, must always be on guard against "the perennial pitfall of an unconsidered word or gesture"—he must constantly police his own perimeters. In this situation, paranoia leads to the overcharging of trifles and a compensatory stance of denaturing or toughness. Since he is being watched simply to determine whether he assumes he is being watched and is, therefore, an American agent, he must also use energy to renaturalize himself and present an easy and relaxed face to the world. He must rearrange himself as ordinary and respectable, with strain—something the enemy does with apparent ease. On the other hand, he must also conduct an anxious scrutiny of his own, since he is also watching others for the same signs of strain: "The light was on Big Ben and as far as Jack could see there was no blankness or surprise. The face was mobile. Honest pleasure rippled over it. . . . Jack had never watched or listened more carefully, but he could detect no flaw" (159–60).

In mystery and detective fiction the attitudes and behavior of the paranoid are appropriate. A character type once restricted to comedy and contempt—the distrusting misanthrope like Tobias Smollett's Matthew Bramble or the elder Martin Chuzzlewit—is recentered in this fiction as an adept and heroic man. Moreover, the novel generally dissipates suspicion: one of the functions of the traditional narrator is to identify villainy for the reader. In Gothic fiction and the sensation novel, villainy is instinctively registered by certain authenticated characters, mostly women, who are able to bore through layers of propriety and make an adequate moral identification: villainy is what makes them shudder, evil is what strikes them as evil.

The protagonists of all three forms of detective fiction are characterized by distrust. The analytic detective suspects everybody (except the Watson, who is exempt from suspicion—and who, by a law of economy, is in turn characterized by a trusting nature that leads to regular outrages), as do the hard-boiled detective and the spy: "It was very wise of you not to trust me, but very unkind," Mr. Peters tells Latimer with continental grace (CD 195); and the nameless protagonist of *The Ipcress File*, after meeting his new assistant, thinks: "It was fine; she was fine, my very first beautiful spy, always presuming, of course, that this was Jean Tonneson's card, and presuming that this was Jean Tonneson. Even if she wasn't, she was still my very first beautiful spy" (IF 84).

"The suspiciousness of the individual with a paranoid perspective on life is well known. It is seen as the paranoid look. . . . This type of patient not only mistrusts the motives of others, he actively searches for clues confirming his mistrust. . . . Every action, every unexplained statement is scrutinized closely" (Swanson 14). The rationale for such unhealthy behavior is an epistemological assumption that is continually validated, that all appearance is deceptive and all utterance is a lie; it is the affective form of the paradox of the obvious. In analytic detective fiction, it results from the design of a clever criminal, while, in the other two forms, distrust is displaced on fictions of history: the world of crime, with its burden of lies and betrayals, and the world of international intrigue.

André Gide praised the dialogue of Dashiell Hammett, where "every character is trying to deceive all the others and . . . the truth slowly becomes visible through the haze of deception" (quoted in Blair 303). Spade tells Gutman that Brigid said she didn't know what the falcon was, "but I took it for granted that she was lying." Spade is as much the subject as the object of lying. The lie is a gambit or ploy in a competitive game everyone is playing. It is the edge a player needs to win. Trust, on the other hand, has come unmoored from its ethical foundation; it is now currency, the medium of exchange in the game of securing one's position:

> "And you know I'd never have placed myself in this position if I hadn't trusted you completely."
>
> "That again!"
>
> "But you know it's so."
>
> "No, I don't know it. . . . My asking for reasons why I should trust you

brought us here. Don't let's confuse things. You don't have to trust me, anyhow, as long as you can persuade me to trust you." (MF 97, 58)

Trust is now a lexical item: Spade's inability to use the language of trust follows its exhaustion on the lips of all the others who preempt this discourse, who glibly quote the old dead language of trust: Brigid ("I've no right to ask you to trust me if I won't trust you. I do trust you, but I can't tell you. . . . I'm afraid of trusting you"), Cairo ("What am I to understand from that, Mr. Spade? I came here in good faith"), and Gutman, who preempts both trust and distrust ("We begin well, sir. . . . I distrust a man that says when. . . . Well, sir, here's to plain speaking and clear understanding. . . . I distrust a close-mouthed man. . . . I do like a man that tells you right out he's looking out for himself. . . . I don't trust a man that says he's not") (MF 31, 58, 94–95).

The protagonist of the amateur thriller is an exception to the law of mistrust but not of suspicion and scrutiny. Like the Watson (with whom I have several times identified him), he is trusting. During the course of his adventures he may, like Kenton, learn slowly and painfully to mistrust, or, like Hannay, continue to trust and somehow blunder through. Nevertheless, as soon as Hannay stumbles upon the existence of the conspiracy and begins his flight from both spies and police, he submits himself to a rhetoric of lies and a succession of false identities. Even the original transmission of the secret—as far back as we are allowed to see it—was a lie: Scudder lies to Hannay, as Hannay lies to the milkman, the innkeeper, and others. When Hannay discovers why Scudder was unable to tell him the truth, he acknowledges the righteousness of lying—because what is at stake is so big, so very important.

Roderick Alleyn thinks, "Is my mere presence in the stalls . . . a cue for homicide? May I not visit the antipodes without elderly theatre magnates having their heads bashed in by jeroboams of champagne before my very eyes?" (VM 42). He imagines it is the act of scrutiny that creates the violence. Max Latin explains that murder "follows me around and comes when I whistle—sometimes even when I don't" ("DGRN" 31); and Marlowe wisecracks, "No cause for excitement whatever. It's only Marlowe finding another body. . . . Murder-a-day Marlowe, they call him. They have the meat wagon following him around to follow up on the business he finds" (LL 94). George Latimer decides it would be fun to write a biography of the criminal Dimitrios, and in the course of pursuing his research from archive to archive brings to life both the criminal and a condition of intrigue and danger of which he is the center.

The hard-boiled and thriller protagonist is like a catalytic agent who creates effects simply by being there. Often, the detective's method is to deliberately "stir things up." In analytic detective fiction, a second murder will occur because the detective has connected someone with the original crime and was intending to question her or him. In *Re-enter Sir John*, a book in which such a circuit takes place, Sir John Suarez expresses a prosaic version of what I call *infectious reality:* "You know, if you leave a pound at compound interest for long it grows into a fortune; and if you leave a single little rolling fact alone it will collect other facts about it, and start bigger facts moving, and at last, long last, the avalanche descends" (RSJ 106). "Extraordinary," thought La Touche, "how, when you get some information about a case, more nearly always comes in" (C 298).

Infectious reality is the trope that lies behind the convention of the "plot thickening" (if you add enough heat and stir things up): "Mystery followed upon the back of mystery. In those brief days, since the advent of the fugitive Italian at Shepherd's Bush, I had become enmeshed in a veritable web of entangled events which seemed to grow more extraordinary and more inexplicable every hour" (MMM 95). Such a narrative condition is also a dynamic form of the solution, where the lines of relatedness act themselves out in time.

The paradigm of infectious reality can be found in a good deal of romance and postmodern fiction. In Thomas Pynchon's *Crying of Lot 49*, for example, the heroine Oedipa Maas stumbles upon the existence of an underground postal service of ancient authority that coincides with and rivals the daytime institution: the symbol of this conspiratorial organization is a muted post horn. Oedipa first sees it on the latrine wall of a bar, The Scope, "among lipsticked obscenities"; then doodled "with a fat felt pencil" by an employee of the Yoyodyne Corporation; on a ring cut from the finger of a dead Indian "back in the gold rush days"; and as the watermark on "a U.S. commemorative stamp, the

Pony Express issue of 1940" (34, 60, 67, 70). Entering the "infected city," Oedipa

> spent the rest of the night finding the image of the Tristero post horn. In Chinatown, in the dark windows of a herbalist, she thought she saw the sign among ideographs. . . . Later on a sidewalk she saw two of them in chalk . . . [in] a drifting dreamy crowd of delinquents in summer-weight gang jackets with the post horn stitched on in thread that looked pure silver . . . scratched on the back of a seat [of a bus] . . . tacked to the bulletin board of a laundromat. . . . Revelations . . . now seemed to come crowding in exponentially, as if the more she collected, the more would come to her, until everything she saw, smelled, dreamed, remembered, would somehow come to be woven into The Tristero." (86–90, 58)

It is as if the discovery of a secret fact calls such facts into being in epidemic proportions so that they eventually redefine the world: Hawthorne's *Scarlet Letter* is threaded through with images of the letter A— Hester Prynne's cloth letter, the coincidence between that letter and Pearl, the unseen letter that may be on the minister's breast, the celestial letter blazing in the night sky, and the letters that Dimmesdale is sure all members of the community bear secretly but proudly beneath their clothes.

This trope is the spatial equivalent of luck, another form of coincidence. The image that infects reality and generates copies of itself is yet another manifestation of the clue: "I had asked about the phrase, the 'Power-House.' Well he had come across it, in the letter of a German friend. . . . [The] correspondent said that in some documents which were seized he found constant allusion to a thing called the *Krafthaus*. . . . And this same word *Krafthaus* had appeared elsewhere—in a sonnet of a poet-anarchist who shot himself in the slums of Antwerp, in the last ravings of more than one criminal, in the extraordinary testament of Professor M___ of Jéna, who . . . took his life after writing a strange mystical message to his fellow citizens" (PH 98).

In the film *Close Encounters of the Third Kind* the blinding appearance of flying saucers seems to implant in a chosen few the image of a mountain with a squashed top, and to generate a frenzy in them to reproduce this image. The character played by Richard Dreyfuss devotes all his energy to this, driving his frightened family away from their home and bringing most of his backyard into the kitchen to give him material to shape the image. Earlier, in a partial return to sanity, he attacks a table-size sculpture of the mountain that he had been staring at all night and pulls its top off. As he stands holding it, his eyes make contact with the television screen, where the morning cartoons have been replaced by a news program, and he finds the image repeated there.

The entire conspiratorial tangle in *The Woman in White* is generated from its opening image. On his first night at Limmeridge House, Walter finds it weaving "itself into the conversation": "The turn of the expression, however, in her last question, or rather the one chance word, 'adventure,' lightly as it fell from her lips, recalled my thoughts to my meeting with the woman in white, and urged me to discover the connection which the stranger's own reference to Mrs. Fairlie informed me must once have existed between the nameless fugitive from the Asylum, and the former mistress of Limmeridge House." Marian is also infected: "Mentioned my mother's name! You interest me indescribably." Marian spends the evening rummaging through old letters and finally finds a text for the image. As the letter names "a sweet little girl about a year older than our darling Laura," Laura passes the glass doors on the balcony where she is making regular rounds of the house. In the letter the girl promises to wear white as long as she lives. Marian then asks if the strange woman was dressed all in white—"While the answer was passing my lips, Miss Fairlie glided into view on the terrace for the third time. . . . My eyes fixed upon the white gleam of her muslin gown and head-dress in the moonlight, and a sensation, for which I can find no name—a sensation that quickened my pulse and raised a fluttering at my heart—began to steal over me. . . . All my attention was concentrated on the white gleam of Miss Fairlie's muslin dress. The moonlight added to all the other uncanny urgencies in the situation." The moonlight, praised by Coleridge and Hawthorne as indispensable for the production of Romantic, or uncanny, images, presses out a reproduction of the original image in a second place: "There stood Miss Fairlie, a white figure, alone in the moonlight; in her attitude, in the turn of her head, in her complexion, in the shape of her face, the living image, at that distance and under those circumstances, of the woman in white!" Walter learns that Laura is to marry and asks who the man is. The answer—"A gentleman of large property in Hampshire"—becomes infected by Anne Catherick's earlier reference to a sinister baronet: " 'Hampshire!' Anne Catherick's native place. Again, and yet again, the woman in white. There *was* a fatality in it. 'Knight or baronet?' I asked, with an agitation that I could hide no longer. . . . I began to doubt whether my own faculties were not in danger of losing their balance. It seemed almost like a monomania to be tracing back everything strange that happened, everything unexpected that was said, always to the same hidden source and the same sinister influence" (Collins 1974, 62, 83, 85–86, 100, 105).

Plague and epidemic are obvious metaphors for infectious reality. The corpse in *A Study in Scarlet* has a copy of the *Decameron* in his pocket; Fergus O'Breen stares at a dead Mexican and bitterly says, "Another one dead. . . . Hell, I'm not a detective. I'm a carrier" (CSS 176). Greene's confidential agent also thinks of himself as a carrier of infection: "Violence went with him everywhere. Like a typhoid carrier, he was responsible for the deaths of strangers" (CA 82); he is like Conrad's Mr. Verloc who arrives in London "like the influenza" (1953, 19).

Alexander Woolcott's anecdote "The Vanishing Lady" brings together coincidence, conspiracy, and infection: an Englishwoman and her daughter are in Paris for the Exposition. The mother falls ill and a physician sends the daughter to fetch a chemical from his house. When she returns, "the very clerk who had handed her a pen to register with that morning look[s] at her without recognition and blandly ask[s]: 'Whom does Mademoiselle wish to see?' " The room she claims as hers is occupied by a long-term French resident; the physician denies ever having seen her. All behave as if she had lost her wits. Only an Englishman chooses to believe her, and there "slowly formed in his mind a suspicion that for some unimaginable reason all these people . . . were part of a plot." He is right; the doctor "had recognized the woman's ailment as a case of the black plague smuggled in from India"; it had "widened into a conspiracy . . . to suppress, at all costs . . . an obituary notice which, had it ever leaked out, would have emptied Paris overnight and spread ruin across a city that had gambled heavily on the great Exposition" (87–94).

What I have been calling the second world is easily identified in hard-boiled detective fiction; it is the underworld into which the quest hero must descend. It is also a paradigm for the lost past; Odysseus encounters his mother and Aeneas his father in that place. "Away behind all the governments and the armies there was a big subterranean movement going on. . . . [Scudder] had come upon it by accident; it fascinated him; he went further; and then got caught" (TS 9); Richard Hannay is qualified for his heroic task of exposing the underworld by his professional credentials as a mining engineer. The rogue male literally goes underground and formalizes it by calling his double, the rogue cat that "could make himself appear the very spirit of hatred and malignity," Asdmodeus (RM 77). The conspiracy that Bond opposes in his early adventures is called SPECTRE.

Milton's underworld is the world of "Old Night," and in detective fiction it is also as a dark or nighttime world that this place exists in opposition to the ordinary world. It is that other world, with its own special uses of the city, that emerges from the cracks and crevices as twilight deepens and respectable citizens go into hiding. More fancifully, it is the world that rises to the top as the earth completes its turn, as though this place were literally the underworld during the day. Such an opposition provides the structure for a work like *Henry IV, Part 1,* which alternates between day and night, court and tavern—episodes in the lives of apparently responsible aristocrats and their criminal counterparts. The plot of Shakespeare's underworld is a robbery and a double cross.

The fantastic presence of such a place lying unknown in the heart of the city and emerging at night or during the holiday is featured in the opening of Hugo's *Hunchback of Notre Dame:* "a magic circle, in which the officers of the Châtelet . . . when they ventured thither, disappeared in morsels—the city of thieves—a hideous wen on the face of Paris—a sink from whence escaped . . . that stream of vice, mendacity, and vagrancy which ever flows through the streets of a capital. . . . The limits of the different races and species seemed to be effaced in this commonwealth as in a pandemonium. . . . It was like a new world, unknown, unheard of, deformed, creeping, swarming, fantastic" (78–79).

Chandler's *Farewell, My Lovely* begins with a racist pun on the nighttime world: the book opens in a black saloon in a black neighborhood. Marlowe's path in this story is upward into a world of light—"a special brand of sunshine, very quiet, put up in noise-proof containers just for the upper classes"—blondness and affluence, but at every level he discovers forms of "blackness" just below the surface. His third stop is at Mrs. Florian's, whose face is "gray and puffy," who had "weedy hair of that vague color which is neither brown nor blond, that hasn't enough life in it to be ginger, and isn't clean enough to be gray." The circuit of his travels is measured by Velma's transformation from a brunette into a "ravishing blond" (FML 101, 20, 78). *The Confidential Agent* also begins in the world of the dead, with a protagonist who journeys to England to try to persuade the government to reopen its dead pits, to start the coal moving again. And crime itself, generally, is a dark business: "It was soothing to catch even that passing glimpse of a tranquil English home in the midst of the wild, dark business which had absorbed us" (SF 116).

The analytic detective is rarely seen wandering through the underworld, although Dupin goes out only at night and Holmes, the major exception, sometimes wanders in disguise through a squalid criminal London. The hard-boiled detective lives in that world and either, like Spade, controls it or, like Marlowe and Archer, drifts through it while the amateur thriller hero suddenly discovers it one day with a shock, and afterward, can never return to ordinary reality. *The Maltese Falcon* is thoroughly informed with the meanings of the underworld, beginning on the first page where Spade is identified as a "blond Satan." There is no context for such a radical identification unless we read Spade as master of the underworld, manipulating his community of thieves, playing them off against one another, and finally betraying them all. The hard-boiled detective as Satan, however, is not uncommon; and in the anthology *Hard-Boiled Dicks* there are also the examples of Satan Hall and Steve Midnight. Like the Christian devil, Spade is a consummate liar. He is regularly associated with fire: and, while smoking was a stock characteristic of the hard-boiled detective, it is extravagantly featured in *The Maltese Falcon*, for example: "Spade put the cigarette in his mouth, set fire to it, and laughed smoke out" (MF 20).

A conventional method of detectives and spies consists of exploding stable situations. The Op practices it: "Plans are all right sometimes. . . . And sometimes just stirring things up is all right—if you're tough enough to survive, and keep your eyes open so you'll see what you want when it comes to the top" (RH 87); so does Spade: "My way of learning is to heave a wild and unpredictable monkey-wrench into the machinery. It's all right with me, if you're sure none of the flying pieces will hurt you" (MF 77); and Inspector Cramer says to Nero Wolfe: "When I heard you were up there today . . . I thought to myself, now the fur's going to fly" (RBx 44). There are other such strategies, mostly associated with heat, for example, putting the heat on—"the pot's beginning to boil," Grave Digger Jones says to his partner, and Coffin Ed Jackson replies, "All I hope is that we don't overcook it" (CK 107)—or grilling people.

This is the strategy of another kind of devil, the protagonists of Mark Twain's late, dark works such as "The Man That Corrupted Hadleyburg," and, earlier, the lineage of southwestern humor that features an almost literal Satan, Sut Lovingood. Sut's adventures consist of repeated moments of stirring or blowing things up, moments of extravagant violence aimed at authority figures like preachers. In Twain, the stirring is directed toward the ordinary in its sanctified form of respectability: "Hadleyburg was the most honest and upright town in all the region round about it. It had kept that reputation unsmirched during three generations, and was prouder of it than of any other of its possessions." Curiously, the mysterious stranger in this tale is associated with the analytic detective—he "looked like an amateur detective gotten up as an impossible English earl"—and his intention is one of criminalizing: "My idea was to make liars and thieves of nearly half a hundred smirchless men and women who had never in their lives uttered a lie or stolen a penny" (Twain 1962, 245, 280, 278).

Many critics have regarded hard-boiled detective fiction as a secularized version of a knightly quest (see Auden 403; Symons 1973, 79,

143). Although this line of allusion is written into these works—in the opening of *The Big Sleep*, Marlowe wearily acknowledges an obligation to substitute himself for a knight in a tapestry—as interpretation it feels too heavy and academic, as if it were itself in armor. Nevertheless, the conjunction of mystery fiction with a tradition stretching back to twelfth-century romance, the sequence provided by Jessie Weston in her book *From Ritual to Romance*, does provide another name for the second world, the *wasteland*. This image is available as a context for the squalid urban settings, but, more pertinently, it is available as a container for the dirt and garbage with which this fiction is filled.

The second world of detective fiction is a dirty or grubby world, the world from which the dirty clues of analytic detective fiction have been displaced: the clue is the seepage. Eric Ambler entitled one of his thrillers *A Dirty Story*, and when Greene's confidential agent tells the story of his adventures to a dead-faced audience, he feels "as if he had told a dirty story in unsuitable company" (CA 75). Quiller thinks, "Here you are again in the thick of a job. . . . It gets in the hair and the eyes and the mouth and you never feel really clean" (QM 124); and McCorkle in *The Cold War Swap* is told, "You're messing around in a potful of crap that's going to spill all over you" (CWS 61). Jules Amthor defines hard-boiled detective fiction when he calls Marlowe a "dirty little man in a dirty little world" (FML 131). Dapper, pink-cheeked Dick Powell, who plays Marlowe in *Murder, My Sweet*, looks too clean for the role, but Elliott Gould in *The Long Goodbye* looks just right: a disheveled man, he produces disorder around him. Hard-boiled detectives wear battered hats and suits that look as if they had been slept in; Bogart's face also looks as if it had been slept in.

The underworld as wasteland is a place of refuse; it is, by virtue of an available pun, a world of shit: Pynchon's underground postal system is named WASTE, and it uses old green trash cans as drops—"On the swinging part were hand-painted the initials W.A.S.T.E. She had to look closely to see the periods" (96). Balzac described the detective as one "who squats in our social sewers" (4), and Hugo wrote that the sewer was "the conscience of the town where all things converge and close. There is darkness here, but no secrets. . . . Every foulness of civilization, fallen into disuse, sinks into the ditch of truth" (Hugo quoted in Stallybrass and White 141). The action of romance often enters those sewers literally; for example, in Hugo's *Les Miserables*, Greene's *The Third Man*, or Gaston Leroux's *Mystery of the Yellow Room:* "At the time of the affair of the woman cut in pieces in the Rue Oberskampf . . . [Rouletabille] had taken to one of the editors of the 'Epoque' . . . the left foot, which was missing from the basket in which the gruesome remains were discovered. For this left foot the police had been vainly searching for a week, and young Rouletabille had found it in a drain where nobody had thought of looking for it. To do that he had dressed himself as an extra sewer-man, one of a number engaged by the administration of the city of Paris" (MYR 8).

The setting of *Dr. No* is a mountain of guano: "Bond stood and gazed at the distant glittering mountain of bird dung. So this was the kingdom of Dr. No! Bond thought he had never seen a more godforsaken landscape in his life." Throughout the adventure, there is a great stress on cleanliness and hygienic technology: "There was everything in the bathroom—Floris Lime bath essence for men and Guerlain bathcubes for women. . . . In a medicine cupboard behind the mirror over the washbasin were toothbrushes and toothpaste, Steradent toothpicks, Rose mouthwash, dental floss, Aspirin and Milk of Magnesia" (DN 83, 119). Bond finally explodes the mountain and Dr. No is buried in it. Bond also saves London from the great rocket of Sir Hugo Drax [*drek*] in *Moonraker*. In *Thunderball*, Blofeld "makes Bond sit on top of a gigantic pipe up which a geyser of boiling mud will shortly come erupting: 'Nanny tells me you haven't been at all regular with your motions lately, James. Permit me to inform you that I propose to deal with the matter drastically and at once' " (Amis 69).

A compelling reading of *The Maltese Falcon* reflects the scatological dimensions of mystery fiction. In this reading, the black bird can be identified through its rhyme, as a black turd—what the French criminologist, Reiss of Lyons, called the "criminal's *carte de visite odorante*" (Reik 1945, 76; Freud 1953 [1908a], 49). In the allegory of the body that is suggested, the magus's name becomes readable as gut-man— that urbane, presumably homosexual fat man who has devoted his life to gaining possession of the bird. The falcon is of "extreme," "immeasurable" value, although, when Spade asks Brigid what "makes it important" she says she doesn't know, they would never tell her. It was originally a tribute to the "father," Emperor Charles V, and, in the film, it comes to Spade as a dying gift from the director's father, Walter Huston. Its blackness—"black as coal and shiny"—is the other side of gold, and, in Perrault's fairy tales and the mythology of modern capitalism, the other side of gold is shit. The bird is a fabulous object that goes underground for years, surfacing from time to time in connection with shady individuals. It is repressed in history as it is repressed in narrative: "Everything happened the way it did happen, but without this dingus"—(feces also, according to a familiar Freudian equation, stand for a dingus or penis). In its disguised and marginalized career, the statuette is treated with disgust—when Effie first sees it, she makes a horrified face and screams—and it is twice identified with smell: "No thickness of enamel could conceal value from his eyes and nose"; and Gutman "gets wind of" the falcon. The image of the falcon generates uncontrollable excitement, but it is always fake, always black, however deeply you chip into it (MF 110, 78, 142, 143, 112).

My final paradigm for the second world of mystery and detective fiction is the *frontier* or *colony*. This is the formula of Conan Doyle's first Holmes novel, where the story of the crime is set not merely in America, but beyond the American frontier in the Mormon colony of Utah. The crime is a strong impulsive movement that is generated in an appropriately lawless setting, the "wilds" of America; and it moves, almost by magnetic attraction, back to the metropolis, where it takes a shocking form. Conan Doyle regularly associates victims or criminals with the frontier or colony (America, South America, India, Australia); mystery and detective fiction is always engaged in a veiled form of colonial discourse.

As it is worked through the imperial imagination, the frontier is also a symbol for the lost past. The scarlet of Conan Doyle's title may or may not be an allusion to the tangled skein, the final image of Sir James Fraser's *Golden Bough*, but the desire that teases those twelve volumes into existence is the delivery to the Victorian gentleman anthropologist of a stunning clue from the past. At the opening of *The Golden Bough*, Fraser proposes that we accompany him on a walking trip into the past—a safe and glorious past, one that supports an exalted sense of the accomplishments of his civilization. He proposes that we visit Augustan Rome and bask in the sunlight of its high culture. A few days later, however, we "gentle and pious pilgrims" journey sixteen miles southeast of Rome to visit a grove consecrated to Diana, and at the grove we catch for a moment a glimpse of a "stern and sinister figure" that arrests and paralyzes us: "the sight of him might well seem to darken the fair landscape, as when a cloud suddenly blots out the sun on a fair day." This grim figure prowls with a drawn sword in hand peering warily about him; he is "a priest and a murderer and the man for whom he looked was sooner or later to murder him" (1–2).

Can this be an image of ourselves? Sixteen miles of continuous space separate Rome from the grove at Nemi, but this conjunction is impossible. Rome is sunlight and high civilization; the grove is darkness, tangle, savagery, and murder. Fraser has had an experience of radical absurdity; he has witnessed a "criminal fact," a clue: the "strange rule of this priesthood has no parallel in classical antiquity and cannot be explained from it," and yet it is a part of classical antiquity. Back in England, Fraser must prepare for a second journey that will not be a vacation; he will fictionalize it as a descent into the underworld to find the impossible connection between the ritual at Nemi and the daylight lineage that justifies him and his civilization (2). It is also the pressure of this darkness in the present—Malthus's urban poor—that necessitates his gentlemanly quest.

Mystery and detective fiction also dramatizes the trauma of a breach with the past. In one standard version of this story—imperialist fictions like *King Solomon's Mines, The Time Machine*, Jack London's *Before Adam* or *The Lost World*, the hero moves from the center to the peripheries, from the present to the past, in order to meet himself in an earlier purer or debased form: Lew Archer, in a moment of despair, thinks of himself as "a slightly earthbound Tarzan in a slightly paranoid jungle. Landscape with figure of a hairless ape" (D 168). E. Phillips Oppenheim's *Great Impersonation* begins in the African bush, where the protagonist meets his degenerate double (they also turn out to be public school pals) who is then, in a manner of speaking, taken back to London and redeemed as an exemplary hero of civilization. In *A Study in Scarlet*, the criminal and the detective, Jefferson Hope and Sherlock Holmes, are old and new versions of the valorous individual.

The other form of the imperialist/anthropological fiction that detective stories play with moves in the opposite direction: it dramatizes an invasion of the center by the margins, an invasion from the past or the frontier. This is the form of much Edwardian horror fiction, which is almost exclusively devoted to the reemergence of the past in the present; for example, Algernon Blackwood's "Willows," E. M. Forster's "Pan," and Oliver Onions's "Beckoning Fair One." The return is dramatized as an infection in works such as W. W. Jacobs's "Monkey's Paw," London's "Scarlet Plague," and the Yellow Peril fiction of the turn of the century. The connection between repression and plague occurs early in Western literature, in Sophocles' *Oedipus Rex*, where Apollo sends a plague to punish the Thebans for hiding a criminal in the city. In the works that generate detective fiction—*The Moonstone, A Study in Scarlet, The Sign of Four*—a secret belonging to an older, "darker" civilization has been brought into the light of the present, where it begins to breed infection and work a curse that leads to murder.

The frontiers are also a dirty world, a world of garbage and ordure. This can take the form of a racist "native" fiction in works like John Buchan's *Prester John* or *The Sign of Four* (where a great mutiny breaks out in a city that is ordinarily "swarming with fanatics and fierce devil-worshippers," and "two hundred thousand black devils [were] let loose, and the country was a perfect hell" [SF 146, 145]). For Claude Lévi-Strauss, the frontiers are dirty because of technological seepage: "The order and harmony of the Western world . . . demand the elimination of a prodigious mass of noxious by-products which now contaminate the globe. The first thing we see as we travel round the world is our own filth, thrown into the face of mankind" (43).

If the inaugural act and meaning of detective fiction is repression, it should come as no surprise. That term has been a discursive silent partner of almost all the conventional tropes that this book has turned to. In the space between *A Study in Scarlet* and *The Sign of Four*, Conan Doyle represses the context and the content of the genre-to-be in order to bring it into being. Conan Doyle makes two mistakes in his first novel: he allows the criminal to be glimpsed as a hero, and he allows the lost past its own place. By the time of his second book, Hope has shrunk into Small, distorted into an ugly, wizened man, and the past history of the community, the history of the crime, has been folded, in a shrunken form, in quotation marks, into the end of the form.

Holmes tells us indirectly in the opening of *The Sign of Four* that the center should be suppressed, not because it is digressive but because it is passionate. Holmes has just finished reading *A Study in Scarlet*, and *The Sign of Four* begins with his criticism of it, his suggestions for revision. He chides Watson for investing the case with romanticism. When Watson answers that the romance was there, Holmes replies that some facts "should be suppressed." Holmes tells Watson that what he did was equivalent to working a love story or an elopement into the fifth proposition of Euclid. This is an allusion to "The Love of the Triangles," a contemptuous rewriting of Erasmus Darwin's "Love of the Tigers." Erasmus is not only the grandfather of Charles, but a writer who advanced a theory of evolution in his own name. And out of this intricate gyre comes a body of fiction that has no antecedents and can only fulfill its function by refusing to evolve.

NOTES

PREFACE

1 Other exemplary works are "Language of Detective Fiction: Fiction of Detective Language," an essay by David A. Miller, and "Clues" by Franco Moretti, a chapter from his book *Signs Taken for Wonders*.

2 Only two of my sample were written in the 1970s; nine were written in the 1960s.

CHAPTER 1: Preliminaries

1 Traditional narrative *is* sexual decency, according to Frank Kermode, for whom both are regulated by the same law of "propriety" (1981, 83). Ironically, the absence of character in the form is what a high modernist like Gertrude Stein applauds: "It is very curious, but the detective story which is as you might say the only really modern novel form that has come into existence gets rid of human nature by having the man dead to begin with; the hero is dead to begin with and so you have so to speak got rid of the event before the book begins" (87–88).

2 Franco Moretti turns this issue around and attaches the throwaway function to contemporary literature: "Watson's function is quantitative in a more profound way: he *accumulates useless details*. His descriptions furnish all—except the essential. He enters a room (in "The Speckled Band") and for two pages describes its furnishings: but he does not even mention the false bell-pull which is the only clue. Thus, through the figure of Watson, detective fiction attacks naturalism" (147).

3 The determinants of detective fiction treated in this section do not distinguish popular from art fiction for long, but they should be put in place nonetheless. So Gerard Genette claims that we read all fiction according to the game of even and odd (77); and Frank Kermode claims that all fiction contains throwaway mass, "disposable noise" (1981, 83).

4 The same charge has been traditionally leveled at the reading of novels: "It may be safely assumed that most of the novel-reading which people fancy an intellectual pastime is the emptiest dissipation,

hardly more related to thought . . . than opium-eating; in either case the brain is drugged, and left weaker and crazier for the debauch" (Howells 94).

5   Addictive reading patterns first belong to adolescence. Havelock Ellis describes his reading of *Boys of England,* which held him in a "kind of fever . . . it was an excitement which overwhelmed all ordinary considerations. My mother forbade me to read these things, but, though I usually obeyed her, in this matter I was disobedient without compunction. But the fever subsided as suddenly as it arose . . . and left not a trace behind. It is an experience which enables me to realize how helpless we are in this matter. If this is the literature a boy needs, nothing will keep him away from it." And the testimony of Robert Louis Stevenson, an addict of "penny dreadfuls" in his youth, reflects on the topic of writing in a particularly graphic metaphor: "Eloquence and thought, character and conversation, were but obstacles to brush aside as we dug blithely after a certain kind of incident, like a pig for truffles" (Ellis and Stevenson quoted in Turner 75–76, 12).

6   See also Chandler 1944, 391; De Voto 36; Wright 47.

CHAPTER 2: Borderlines and Boundaries

1   One of the common explanations for the emergence of detective fiction is the development of the urban police force: "Until there was a well-organized police, until the science of detection had been systematized, until, finally, murder . . . had become the rare and shocking thing it is today, anything in the nature of a detective story as we understand it is impossible" (Hare 59; see also Kayman 61–80). In repudiation of this sociological thesis, Richard Alewyn points out that representatives of the agencies in question are amply present in detective fiction—as outsiders and blunderers (66–67).

2   *Newsweek,* 22 March 1971, 108.

3   Knight "points out that though Chandler may seem to be a social realist, the 'outer' plot concerned with corrupt links between respectable and criminal worlds always gives way (often via a moment when the main gangster turns out to be a kind of gentleman) to an 'inner' purely private plot where a woman threatens Marlowe and then kills or turns out to have killed the male *alter ego* he is seeking" (76).

4   See the literature surveyed by Richard Altick and Joel Black. On the

other hand, these borders are not logical but conventional, and there is nothing to present a hybrid form emerging, like Gardner's Perry Mason stories.

5   Dorothy Sayers and Margery Allingham add their voices to this ghoulish chorus: the reader "looks upon death and mutilation with a dispassionate eye" (Sayers 1929b, 22); and detective fiction is "almost entirely cerebral, since it aims to provide a means of escape for those who do not wish, for some excellent private reasons, to take their emotions for a ride with the novelist. . . . Death is merely a cipher for the most important happening" (Allingham 31).

6   Other boundary fictions can be provided for the historical emergence of detective literature, for example, that of a prior history of the novel dominated by crime: "The nineteenth century witnesses a decisive transformation: the replacement of the (reformed) criminal as the narrative authority by the detective—the substitution, in other words, of the first-person confession by the master's solution" (Kayman 60).

7   According to Antonini, the Bond villains inhabit hermetically sealed boxes as well (117–18).

CHAPTER 3: The Constant Character

1   The thriller also stresses character as mechanism: "Bond is a 'cybernetic' hero as well as a behaviorist; he reacts to stimuli selecting precisely those that are useful from those that are useless or harmful; he can estimate, evaluate, measure any circumstances, any action, with the accuracy of an electronic computer" (Antonini 105). The image of the computer is sharper in Adam Hall's *Warsaw Document*, where the language slides into science-fiction compounds: "stay on brain-think because there's a lot coming up"; "a fair percentage of the place-feel had reached the brain through the feet"; "purpose-tremor was setting up in the muscles, normal but hazardous" (148, 183–84, 179).

2   Todorov saw the detective's immunity as a rule of the genre (1977, 44), whereas Freud wrote that "through this revealing characteristic of invulnerability, we can immediately recognize His Majesty the Ego, the hero alike of every day-dream and of every story" (1953 [1908b], 150).

CHAPTER 5: The Pleasures of Being Merely Male

1   A feature of masochism that Reik was tempted to list as a fourth primary characteristic is the "provocative factor": "the provocation easily assumes the form of teasing, of jeering, or quarreling or tormenting. . . . This behavior can progress from slight irony to impudent challenge of the object, from apparently harmless teasing to rude abuse" (1957, 248–50). This is a sadistic detour, where the masochist is forced to act like his supposed opposite in order to gain passive satisfaction.

2   The narrow escape of King Arthur from hanging in Twain's novel, by the way, is a version of the "Aztec cycle" of masochistic fantasy as recorded by Reik (1957, 225).

3   Toward the end of the book, the hero admits that he had intended to shoot and then rings in a story of a true love previously tortured and executed by this secret service, but this does not inform the novel.

4   Actually masochism and sadism are not related as cover and depth, appearance and reality, but rather as cover and cover. They dance to the rhythms of a form of convolution that appeared early in detective fiction, as the game of "even and odd" in Poe's "Purloined Letter." Which is the disguise, Sir Percy Blakeney or the Scarlet Pimpernel? The work tells us that the real self is the representation most obviously in disguise: the Pimpernel, Zorro, Superman, and Batman, characters who look as if they have just come from a masquerade or staged performance.

5   The masochist "shows a tenacity, and adhesion, which is characteristic of no other perversion" (Reik 1957, 255). A similar hero appears two years later in Kingsley's *Water-Babies:* "But Tom was always a brave, determined little English bull-dog, who never knew when he was beaten" (85).

6   The heroes of Len Deighton's hard-boiled spy thrillers, however, are definitely not public school boys, so definitely not that his work is informed by this tension. Merry writes that this type of thriller "places a particular emphasis on the non-privileged boy's desire to make good in an expensive environment. We are back to the old state school vs. public school dichotomy which has loomed so large in post-war British writing. More often than not, the agent is a grammar school man, while his boss in London comes from the upper crust" (60). Nevertheless the underlying ethos is unchanged.

CHAPTER 6: The Texture of Femininity

1   The pal and the bitch are opposite types, however. This is made clearer
in *Murder, My Sweet,* the film by Edward Dmytryk made from *Farewell, My Lovely.* There Anne Riordan is Velma's stepdaughter, and
"Marlowe consistently repels Mrs. Grayle's advances and seeks the
domestic shelter of Anne's maternal affection" (Buchsbaum 44–45).

CHAPTER 7: The Crime, the Criminal, the Community

1   I suggested earlier that the amateur thriller protagonist resembled
Watson without Holmes. I now identify one type of thriller criminal,
the spy-master, as the missing Holmes, manipulating and torturing
his old friend just as he used to tease and insult him in their rooms in
Baker Street.

CHAPTER 8: Detective Solutions and Their Fictions

1   By way of contrast, heroes of Western and jungle fiction possess an
instinctive map of their unmapped territories. The paradigm for these
forms can be found in *Moby-Dick:* "Now, to any one not fully acquainted with the ways of the leviathans, it might seem an absurdly
hopeless task thus to seek out one solitary creature in the unhooped
oceans of this planet. But not so did it seem to Ahab, who knew the
sets of all tides and currents . . . could arrive at reasonable surmises,
almost approaching to certainties, concerning the timeliest day to be
upon this or that ground in search of his prey" (Melville 1964, 267).

2   For the relationship between the psychoanalyst and the detective, see
Stanley Hyman, Carlo Ginzburg, and Peter Brooks: "It is in fact the
Wolfman himself . . . who tells us what we might have suspected all
along: that Freud was a faithful reader of Sherlock Holmes, and fully
aware of the analogies between psychoanalytic investigation and detective work. . . . In his earliest case histories . . . he almost explicitly
assumes the posture of the detective, pressing for the symptomatic
clues, reaching back to uncover a moment of trauma, a scene of crime
which makes sense of all subsequent events" (Brooks 74).

3   Martin Priestman traces this figure through Wilde's *Picture of Dorian
Gray* and Gaboriau's *Widow Lerouge* (144).

4   In an earlier piece, "The Ghostly Rental," the resemblance to detec-

tion is more pointed: "When I asked her how she had acquired her learning, she said simply—'Oh, I observe!' 'Observe closely enough,' she once said, 'and it doesn't matter where you are. . . . Shut me up in a dark closet and I will observe after a while, that some places in it are darker than others. After that (give me time) and I will tell you what the President of the United States is going to have for dinner' " (James 1963, 84–85).

5   "The solution must account for everything" (Hare 60). The term *account*, as either a verb or noun, is yet another synonym for narrative although it is frequently used in opposition to narrative to refer to everything that is not narrative—all the talk, explanation, and analysis that a narrator claims is necessary because of gaps in the narrative. It is an extremely frequent word in Henry Fielding's *Tom Jones*, for example: "To account in some measure for this to the reader, I think proper to inform him"; "for which, as it renders him liable to the charge of stupidity, or at least of want of taste, we shall now proceed to account"; "before we proceed any farther in our history, it may be proper to look a little back, in order to account for the extraordinary appearance of Sophia and her father at the inn"; and "before we attend him to this intended interview with the lady, we think proper to account for both the preceding notes" (58, 125, 475, 635). "Surely an unaccountable sort of expedition!" is the refrain that runs through Dickens's account of Durdles and Jasper's nocturnal foray into the Cloisterham Crypt in a "detective" novel that does not close and needs to be resolved at various intervals (1961 [1870], 131).

CHAPTER 9: Methodological Items

1   This, according to Alethea Hayter, is also the method of addicts. Speaking of Baudelaire, she writes that "both heroin and opium . . . rivetted the attention inescapably on trivial and minute details" (152).

2   The other side of this paradigm shift has been advanced as the origin of detective fiction as well: Gillian Beer suggests that "the short span of time previously allowed to events has implied, said Lyell, a narrative of catastrophe and revolution, of upheaval and reversal, a magical or nightmare romance. . . . Here we have possible incentives within the culture for the rise of the detective story, with its emphasis on false clues, determined reading, recuperable losses, the deciphering

of traces: a way of controlling the hermeneutic plethora, the impo-
sition of a certain formal coherence on a virtual chaos of 'events'"
(71, 75).

CHAPTER 10: Methodological Moves

1   See also Hawthorne's *Marble Faun:* "And the sculptor here noted
a circumstance, which, according to the interpretation he might put
upon it, was either too trivial to be mentioned, or else so mysteriously
significant that he found it difficult to believe his eyes" (1968, 409).

BIBLIOGRAPHY

PRIMARY WORKS

AA   G. K. Chesterton. 1958 [1935]. *The Amazing Adventures of Father Brown.* New York: Dell.

ABC   Agatha Christie. 1948 [1936]. *The ABC Murders.* Harmondsworth, Middlesex: Penguin.

AJ   Samuel Hopkins Adams. 1911. *Average Jones.* New York: Grosset & Dunlap.

ASH   Sir Arthur Conan Doyle. [1891]. *The Adventures of Sherlock Holmes.* In CSH, 159–332.

"BBM"   Israel Zangwill. 1978 [1891]. "The Big Bow Mystery." In *Three Victorian Detective Novels.* New York: Dover, 199–302.

BC   Ross Macdonald. 1956. *The Barbarous Coast.* New York: Knopf.

BD   Eric Ambler. 1945 [1939]. *Background to Danger.* In *Double Decker.* New York: World, 1–178.

BDT   R. Austin Freeman. 1973 [1909–12]. *The Best Dr. Thorndyke Detective Stories.* New York: Dover.

BMC   S. S. Van Dine. 1926 [1925]. *The Benson Murder Case.* New York: A. L. Burt.

BMD   Nicholas Blake. 1938. *The Beast Must Die.* New York: Harper & Brothers.

BS   Raymond Chandler. 1957 [1939]. *The Big Sleep.* In *A Treasury of Great Mysteries.* Vol. 2, 4–130. Ed. Howard Haycraft and John Beecroft. New York: Simon & Schuster.

BTM   Jacques Futrelle. 1973 [1905–7]. *Best "Thinking Machine" Detective Stories.* New York: Dover.

C   Freeman Wills Crofts. 1977 [1920]. *The Cask.* New York: Dover.

"C"   T. S. Stribling. 1941. "The Cablegram." *EQMM,* Fall, 42–57.

CA   Graham Greene. 1943 [1939]. *The Confidential Agent.* In *3 by Graham Greene.* New York: Viking, 1–170.

CBSH   Sir Arthur Conan Doyle. [1927]. *The Casebook of Sherlock Holmes.* In CSH, 983–1122.

CC   *Cosmopolitan Crimes.* 1972. Ed. Hugh Greene. Harmondsworth, Middlesex: Penguin.

CD   Eric Ambler. 1972 [1937]. *A Coffin for Dimitrios.* New York: Bantam.

CGF William Hope Hodgson. 1973 [1910]. *Carnacki the Ghost Finder.* London: Granada.

CK Chester Himes. 1973 [1959]. *The Crazy Kill.* Chatham, N.J.: Chatham Bookseller.

CM *Crime on Her Mind.* 1977. Ed. Michelle B. Slung. Harmondsworth, Middlesex: Penguin.

CO Dashiell Hammett. 1975 [1924–30]. *The Continental Op.* London: Macmillan.

CP Earl Derr Biggers. 1974 [1926]. *The Chinese Parrot.* New York: Bantam.

CQ Michael Gilbert. 1947. *Close Quarters.* London: Hodder & Stoughton.

CR Ian Fleming. 1971 [1953]. *Casino Royale.* New York: Bantam.

CSH Sir Arthur Conan Doyle. 1930. *The Complete Sherlock Holmes.* Garden City, N.Y.: Doubleday.

CSS Anthony Boucher. 1942. *The Case of the Seven Sneezes.* New York: Dell.

CVC Erle Stanley Gardner. 1940 [1933]. *The Case of the Velvet Claws.* New York: Pocket.

CWS Ross Thomas. 1966. *The Cold War Swap.* New York: Avon.

D Ross Macdonald. 1959 [1958]. *The Doomsters.* New York: Bantam.

"D" Eugène Sue. "The Detective." In WG, 438–50.

DC Dick Francis. 1962. *Dead Cert.* New York: Avon.

"DGRN" Norbert Davis. [1941]. "Don't Give Your Right Name." In HD, 1–41.

DI Peter Cheyney. 1957. *Dark Interlude.* London: Pan.

DN Ian Fleming. 1959 [1958]. *Doctor No.* New York: Signet.

DP T. H. White. 1978 [1932]. *Darkness at Pemberley.* New York: Dover.

"EMS" Grant Allen. [1897]. "The Episode of the Mexican Seer." In CC, 19–35.

ES Eric Ambler. 1953 [1952]. *Epitaph for a Spy.* New York: Bantam.

ESJ Clemence Dane and Helen Simpson. 1928. *Enter Sir John.* New York: Cosmopolitan.

FB Len Deighton. 1965. *A Funeral in Berlin.* New York: Putnam.

FD Ben Hecht. 1923. *The Florentine Dagger.* New York: Boni & Liveright.

FML Raymond Chandler. 1971 [1940]. *Farewell, My Lovely.* New York: Ballantine.

"FP"   Dashiell Hammett. 1949 [1929]. "Fly Paper." In CO, 5–35. New York: Jonathan Press.

FPM   Ellery Queen. 1969 [1930]. *The French Powder Mystery*. New York: Signet.

FSCC   *Famous Stories of Code and Cipher*. 1965. Ed. Raymond T. Bond. New York: Collier.

FSO   Leslie Charteris. 1939 [1930–39]. *The First Saint Omnibus*. Garden City, N.Y.: Sun Dial.

FT   Desmond Bagley. 1971. *The Freedom Trap*. London: Fontana.

"FW"   Ross Macdonald. [1946]. "Find the Woman." In Allen and Chako, 226–44.

GC   Ross Macdonald. 1960 [1959]. *The Galton Case*. New York: Bantam.

"GC"   Melville Davisson Post. [1929]. "The Great Cipher." In FSCC, 57–74.

GCM   Margery Allingham. 1963 [1931]. *The Gyrth Chalice Mystery*. New York: McFadden.

GI   E. Phillips Oppenheim. 1920. *The Great Impersonation*. New York: A. L. Burt.

GK   Dashiell Hammett. 1972 [1931]. *The Glass Key*. New York: Vintage.

GN   Dorothy L. Sayers. 1968 [1935]. *Gaudy Night*. New York: Avon.

"GS"   Frank L. Packard. [1917]. "The Gray Seal." In WG, 251–65.

GSM   Gypsy Rose Lee. 1941. *The G-String Murders*. New York: Simon & Schuster.

HB   Sir Arthur Conan Doyle. [1902]. *The Hound of the Baskervilles*. In CSH, 667–766.

HD   *The Hardboiled Dicks*. 1967. Ed. Ron Goulart. New York: Pocket.

HLB   Sir Arthur Conan Doyle. [1917]. *His Last Bow*. In CSH, 869–980.

HN   John Dickson Carr. 1963 [1933]. *Hag's Nook*. New York: Collier.

HR   Michael Innes. 1961 [1949]. *Hamlet, Revenge!* Harmondsworth, Middlesex: Penguin.

HT   Nicholas Blake. 1964 [1949]. *Head of a Traveler*. New York: Berkeley.

HW   Raymond Chandler. 1951 [1943]. *The High Window*. Harmondsworth, Middlesex: Penguin.

IF   Len Deighton. 1968 [1962]. *The Ipcress File*. Greenwich, Conn.: Fawcett.

IFB G. K. Chesterton. 1975 [1911]. *The Innocence of Father Brown.* New York: Penguin.

IJ Mickey Spillane. 1964 [1947]. *I, the Jury.* New York: Signet.

JJ Anthony Berkeley. 1941 [1933]. *Jumping Jenny.* Harmondsworth, Middlesex: Penguin.

LG Raymond Chandler. 1971 [1953]. *The Long Goodbye.* New York: Ballantine.

LGW John le Carré. 1965. *The Looking Glass War.* London: Heinemann.

"LH" Maurice Leblanc. [1922]. "The Lady with the Hatchet." In WG, 225–39.

LL Raymond Chandler. 1976 [1943]. *The Lady in the Lake.* New York: Vintage.

LS Raymond Chandler. 1950 [1949]. *Marlowe [The Little Sister].* New York: Pocket.

LW Louis Joseph Vance. 1914. *The Lone Wolf.* New York: A. L. Burt.

"MA" E. C. Bentley. "The Ministering Angel." In FSCC, 75–91.

MAS Agatha Christie. 1961 [1921]. *The Mysterious Affair at Styles.* New York: Bantam.

MB Lynn Brock. 1930. *Murder on the Bridge.* London: Crime Club.

MCC Agatha Christie. [1933]. *Murder in the Calais Coach.* In *A Treasury of Great Mysteries*, Vol. 1, 9–146. Ed. Howard Haycraft and John Beecroft. New York: Simon & Schuster.

MCH G. D. H. Cole and Margaret Cole. 1927. *The Murder at Crome House.* Harmondsworth, Middlesex: Penguin.

"MDUR" Baroness Orczy. [1901]. "The Mysterious Death on the Underground Railway." In ROSH, 206–25.

MF Dashiell Hammett. 1972 [1930]. *The Maltese Falcon.* New York: Vintage.

MHM John Dickson Carr. 1933. *The Mad Hatter Mystery.* New York: Harpers.

MK R. A. J. Walling. 1939 [1929]. *Murder at the Keyhole.* London: Methuen.

MKF John Stephen Strange. 1928. *The Man Who Killed Fortescue.* Garden City, N.Y.: Collier.

ML Agatha Christie. 1967 [1923]. *Murder on the Links.* New York: Dell.

MLq Émile Gaboriau. 1975 [1869]. *Monsieur Lecoq.* New York: Dover.

MMA Dorothy L. Sayers. 1959 [1933]. *Murder Must Advertise.* London: New English Library.

MMF   H. C. Bailey. 1942 [1932–42]. *Meet Mr. Fortune.* New York: Book League of America.

MMM   William Le Queux. n.d. *The Mysterious Mr. Miller.* London: Skeffington.

"MNL"   Hugh C. Weir. [1914]. "The Man with Nine Lives." In CM, 131–64.

"MPT"   Anna Katherine Green. [1888]. "Missing: Page Thirteen." In WG, 12–37.

MSH   Sir Arthur Conan Doyle. [1893]. *Memoirs of Sherlock Holmes.* In CSH, 335–480.

MSY   David Frome. 1942 [1932]. *The Man from Scotland Yard.* New York: Pocket.

MYR   Gaston Leroux. 1977 [1908]. *The Mystery of the Yellow Room.* New York: Dover.

NMW   Carter Dickson. 1959 [1951]. *Night at the Mocking Widow.* London: Pan.

NRM   Agatha Christie. 1989 [1970]. *The Nursery Rhyme Murders.* New York: Putnam.

OA   Dick Francis. 1965. *Odds Against.* New York: Pocket.

OD   Ngaio Marsh. 1943 [1939]. *Overture to Death.* New York: Pocket.

OLN   Mickey Spillane. 1951. *One Lonely Night.* New York: Signet.

PCC   Anthony Berkeley. 1951 [1929]. *The Poisoned Chocolate Case.* New York: Pocket.

PH   John Buchan. 1954 [1916]. *The Power House.* London: Longmans, Green.

PL   Cornell Woolrich. 1942. *The Phantom Lady.* New York: Ace.

QM   Adam Hall. 1967 [1965]. *The Quiller Memorandum.* London: Fontana.

R   Phillip Macdonald. 1940 [1924]. *The Rasp.* New York: Penguin.

RB   Rex Stout. 1943 [1936]. *The Rubber Band.* New York: Pocket.

RBx   Rex Stout. 1964 [1936]. *The Red Box.* New York: Pyramid.

RH   Dashiell Hammett. 1943 [1929]. *Red Harvest.* New York: Pocket.

RHM   A. A. Milne. 1922. *The Red House Mystery.* New York: E. P. Dutton.

RM   Geoffrey Household. 1963 [1939]. *Rogue Male.* New York: Pyramid.

ROSH   *The Rivals of Sherlock Holmes.* 1971. Ed. Hugh Greene. Harmondsworth, Middlesex: Penguin.

RS   Erskine Childers. 1976 [1903]. *The Riddle of the Sands.* New York: Dover.

RSH Sir Arthur Conan Doyle. [1905]. *The Return of Sherlock Holmes.* In CSH, 483–666.

RSJ Clemence Dane. 1932. *Re-enter Sir John.* London: Hodder & Stoughton.

RWM Carter Dickson. 1951 [1935]. *The Red Widow Murders.* Harmondsworth, Middlesex: Penguin.

SC John Le Carré. 1963. *The Spy Who Came In from the Cold.* New York: Coward-McCann.

SF Sir Arthur Conan Doyle. [1889]. *The Sign of Four.* In CSH, 89–158.

SI Eric Ambler. 1953. *The Schirmer Inheritance.* New York: Knopf.

"SIS" John K. Butler. [1941]. "The Saint in Silver." In HD, 43–89.

SIW John Creasey. 1956. *Send for Inspector West.* London: Hodder & Stoughton.

SP Dorothy L. Sayers. 1967 [1930]. *Strong Poison.* New York: Avon.

SS Michael Innes. 1965 [1937]. *Seven Suspects.* New York: Berkeley.

SSt Sir Arthur Conan Doyle. [1887]. *A Study in Scarlet.* In CSH, 15–86.

ST John P. Marquand. 1956. *Stopover Tokyo.* Boston: Little, Brown.

TF Craig Rice. 1942 [1941]. *Trial by Fury.* Cleveland: World.

TH John Buchan. n.d. [1924]. *The Three Hostages.* New York: Popular Library.

ThM Graham Greene. 1971 [1949]. "The Third Man." In *Triple Pursuit!* New York: Viking, 161–244.

TLC E. C. Bentley. 1970 [1913]. *Trent's Last Case.* New York: Avon.

TM Dashiell Hammett. 1965 [1934]. *The Thin Man.* In *The Novels of Dashiell Hammett.* New York: Knopf, 589–726.

TOC E. C. Bentley and H. Warner Allen. 1936. *Trent's Own Case.* London: Constable.

TS John Buchan. n.d. [1915]. *The Thirty-Nine Steps.* New York: Popular Library.

TTSS John le Carré. 1974. *Tinker, Tailor, Soldier, Spy.* New York: Knopf.

UD Dorothy L. Sayers. 1964 [1927]. *Unnatural Death.* New York: Avon.

"UM" Frederick Irving Anderson. 1942. "The Unknown Man." *EQMM,* July, 34–39.

VM Ngaio Marsh. n.d. [1937]. *Vintage Murder.* New York: Berkeley.

"WBH" Baroness Orczy. [1910]. "The Woman in the Big Hat." In ROSH, 254–77.

WES Lawrence Durrell. 1980 [1957]. *White Eagles over Serbia.* Harmondsworth, Middlesex: Penguin.

WG   *World's Greatest Detective Stories.* 1928. New York: Walter J. Black.

WM   James Hilton. 1979 [1931]. *Was It Murder?* New York: Dover.

WMLE   Roy Fuller. 1963. *With My Little Eye.* Harmondsworth, Middlesex: Penguin.

SECONDARY WORKS

Adams, Sir John. 1932. "The Detective-Fiction Game." *Overland Monthly,* August.

Ade, George. 1928. "The Glendon Mystery; Or, Eddie Parks, the Newsboy Detective." In *Bang! Bang!,* 17–30. New York: J. H. Sears.

Aldrich, T. B. 1968 [1880]. *The Stillwater Tragedy.* Ridgewood, N.J.: Gregg Press.

Alewyn, Richard. 1983. "The Origin of the Detective Novel." In Most and Stowe, 62–78.

Allen, Dick, and David Chako. 1974. *Detective Fiction/Crime and Compromise.* New York: Harcourt Brace Jovanovich.

Allingham, Margery. 1950. "Mysterious Fun for Millions of Innocent Escapists." *New York Times Book Review,* 4 June, 3.

Altick, Richard D. 1970. *Victorian Studies in Scarlet.* New York: W. W. Norton.

Alvarez, A. 1966. "The Thin Man." *Spectator,* 11 February, 169–70.

Amis, Kingsley. 1965. *The James Bond Dossier.* London: Jonathan Cape.

Andersen, Margaret L. 1987. "Changing the Curriculum in Higher Education." *Signs* 12 (winter): 222–54.

Antonini, Fausto. 1966. "The Psychoanalysis of 007." In Del Buono and Eco, 103–21.

Arnold, Edwin Lester. 1976. *Lieut. Gulliver Jones: His Vacation.* London: New English Library.

Auden, W. H. 1974. "The Guilty Vicarage." In Allen and Chako, 400–410.

Auerbach, Nina. 1982. "Magi and Maidens: The Romance of the Victorian Freud." In *Writing and Sexual Difference,* 111–30. Ed. Elizabeth Abel. Brighton, Sussex: Harvester.

Austen, Jane. 1970 [1813]. *Pride and Prejudice.* London: Oxford University Press.

Balzac, Honoré de. 1960 [1831]. *The Wild Ass's Skin.* New York: E. P. Dutton.

Barthes, Roland. 1975. *The Pleasure of the Text.* New York: Hill & Wang.

———. 1977. "Textual Analysis of a Tale by Edgar Poe." *Poe Studies* 10 (June): 1–12.

Batsleer, Janet, Tony Davies, Rebecca O'Rourke, and Chris Weedon. 1985. *Rewriting English: Cultural Politics of Gender and Class.* London: Methuen.

Beer, Gillian. 1986. "Origins and Oblivion in Victorian Narrative." In *Sex, Politics, and Science in the Nineteenth-Century Novel,* 63–87. Ed. Ruth Bernard Yeazell. Baltimore: Johns Hopkins University Press.

Bell, Ian A., and Graham Daldry. 1990. *Watching the Detectives.* New York: St. Martin's.

Benjamin, Walter. 1969. *Illuminations.* New York: Schocken.

Bennett, Arnold. 1938. *The Grand Babylon Hotel.* Harmondsworth, Middlesex: Penguin.

Bishop, John Peale. 1941. "Georges Simenon." *New Republic,* 10 March, 345–46.

Black, Joel. 1991. *The Aesthetics of Murder: A Study in Romantic Literature and Contemporary Culture.* Baltimore: Johns Hopkins University Press.

Blair, Walter. 1967. "Dashiell Hammett: Themes and Techniques." In *Essays on American Literature in Honor of Jay B. Hubbell,* 295–306. Ed. Clarence Gohdes. Durham, N.C.: Duke University Press.

Blake, Nicholas. 1974. "The Detective Story—Why?" In Haycraft, 398–405.

Bloom, Harold. 1984. "Inescapable Poe." *New York Review of Books,* 11 October.

Bogan, Louise. 1944. "The Time of the Assassins." *Nation,* 27 May, 475–78.

Bonaparte, Marie. 1949. *The Life and Works of Edgar Allan Poe: A Psycho-Analytic Interpretation.* London: Imago.

Braudy, Leo. 1977. *The World in a Frame.* Garden City, N.Y.: Doubleday, Anchor.

Brooks, Peter. 1979. "Fictions of the Wolfman: Freud and Narrative Understanding." *Diacritics* (spring): 72–83.

Brophy, Brigid. 1965. "Detective Fiction: A Modern Myth of Violence?" *Hudson Review* 18 (spring): 11–30.

Buchan, John. n.d. Preface to *A Book of Escapes and Hurried Journeys.* New York: Houghton Mifflin.

Buchsbaum, Jonathan. 1986. "Tame Wolves and Phony Claims: Paranoia in Film Noir." *Persistence of Vision* 3/4 (summer): 35–47.

Burroughs, Edgar Rice. 1963 [1912]. *Tarzan of the Apes.* New York: Ballantine.

Butor, Michel. 1969. *Passing Time.* New York: Simon & Schuster.

Carroll, Lewis. 1971 [1865]. *Alice in Wonderland.* Ed. Donald J. Gray. New York: Norton Critical Editions.

Chandler, Raymond. 1984 [1962]. *Raymond Chandler Speaking.* Ed. Dorothy Gardiner and Katherine Sorley Walker. London: Allison & Busby.

———. [1944]. "The Simple Art of Murder." In Allen and Chako, 387–99.

Chesterton, G. K. [1902]. "A Defense of Detective Stories." In Haycraft, 3–6.

———. 1921. "The Domesticity of Detectives." In *The Uses of Diversity*, 24–29. London: Methuen.

———. 1929. "Detective Stories." In *G.K.C. as M.C.*, 173–77. Ed. J. P. de Fonseka. London: Methuen.

Clover, Carol J. 1987. "Her Body, Himself: Gender in the Slasher Film." *Representations* 20 (Fall): 187–228.

Cohen, Morton. 1960. *Rider Haggard*. London: Hutchinson.

Collins, Wilkie. 1966 [1868]. *The Moonstone*. Harmondsworth, Middlesex: Penguin.

———. 1974 [1860]. *The Woman in White*. Harmondsworth, Middlesex: Penguin.

Columbo, Furio. 1966. "Bond's Women." In Del Buono and Eco, 86–102.

Conrad, Joseph. 1953 [1907]. *The Secret Agent*. Garden City, N.Y.: Anchor.

———. 1976 [1910]. "The Secret Sharer." In *The Portable Conrad*, 648–99. Ed. Morton Dauwen Zabel. New York: Penguin.

Cooper, James Fenimore. 1961 [1840]. *The Pathfinder*. New York: Signet.

———. 1962 [1826]. *The Last of the Mohicans*. New York: Signet.

Cowley, Malcolm. 1951. *Exile's Return*. New York: Viking.

Darwin, Charles. n.d. [1859]. *On the Origin of Species by the Means of Natural Selection*. New York: Modern Library.

Defoe, Daniel. 1975 [1719]. *Robinson Crusoe*. New York: W. W. Norton.

Del Buono, Oreste, and Umberto Eco. 1966. *The Bond Affair*. London: Macdonald.

Descartes, René. 1960 [1641]. *Meditations on First Philosophy*. New York: Bobbs-Merrill.

De Voto, Bernard. 1944. "Easy Chair." *Harper's Magazine*, December, 34–37.

Dickens, Charles. 1961 [1870]. *The Mystery of Edwin Drood*. New York: Signet.

———. 1966 [1841]. *Barnaby Rudge*. New York: Everyman's Library.

Docherty, Brian. 1988. *American Crime Fiction*. New York: St. Martin's.

Doyle, Arthur Conan. n.d. *Uncle Bernac*. London: George Newnes.

Eco, Umberto. 1966. "The Narrative Structure in Fleming." In Del Buono and Eco, 35–75.

Eco, Umberto, and Thomas A. Sebeok. 1983. *The Sign of Three: Dupin, Holmes, Pierce*. Bloomington: Indiana University Press.

Edwards, P. D. 1971. *Some Mid-Victorian Thrillers*. Queensland, Australia: University of Queensland Press.

Edwards, Thomas R. 1976. "Tough Guys." *New York Review of Books*, 30 September, 13–15.

Elliott, George. 1960. "Country Full of Blondes." *Nation*, 23 April, 354–60.

Fiedler, Leslie. 1979. "Giving the Devil His Due." *Journal of Popular Culture* 12: 197–207.

Fielding, Henry. n.d. [1749]. *The History of Tom Jones: A Foundling*. New York: Modern Library.

Ford, Ford Madox. 1938. *The March of Literature*. New York: Dial.

Fraser, Sir James. 1955 [1922]. *The Golden Bough*. New York: Macmillan.

Freeman, R. Austin. 1974 [1924]. "The Art of the Detective Story." In Haycraft, 7–17.

Freud, Anna. 1966. "The Ego and the Id at Puberty." In *Writings*, 2:137–51. New York: International Universities Press.

Freud, Sigmund. 1953 [1905]. "Fragment of an Analysis of a Case of Hysteria." In *The Standard Edition*, 7:7–122. London: Hogarth.

———. 1953 [1908a]. "Character and Anal Eroticism." In *The Standard Edition*, 9:167–76. London: Hogarth.

———. 1953 [1908b]. "Creative Writers and Day-dreaming." In *The Standard Edition*, 9:141–54. London: Hogarth.

———. 1953 [1910]. "The Antithetical Meaning of Primal Words." In *The Standard Edition*, 11:153–62. London: Hogarth.

———. 1953 [1919]. "The 'Uncanny'." In *The Standard Edition*, 17:217–52. London: Hogarth.

———. 1953 [1920]. *A General Introduction to Psychoanalysis*. New York: Pocket.

———. 1953 [1924]. "The Economic Problem of Masochism." In *The Standard Edition*, 19:155–72. London: Hogarth.

Freud, Sigmund, and Josef Breuer. 1966 [1893–1895]. *Studies on Hysteria*. New York: Avon.

Frye, Northrop. 1968. *Anatomy of Criticism*. New York: Atheneum.

Gardner, Erle Stanley. 1974. "The Case of the Early Beginning." In Haycraft, 203–7.

Genette, Gerard. 1980. *Narrative Discourse: An Essay on Method*. Ithaca: Cornell University Press.

Gerber, Richard. 1975. "Name as Symbol: On Sherlock Holmes and the Nature of the Detective Story." *Armchair Detective*, August, 280–87.

Gilbert, Michael. 1959a. *Crime in Good Company*. London: Constable.

———. 1959b. "The Moment of Violence." In Gilbert, 105–25.

Ginzburg, Carlo. 1966. "Morelli, Freud, and Sherlock Holmes: Clues and Scientific Method." In Eco and Sebeok, 81–118.

Godwin, William. n.d. [1797]. *Caleb Williams.* New York: Rinehart.

Green, Martin. 1979. *Dreams of Adventure, Deeds of Empire.* New York: Basic.

Grella, George. 1974. "Murder and the Mean Streets." In Allen and Chako, 411–29.

Hammett, Dashiell. 1974 [1927]. "The Benson Murder Case." In Haycraft, 382–83.

Hare, Cyril. 1959. "The Classic Form." In Gilbert, 55–84.

Hartman, Geoffrey. 1975. "Literature High and Low." In *The Fate of Reading,* 203–22. Chicago: University of Chicago Press.

Hawthorne, Nathaniel. 1964 [1852]. *The Blithedale Romance.* Centenary Edition. Columbus: Ohio State University Press. Vol. 3.

———. 1968 [1860]. *The Marble Faun.* Vol. 4.

Haycraft, Howard. 1974. *The Art of the Mystery Story.* New York: Carroll & Graf.

Hayter, Alethea. 1988. *Opium and the Romantic Imagination: Addiction and Creativity in De Quincey, Coleridge, Baudelaire, and Others.* Wellingborough, Northants: Crucible.

Heissenbüttel, Helmut. 1983. "Rules of the Game of the Crime Novel." In Most and Stowe, 79–92.

Henty, G. A. 1895. *Through Russian Snows.* London: Atlantic.

Hilfer, Tony. 1990. *The Crime Novel: A Deviant Genre.* Austin: University of Texas Press.

Hoffmann, E. T. A. 1967. *The Best Tales.* New York: Dover.

Holquist, Michael. 1983. "Whodunit and Other Questions: Metaphysical Detective Stories in Post-War Fiction." In Most and Stowe, 149–74.

Horney, Karen. 1937. *The Neurotic Personality of Our Time.* New York: W. W. Norton.

Howells, William Dean. 1891. *Criticism and Fiction.* New York: Harper.

Hughes, Thomas. 1906. *Tom Brown's Schooldays.* London: J. M. Dent.

Hugo, Victor. 1965 [1831]. *The Hunchback of Notre Dame.* London: Everyman's Library.

Hutter, Albert. 1983. "Dreams, Transformations, and Literature." In Most and Stowe, 230–51.

Hyman, Stanley Edgar. 1959. *The Tangled Bank: Darwin, Marx, Fraser, & Freud as Imaginative Writers.* New York: Grosset & Dunlap.

Irwin, John T. 1980. *American Hieroglyphics.* New Haven: Yale University Press.

James, Clive. 1979. "The Country behind the Hills: Raymond Chandler"; "The Sherlockologists." In *At the Pillars of Hercules*, 127–38; 117–26. London: Faber & Faber.

James, Henry. 1956 [1884]. "The Art of Fiction." In *The Future of the Novel*, 3–27. Ed. Leon Edel. New York: Vintage.

———. 1963 [1876]. "The Ghostly Rental." In *Ghostly Tales of Henry James*, 69–106. Ed. Leon Edel. New York: Universal Library.

Jameson, Fredric. 1970. "On Raymond Chandler." *Southern Review* 6 (July): 624–50.

Kaemmel, Ernst. 1983. "Literature under the Table: The Detective Novel and Its Social Mission." In Most and Stowe, 55–61.

Kayman, Martin A. 1992. *From Bow Street to Baker Street: Mystery, Detection, and Narrative.* New York: St. Martin's.

Kermode, Frank. 1972. *Novel and Narrative.* Glasgow: University of Glasgow.

———. 1981. "Secrets and Narrative Sequence." In *On Narrative*, 79–97. Ed. W. J. T. Mitchell. Chicago: University of Chicago Press.

Kingsley, Charles. n.d. *The Water-Babies.* London: J. M. Dent.

Kipling, Rudyard. 1930 [1890]. *The Light That Failed.* Garden City, N.Y.: Doubleday, Doran.

Klein, Kathleen Gregory. 1988. *The Woman Detective: Gender & Genre.* Urbana: University of Illinois Press.

Knight, Stephen. 1988. "'A Hard Cheerfulness': An Introduction to Raymond Chandler." In Docherty, 71–87.

Knox, Ronald. 1974. "A Detective Story Decalogue." In Haycraft, 194–96.

Krutch, Joseph Wood. 1988. "'Only a Detective Story.'" In Winks, 41–46.

Kubie, Lawrence S. 1937. "The Fantasy of Dirt." *Psychoanalytic Quarterly* 6: 388–425.

Leacock, Stephen. 1942. "Twenty Cents' Worth of Murder." In *The Pocket Mystery Reader*, 215–19. New York: Pocket.

———. 1946. "The Great Detective." In *Laugh with Leacock*, 25–43. New York: Pocket.

———. 1974 [1938]. "Murder at $2.50 a Crime." In Haycraft, 327–37.

Leger, Fernand. 1926. "A New Realism—The Object." *Little Review* 11 (Winter): 7–8.

Lehman, David. 1989. *The Perfect Murder.* New York: Free Press.

Lévi-Strauss, Claude. 1978 [1955]. *Tristes Tropiques.* Harmondsworth, Middlesex: Penguin.

Linker, Kate. 1984. "From Imitation, to the Copy, to Just Effect: On Reading Jean Baudrillard." *Artforum* 22 (April): 44–47.

Lyell, Charles. 1976. "Man in the Geological Record." In *The Portable Victorian Reader*, 497–506. Ed. Gordon S. Haight. Harmondsworth, Middlesex: Penguin.

Macdonald, Dwight. 1962. *Against the American Grain*. New York: Random House.

Madden, David. 1968. *Tough Guy Writers of the Thirties*. Carbondale: Southern Illinois University Press.

Marcus, Steven. 1975. Introduction to *The Continental Op*. London: Macmillan.

Mason, Michael. 1976. "Deadlier Than the Male." *TLS*, 17 September, 1147.

Maugham, W. Somerset. 1940. "Give Me A Murder." *Saturday Evening Post*, 28 December, 46–49.

Mehlman, Jeffrey. 1972. "The 'Floating Signifier': From Lévi-Strauss to Lacan." *Yale French Studies* 48: 10–37.

Melville, Herman. 1962. *Billy Budd, Sailor*. Ed. Harrison Hayford and Merton M. Scalts, Jr. Chicago: University of Chicago Press.

———. *Moby-Dick*. 1964 [1851]. Indianapolis: Bobbs-Merrill.

Merry, Bruce. 1977. *Anatomy of the Spy Thriller*. Montreal: McGill-Queen's University Press.

Mierow, Charles C. 1933. "Through Seas of Blood." *Sewanee Review* 41 (January–March): 1–22.

Miller, David A. 1979. "Language of Detective Fiction: Fiction of Detective Language." *Antaeus* 35 (Autumn): 99–106.

———. 1980. "From *roman policier* to *roman-police*: Wilkie Collins' *The Moonstone*." *Novel* 13 (Winter): 153–70.

Milne, A. A. 1929. "Introducing Crime." In *By Way of Introduction*, 38–42. London: Methuen.

Moretti, Franco. 1983. "Clues." In *Signs Taken for Wonders: Essays in the Sociology of Literary Forms*, 130–56. London: Verso.

Moss, Leonard. 1966. "Hammett's Heroic Operative." *New Republic*, 8 January, 32–34.

Most, Glenn, and William W. Stowe. 1983. *Poetics of Murder*. New York: Harcourt Brace Jovanovich.

Nicolson, Marjorie. 1974. "The Professor and the Detective." In Haycraft, 110–27.

O'Faolain, Sean. 1935. "Give Us Back Bill Sikes." *Spectator*, 15 February, 242–43.

Orczy, Baroness. 1960 [1905]. *The Scarlet Pimpernel*. New York: Pyramid.

Orwell, George. 1954. *A Collection of Essays*. Garden City, N.Y.: Doubleday.

Palmer, Jerry. 1978. *Thrillers.* London: Edward Arnold.

Perelman, S. J. 1962. "Farewell, My Lovely Appetizer." In *The Most of . . .* 191–96. New York: Simon & Schuster.

Phillips, Walter C. 1919. *Dickens, Reade, and Collins: Sensation Novelists.* New York: Columbia University Press.

Poe, Edgar Allan. 1902. *The Complete Works of Edgar Allan Poe.* Ed. James A. Harrison. 17 volumes. New York: Thomas Y. Crowell.

———. 1960 [1838]. *The Narrative of Arthur Gordon Pym.* New York: Hill & Wang.

Porter, Dennis. 1981. *The Pursuit of Crime: Art and Ideology in Detective Fiction.* New Haven: Yale University Press.

———. 1988. "Detection and Ethics: The Case of P. D. James." In Rader and Zettler, 11–18.

Priestman, Martin. 1991. *Detective Fiction and Literature: The Figure on the Carpet.* New York: St. Martin's.

Pykett, Lyn. 1990. "Investigating Women: The Female Sleuth after Feminism." In Bell and Daldry, 48–67.

Pynchon, Thomas. 1965. *The Crying of Lot 49.* New York: Bantam.

Rader, Barbara A., and Howard G. Zettler. 1988. *The Sleuth and the Scholar: Origins, Evolution, and Current Trends in Detective Fiction.* New York: Greenwood Press.

Reddy, Maureen T. 1988. *Sisters in Crime: Feminism and the Crime Novel.* New York: Continuum.

Redman, Ben Ray. 1932. "Murder Will Out." *Saturday Review of Literature,* 10 December, 306.

Reik, Theodor. 1945. *The Unknown Murderer.* New York: Prentice-Hall.

———. 1957. "Masochism in Modern Man." In *Of Love and Lust: On the Psychoanalysis of Romantic and Sexual Emotions,* 195–366. New York: Farrar, Straus & Cudahy.

Ricardou, Jean. 1976. "Gold in the Bug." *Poe Studies* 9 (December): 33–39.

Ricoeur, Paul. 1970. *Freud and Philosophy.* New Haven: Yale University Press.

Riddel, Joseph N. 1979. "The 'Crypt' of Edgar Poe." *Boundary 2* 7 (spring): 117–41.

Rodell, Marie F. 1974. "Clues." In Haycraft, 264–72.

Rosenberg, Samuel. 1975. *Naked Is the Best Disguise.* New York: Penguin.

Roth, Marty. 1990. "Sherlock Holmes and the Madness of Representation." *North Dakota Quarterly* 58 (summer): 159–68.

Ruskin, John. 1963. "Fiction, Fair and Foul." In *The Genius of John Ruskin,* 435–44. Ed. John D. Rosenberg. New York: George Braziller.

Russell, D. C. 1945. "The Chandler Books." *Atlantic Monthly*, March, 123–24.

Rycroft, Charles. 1968. "The Analysis of a Detective Story." In *Imagination and Reality*, 114–28. London: Hogarth.

Sanders, Dennis, and Len Lovallo. 1984. *The Agatha Christie Companion*. New York: Delacorte.

Sayers, Dorothy L. 1929a. *The Omnibus of Crime*. Garden City, N.Y.: Garden City.

———. 1929b. "A Sport of Noble Minds." *Saturday Review of Literature*, 3 August, 22–23.

———. 1947. "Aristotle on Detective Fiction." In *Unpopular Opinions*, 222–36. New York: Harcourt, Brace.

———. 1974 [1937]. "Gaudy Night." In Haycraft, 208–21.

Schwartz, Hillel. 1989. "The Three-Body Problem and the End of the World." In *Fragments for a History of the Human Body, Part Two*, 406–65. Ed. Michel Feher. New York: Zone.

Scott, Sir Walter. *Rob Roy*. 1956 [1817]. Boston: Riverside.

———. 1966 [1811]. Introduction to *The Castle of Otranto* . . . Ed. E. F. Bleiler. New York: Dover.

———. *Waverley*. 1980 [1814]. Harmondsworth, Middlesex: Penguin.

See, Carolyn. 1968. "The Hollywood Novel: The American Dream Cheat." In Madden, 199–217.

Sennett, Richard. 1977. *The Fall of Public Man*. New York: Knopf.

Slung, Michele. 1988. "Let's Hear It for Agatha Christie: A Feminist Appreciation." In Rader and Zettler, 63–68.

Southern, Terry. 1960. "An Investigation . . ." *Esquire*, July.

Stallybrass, Peter, and Allon White. 1986. *The Politics and Poetics of Transgression*. Ithaca: Cornell University Press.

Starrett, Vincent. 1974. "The Private Life of Sherlock Holmes." In Haycraft, 146–57.

Steeves, Harrison R. 1974. "A Sober Word on the Detective Story." In Haycraft, 513–26.

Stein, Gertrude. 1940. *What Are Master-pieces and Why Are There So Few of Them?* Los Angeles: Conference Press.

Steiner, George. 1977. "Sleuths." *New Yorker*, 25 April, 141–48.

Stern, Philip Van Doren. 1974. "The Case of the Corpse in the Blind Alley." In Haycraft, 527–35.

Sterne, Laurence. 1967 [1768]. *A Sentimental Journey*. Harmondsworth, Middlesex: Penguin.

Stevenson, Robert Louis. 1946 [1883]. *Treasure Island.* Harmondsworth, Middlesex: Penguin.

———. 1967 [1886]. "Dr. Jekyll and Mr. Hyde." In *Minor Classics of 19th-Century Fiction.* Vol. 2, 57–109. Ed. William E. Buckler. New York: Houghton Mifflin.

———. *The Dynamiter.* n.d. [1885]. Chicago: Standard Education Society.

———. *Kidnapped.* n.d. [1886]. London: Thomas Nelson.

Stevenson, Robert Louis [and Lloyd Osbourne]. 1909 [1891]. *The Wrecker.* New York: Scribner.

Strong, L. A. G. 1959. "The Crime Short Story—An English View." In Gilbert, 149–62.

Swanson, David, Philip J. Bohnert, and Jackson A. Smith. 1970. *The Paranoid.* Boston: Little, Brown.

Symons, Julian. 1973. *Mortal Consequences.* New York: Schocken.

———. 1981. "The Tough Guy at the Typewriter." *TLS,* 5 June, 619–20.

Thompson, H. Douglas. 1974. "Masters of Mystery." In Haycraft, 128–45.

Todorov, Tzvetan. 1973. *The Fantastic.* Ithaca: Cornell University Press.

———. 1977. *The Poetics of Prose.* Ithaca: Cornell University Press.

Tornabuoni, Lietta. 1966. "A Popular Phenomenon." In Del Buono and Eco, 13–34.

Trollope, Anthony. n.d. [1883]. *An Autobiography.* Garden City, N.Y.: Doubleday, Dolphin.

Truzzi, Marcello. 1983. "Sherlock Holmes: Applied Social Psychologist." In Eco and Sebeok, 55–80.

Turner, E. S. 1976. *Boys Will Be Boys.* Harmondsworth, Middlesex: Penguin.

Twain, Mark. 1948 [1889]. *A Connecticut Yankee in King Arthur's Court.* New York: Washington Square.

———. 1958. *The Complete Short Stories.* Ed. Charles Neider. New York: Bantam.

———. 1962. *Selected Shorter Writings.* Ed. Walter Blair. Boston: Houghton Mifflin.

Van Dine, S. S. 1974. "Twenty Rules for Writing Detective Stories." In Haycraft, 189–93.

'Veendam, S. S.' 1974. "The Pink Murder Case." In Haycraft, 321–26.

Vickers, Roy. 1959. "Crime on the Stage—The Criminological Illusion." In Gilbert, 178–91.

†Walker, Ronald G., and June M. Frazer. 1990. *The Cunning Craft.* Macomb: Western Illinois University Press.

†Watson, Colin. 1971. *Snobbery with Violence.* London: Eyre & Spottiswoode.

Weberman, A. J. 1971. "The Art of Garbage Analysis." *Esquire*, November, 113–17.

Wells, H. G. 1960. *Best Stories* . . . New York: Ballantine.

———. n.d. [1897]. *The Invisible Man.* In *Seven Science Fiction Novels*, 183–306. New York: Dover.

Welty, Eudora. 1971. "The Stuff That Nightmares Are Made Of." *New York Times Book Review*, 14 February.

Widmer, Kingsley. 1968. "The Way Out: Some Life-Style Sources of the Literary Tough Guy and the Proletarian Hero." In Madden, 3–12.

Wilbur, Richard. 1962. "Edgar Allan Poe." In *Major Writers of America.* Ed. Perry Miller. Vol. 1, 369–82. New York: Harcourt, Brace & World.

Wilson, Edmund. 1952. *A Literary Chronicle: 1920–1950.* Garden City, N.Y.: Doubleday.

———. 1974 [1945]. "Who Cares Who Killed Roger Ackroyd?" In Haycraft, 390–97.

✗ Winks, Robin. 1988. *Detective Fiction: A Collection of Critical Essays.* Woodstock, Vt.: Countryman.

Wister, Owen. 1902. *The Virginian.* New York: Grosset & Dunlap.

Wodehouse, P. G. 1942 [1929]. "About These Mystery Stories." In *The Pocket Mystery Reader*, 238–45. New York: Pocket.

Woods, Robin. 1990. " 'His Appearance Is against Him': The Emergence of the Detective." In Walker and Frazer, 15–24.

Woollcott, Alexander. 1937. *While Rome Burns.* New York: Grosset & Dunlap.

Wright, Willard Huntington. 1974. "The Great Detective Stories." In Haycraft, 33–70.

Wrong, E. M. 1974. "Crime and Detection." In Haycraft, 18–32.

Wu, William F. 1982. *The Yellow Peril.* Hamden, Conn.: Archon.

Wyndham, Francis. 1979. "Deadly Details." *TLS*, 8 September, 626.

Zangwill, Israel. *Pall Mall Magazine.* 1 (1893).

INDEX

149; *Ipcress File, The*, 61, 65, 169, 186, 187, 235
De Quincey, Thomas, 97
Derr Biggers, Earl, 62, 74–76
Descartes, René, 225
Detection: as game or puzzle, xiii, 43, 50, 52, 101–2, 108, 226
Detective, 43–44, 68–87; adolescent, 45–67, 112; amateur, 61, 65, 69, 101, 117; aristocrat, xiii, 71, 73; artist, 44, 71, 72, 174–75; exhibitionist, xiii, 52–61, 92, 232; and police, 37, 61–67, 133–34, 179, 195–96, 252 (n.1); from public school, 98–105; as scientist, xiii, 71, 72; as thinking machine, xiii, 43, 56–57, 156, 231; tough, 68–69, 80–87, 196; the Watson, 30–31, 36, 37, 75, 105–7, 175, 180–81, 185, 195–96, 236, 251 (n. 2); wisecracking and banter, 75, 84–85
Detective fiction: without affect, 32–33, 35; fair play rule, xi, 29–31, 54, 82, 101, 196, 209; language, 40–41, 53, 119; parody, 24–25, 28, 37, 45, 115, 144; and psychoanalysis, 20, 138–40, 141, 153, 154, 161; realism, 23–29; rules, 30–33, 113–14; solution, 20–21, 137, 162–78, 231; structure, xiii, 6–7, 156, 174
Detective films, 49, 64, 68, 105, 106, 116, 166, 167, 170, 233, 244, 246, 255 (n. 1)
De Voto, Bernard, 5, 16
Dickens, Charles, xiii, 13, 21, 46, 142, 149, 193, 210, 211, 228–29, 256 (n. 5)

Disraeli, Benjamin, 71
Dostoyevsky, Fyodor, 2, 21, 85
Doyle, Arthur Conan, 4, 18–27 passim, 41, 42, 46, 53–61 passim, 68, 69, 70, 72, 95, 97, 105–6, 114–15, 124, 133, 141–57 passim, 164–202 passim, 223, 227, 229, 242–48 passim; *Hound of the Baskervilles, The*, 17, 35, 50, 106, 155, 156; *Sign of Four*, 10, 35–36, 44, 53, 54, 58–59, 71, 72, 102, 106–7, 132, 143, 147–48, 153, 154, 167–68, 174, 180, 189, 194, 196, 199, 204, 242, 248; *Study in Scarlet, A*, 10, 27, 43–44, 54, 62, 64, 144, 146–47, 152, 165, 167–68, 174, 181, 199, 232, 240, 246, 247–48
Dreiser, Theodore, 44, 72, 145
Dumas, Alexandre, 221
du Maurier, George, 151
Durrell, Lawrence, 105, 193

Eco, Umberto, 10–11, 13, 15
Einstein, Albert, 192, 197
Eliot, T. S., 17, 202
Elliott, George, 12, 21, 120–21
Ellis, Havelock, 252 (n. 5)
Emerson, Ralph Waldo, 201
Epistemology: clue, 133, 187–93, 214; coincidence, xiii, 205–14, 238; convolution, xiii, 214–22; dirt and garbage, xiii, 199–204, 244–46, 248; evidence, 179–84; paranoia, 184–87, 226, 228–30; suspicion, 65, 158–61, 215; trifle, xiii, 193–99; trust and mistrust, 103, 224, 233–36